English Electric Lightning

English Electric Lightning

Martin W. Bowman

First published in 1997 by
The Crowood Press Ltd
Ramsbury, Marlborough
Wiltshire SN8 2HR

**British Library
Cataloguing-in-Publication Data**

A catalogue record for this book is
available from the British Library.

ISBN 1 86126 099 7

Frontispiece: A formation of Lightning
F.2As of 19 Squadron. *Aeroplane*

Typeset by Phoenix Typesetting, Ilkley,
West Yorkshire

Printed and bound in Great Britain by
Butler & Tanner, Frome

Contents

Introduction

There have been several books published on the superlative Lightning, but not every aspect has been covered fully, or indeed accurately. This book offers a refreshingly different approach, benefitting from the most detailed research on the Lightning yet. Lightnings were not always stationed at Binbrook, and not all were painted green. In fact, for many years, Norfolk and Suffolk (Coltishall and Wattisham respectively) were the hub of Lightning operations and many now opine that the only true 'Frightenings' were the natural metal-clad steeds, the ones that gleamed like polished silver. I am all of these. Reminiscent of knights in shining armour, their tail fins bedecked in tigerish yellow and black and Crusader red and white, their refuelling probe was their jousting lance, the pitot tube their foil, air brakes and wheel-well doors their 'shields'; and their weaponry, well, it was just evil!

It is difficult for younger readers reared on the Jaguar and Tornado to believe that the Lightning was born of an idea in 1946 and that it progressed as a result of fifties and sixties airframe, engine and weapons technology – all of them British – into the thoroughbred that it is. If, during school holidays, in the far off, halycon days of the sixties, you stood, like me, at the end of the brick road by the yellow crash gate to witness the last all-British fighter take off with full reheat, then you too would recall these times with affection. This was in the days before political correctness, when the sounds of the sixties were easy on the airwaves, the only foreign footballers came from Wales, Ireland and Scotland, car tyres were only £3 17s 6d in real money, a new 1968 Vauxhall Viva 90 (de luxe!) just £744, and your Morris Oxford Traveller came in Trafalgar Blue. A Lightning pilot, though, was earning over £2,750 per annum and in Norwich in 1968 a 'modern detached bungalow', just three years old, retailed at 'only' £3,350, while a 'spacious' detached house cost just £750 more.

All right, so you were on £14 a week and probably you had to work for two or three months to buy a decent camera. Let us not forget that the Cold War years were dangerous years, too. No one though, can ever take away the vivid memories and the cacophony of sound generated by the twin Avon engines that reverberated around an airfield at take off time like a violent storm. Visions such as this, albeit in words and pictures, are featured together with pictorial images and vivid recollections of the pilots and their ground crews in what I hope you will agree is a refreshingly different approach. The Lightning may be gone, but it certainly is not forgotten. There never has been and never will be, another aircraft like it. Without doubt it is the best of the best of British!

Acknowledgements

'From the skies came this almighty streak of Lightning,' recalls retired drill sergeant Bill Mathews. Like the hundred other contributors who graciously swamped me with material, all of it superb, Bill said that he hoped the contents of his letter could be used in this book. However, it referred to his pal being knocked to the ground by a bolt of lightning in Malta, 1941! But what enthusiasm – the trademark of all of the following: J. Adams; Captain A.M. Aldridge; Brian Allchin RAF (Retd); John Arnold; Diana Barnato Walker MBE; Rex Barrett; Gp Capt Antony J. Barwood OBE RAF (Retd); Richard G. Basey; Chris Bassham; Mike Baxter; Capt Martin Bee; Sqn Ldr Dick Bell RAF (Retd); John Bexfield; Ray Biddle MBE; AVM George P. Black RAF (Retd); Steve Bowes; Alan A. Brain; Roly Bray; Wg Cdr John Bryant RAF (Retd); John Brindle; Colin W. Brock; Ray Brooks; Flt Lt Peter Brown; Trevor Brucklesby; Sqn Ldr E.H. Bulpett RAF (Retd), CRO, RAF Marham; Wg Cdr Ken Burford RAF (Retd) RAF Flight Safety Magazine; Dave Bussey; A.G. Calver; Denis Calvert; Sqn Ldr Brian Carroll RAF (Retd); Edwin Carter; Mick Cartwright; Derek Chilvers; Martin Chorlton; John Church; AVM Peter S. Collins CB AFC BA RAF (Retd); Mike Cooke; Bob Cossey; Ray Cossey; Alec B. Curtis; Sqn Ldr Dick Doleman RAF (Retd); Tony Dossor; John Dunnell; Gp Capt Ed Durham RAF (Retd); Barry J. Dye; *Eastern Daily Press*; *East Anglian Daily Times*; J. Malcolm English; Jonathan Falconer; Kevin C. Farrow; Nigel Farrow; Daniel and Tony Fishlock; Mike Flowerday; Dave Freeman; D.E. Freeman; John Fuller, 432 (Woodbridge) Squadron ATC; Caroline Galpin; ACM Sir Joseph Gilbert RAF (Retd); Ron Godbold; Tony and Breet Goodyear; Air Cdre Ken J. Goodwin CBE AFC; A.L.S. 'Les' Hall; Joan Hammond; Ken Hayward; Peter Hayward; Ken Hazell; Gp Capt Tim Hewlett; Mike Hillier; Gp Capt Mike Hobson CBE; Del Holyland, Martin Baker Aircraft Co. Ltd.; J.R. 'Robbie' Honnor; Gp Capt W.B.G. Hopkins AFC RAF (Retd); AVM John Howe CB CBE AFC RAF (Retd); Mike Indge; W/O Mick Jennings RAF; Sqn Ldr Jimmy Jewell; Ken Johnson; Robert Johnson; Ronald Johnson; the late Roy Johnson; Tony Kemp; Brian Knight, Prospect Litho Ltd; Douglas Knights; Jim Lilley; Paul Lincoln; Sqn Ldr Jack Love RAF (Retd), CRO, RAF Coltishall; Barry J. Madden; Alec Michael; Vernon Miller; Captain Bruce Monk RAF (Retd); Sqn Ltd Gordon Moulds MBE; Captain Ted J. Nance; Pete W. Nash; Gp Capt Hans Neubroch OBE RAF (Retd); Air Marshal Sir John Nicholls KCB CBE DFC AFC RAF (Retd); Mick Oakey, *Aeroplane Monthly*; Flt Lt R.E. Offord RAF (Retd); Wg Cdr George Parry DSO* DFC* OBE; Simon Parry; Tony

Paxton RAF (Retd); Gerald Pearson; Sqn Ldr Henry Ploszek AFC RAF (Retd); Steve Pope, Norwich Aviation Museum; Pete Purdy; Richie Pymar; Sarita Rao, Assistant Editor, *Rolls-Royce Magazine*; Wg Cdr Alex Reed OBE RAF (Retd); Richard Reeve; Jeremy Richards; Captain Mike Rigg; Captain Ian H.R. Robins; Mike Rondot, RAF (Retd); Sqn Ldr Derek Rothery RAF (Retd); Gp Capt Dave C. Roome OBE MRAeS; Ray Reed; Gary Revell; Richard Riding, Editor, *Aeroplane Monthly*; Graham Rollins; Charles Ross; Adrian Savage; Gp Capt Dave Seward AFC RAF (Retd); Gp Capt Mike J.F. Shaw CBE RAF (Retd); Kelvin Sloper, Norwich Aviation Museum; Patrick and Lionel Snell; Steve Snelling; Laury Squibb; Jean Stangroom; Geoff Syrett; Air Cdre M.J.E. Swiney RAF (Retd); Flt Lt Andy Thomas; Eric Thomas; Hugh Trevor, Lightning Preservation Group, Bruntingthorpe; Vic Yorath RAF (Retd); Graham Vernon; S. Wade; John Ward; Sid Watkinson; John Watson; W.H. Welham; C.A. Wheatland; David Williams; Peter Winning; Andrew Woodroof; Gp Capt P.T.G. Webb OBE DL RAF (Retd); Arthur Wright; Ian Wright, 222 (Broadland) Sqn ATC.

CHAPTER ONE

Formula One Fighter

'I first heard of the Lightning in 1953,' recalls Sqn Ldr (later Gp Capt) Dave Seward,

> when a wing commander from the Central Fighter Establishment visited No.1 Squadron at RAF Tangmere to give us a talk on fighter development. He discussed the problems with the Swift, the introduction of the Hunter and Javelin, and then went on to describe the fighter of the future. At the time, rumours were rife that we were going to get a jet-rocket fighter that took off on a trolley and landed on skids. To us this sounded too much like the Me 163 [a German World War Two rocket-powered interceptor] and we were not too enthusiastic. Also, this was the same time that the so called 'moving runway' was in vogue. We reckoned that if you landed a bit too slow, the runway could be rotating too fast and you would end up through the windscreen. So, to get the real 'poop' from the horse's mouth for a change was eagerly awaited.

The 'poop' that Sqn Ldr Seward, and others like him, received centred on a radical and revolutionary new design by the English Electric Company, the result of Experimental Requirement 103, issued by the Ministry of Supply in May 1947, for a research aircraft capable of exploring transonic and low supersonic speeds of up to Mach 1.5. A year earlier, in 1946, the de Havilland Vampire was entering RAF service, both Hawker and Supermarine were studying schemes for swept-wing jet fighters which would eventually emerge as the Hunter and Swift, and which would be capable, just, of exceeding Mach 1 in a dive. At English Electric, chief engineer W.E.W. 'Teddy' Petter began sketching possible fully supersonic designs.

One of the immediate problems was finding a suitable engine, even though Britain had established her jet pedigree as far back as 1937, when Frank (later Sir Frank) Whittle had run the first gas turbine aero-engine in this country. Jet fighter development accelerated in World War Two, not least in Germany, where the Messerschmitt Me 262, powered by Jumo 004-0 jet engines, became operational on 3 October 1944. Britain's first operational jet fighter, the Gloster Meteor I, powered by centrifugal-flow engines, entered squadron service in July 1944, and on 7 November 1945 a Meteor F.4 of the High Speed Flight established a new world air speed record of 606mph (970kph). On 7 September the record increased to 616mph (986kph).

In 1947 Britain's world lead in jet fighter design was seriously challenged for the first time, by America. Early American jet aircraft had not proved successful, but in June 1947 America captured the world speed record when the Lockheed P-80R Shooting Star raised the record to 623.74mph (998kph). Douglas Skystreak raised it even further later that year, to 650.92mph (1,042kph). Jet aircraft at this time were all of conventional straight-winged design, but then the results of German wartime research into high-speed aerodynamics became available and it was the American aviation and space industries which benefitted most.

German designers had explored ways of avoiding the problems of 'compressibility'. As an aircraft approaches the speed of sound, the air it displaces is compressed into a series of high-pressure waves that stream back in a cone from the nose. As these hit the wing, they cause the airflow over that part of the aircraft to break up, and cause added drag. They also create extreme buffeting, with harmful effects to the structure of the wing. The German designers discovered that if they swept back the wing, this delayed the onset of compressibility problems and allowed higher subsonic speeds to be attained.

On 14 October 1947, Captain Charles 'Chuck' Yeager, in the Bell X-1, became the first man to break the sound barrier, when he attained a level speed of 670mph (1,072kph), or Mach 1.015, at a height of 42,000ft (13,000m). America's F-86 Sabre, the first transonic, swept-wing jet fighter to see service in the West, had flown for the first time on 1 October 1947, and on 15 September 1948, an F-86a established a new world air speed record of 670.98mph (1,074kph). By July 1953, the Sabre had increased the record speed to 715.75mph (1,146kph). On 29 October 1953, the F-100 Super Sabre, the world's first operational fighter capable of supersonic performance, established yet another new world air speed record of 755.15mph (1,210kph). In Russia, the MiG-17, an updated version of the swept-wing MiG-15, also appeared in 1953, and was claimed to have exceeded Mach 1 in level flight some three years before.

Britain could therefore be forgiven for the onset of despondency. She could also be accused of shooting herself in the foot. In February 1946, British technology was seriously jeopardised when, just as construction was about to start, the Miles M.52 supersonic research aircraft was disastrously cancelled; theoretically, this aircraft would have been capable of reaching 1,000mph (1,600kph) at 36,000ft (11,000m). By 1948 it was quite apparent that the lead in supersonic design had passed to America. The first British supersonic flight was made on 9 September 1948 by John Derry in the de Havilland DH 108, but only in a dive. Conceived in 1953, the delta-winged Avro 720, powered by an Armstrong Siddeley Viper engine and Armstrong Siddeley Screamer rocket unit, was theoretically capable of Mach 2 at 40,000ft (12,000m); it was cancelled in 1957 just as the prototype neared completion. Although her Canberra and Hunter aircraft established speed records in 1953 (the latter raised the world speed record to 726.6mph (1,163kph) on 7 September), it must have seemed that Britain had thrown away what could have been a world lead in supersonic research.

However, Specification 103, which had called for a high speed research aircraft, had already prompted both the Fairey and English Electric companies to initiate design studies. Fairey was to respond with the delta-winged FD.2, while at English Electric, Teddy Petter and his young, talented design team, started work on two prototypes and a third airframe for static test. In mid-1949, Specification F.23/49 was issued for a structural test specimen and two 7g research aircraft with guns and

a sighting system, 'to investigate the practicality of supersonic speed for military aircraft', and English Electric developed the P.1 supersonic day fighter to meet it.

The P.1

Although the company had no direct research and experience to call upon – indeed, English Electric's experience of aircraft production had been limited to producing Hampdens and Halifaxes in World War Two, then Vampires after the

War, Petter's genius and the technical expertise of his team, already heavily engaged in bringing the EE.A1 jet bomber design to reality as the Canberra, were ready to overcome all obstacles. They were helped greatly by data provided by the Short S.B.5. (WG768), a scaled down test-bed powered by a 3,500lb (1,600kg) thrust Rolls-Royce Derwent jet engine and fitted with a non-retractable undercarriage, adjustable for centre of gravity variations. The S.B.5 first flew on 2 December 1952. Various wing designs with a sweepback of 50, 60 and 69 degrees were tested, and a variable incidence tailplane positioned either at the top of the fin or on the rear fuselage was also experimented with by Short Brothers.**Pic 1 in para above**

Further data was provided by the installation at the Warton Factory of both water and transonic wind tunnels (the first in Britain), including equipment capable of operating at Mach 4 and Mach 6. Some fifty-one models were tested, and in excess of 4,600 runs were made in the various wind tunnels. Even so, to produce an operational front-line fighter capable not only of sustaining supersonic flight, but also of reaching Mach 2, was a challenge so daunting that in 1949 it was akin to trying to be the first to put a man on the moon.

A decision was taken to use two Hawker Siddeley Sapphire AS-Sa5 axial flow engines. These had a lower frontal area than the centrifugal flow engines that powered the older Meteor and Vampire, and were each capable of providing 7,200lb (3,300kg) dry thrust with no re-heat. By this method, less fuel would be used than with a single large engine combined with afterburning, and if the two engines were 'stacked' one above and behind the other, double the thrust of a single unit could be obtained while the frontal area was increased by only fifty per cent. Most Soviet and American designers had tried to design a fighter capable of achieving supersonic speeds in level flight without the use of afterburners, but without success. (The Sapphires were later supplemented by more than 2,000lb (900kg) of re-heat thrust.)

Even more radical were the wings, with 60 degrees of sweep to minimize wave drag; had the trailing edge been continuous they would have been of delta form like those of the FD.2. Petter rejected the delta wing, however, because it would not provide sufficient control during certain flight contingencies and the positive control

English Electric were helped greatly in the development of the P.1 by data provided by WG768, the Short SB.5, a scaled down test-bed powered by a 3,500lb (1,600kg) thrust Rolls-Royce Derwent and fitted with a non-retractable undercarriage, adjustable for centre of gravity variations. The SB.5 first flew on 2 December 1952. *Aeroplane*

provided by a tailplane would not then have been available. A deep notch was cut into the trailing edge of the shoulder wings at about fifty per cent of each half span, with the ailerons being carried along the outer transverse trailing edge to the tips. To avoid pitch-up problems, the sharply swept-back, all-moving tailplane was mounted below the level of the wing (beneath the lower tailpipe) on the slab-sided fuselage. Advanced avionics, powered controls and a very clever retraction of the main undercarriage wheels into the thin wings were other notable aspects of the design. The wings, despite having a thickness/chord ratio of only five per cent, gave a very reasonable fuel storage area, and kept the fuselage free of fuel tanks – a feature which would hamper the Lightning in later years. However, in 1947 the RAF wanted only a short-range, rapid climb interceptor. Fuel was not then the main consideration.

WG760, the first prototype P.1, was fitted with two 7,500lb static thrust sapphires fed throough the single nose intake which was bifurcated internally to each engine. It had a delta fin with a rounded tip, and an uncranked wing leading edge. To minimize wave drag, the top of the hood was virtually flush with the upper line of the fuselage. In 1950, Petter left English Electric to join Folland

WG763, the second F23/49 P.1A prototype, with ventral tank fitted, rolled out at Warton in July 1955. Roland Beamont first flew this aircraft on 18 July and it made its first public appearance at Farnborough in September that year. BAe via Hugh Trevor

Aircraft and responsibility for the design and subsequent development of the P.1 passed to F.W. (later Sir Freddie) Page.

The first indications that Britain had a world beating supersonic design which could catapult the RAF into the supersonic age sparked understandable euphoria, as Sqn Ldr Dave Seward confirms:

'It has an air intake right in the nose,' the wing commander from the CFE said. 'Wings swept so far back that the ailerons are on the wingtips, and it has two engines – one on top of the other,' he added. 'Furthermore, it can climb to 36,000ft in under five minutes and it flies at one and a half times the speed of sound.' Then he said, 'It's so secret, that you should forget what I've told you.' Well, how could we forget such an aircraft when we were flying Meteor 8s which could just about achieve Mach 0.82, almost out of control? The idea was to have a rocket pack fitted underneath the fuselage to give extra thrust for acceleration and combat. Thankfully the rocket pack, which seemed to have a habit of blowing up no matter which firm made them, was dispensed with, and a ventral fuel tank was installed in its place.

The P.1 prototype was finished in the spring of 1954 and was transferred by road to the A&AEE, Boscombe Down, for its first flight on 4 August 1954 in the hands

P1.A WG760, the F23/49 prototype at Boscombe Down in July 1954 for final checking before engine runs. BAe via Hugh Trevor

Test pilot Roland 'Bee' Beamont first flew WG760 on 4 August 1954 from Boscombe Down. It is seen here taking off at Farnborough during the September 1955 show. *Aeroplane*

of English Electric's chief test pilot, Wg Cdr Roland P. 'Bee' Beamont. Beamont reached Mach 0.85 on the first flight. On the third flight, on 11 August, WG760 became the first British aircraft to exceed Mach 1 in level flight, but it was not realized that this had been achieved until the following day when the aircraft's speed was accurately computed! On 18 July 1955, P.1A WG763, the second prototype, flew for the first time, and that September it gave its first public demonstration when it performed at the SBAC Display at Farnborough. The P.1A differed from the P.1 in having a pair of 30mm Aden cannon in the nose and American-style toe-brakes. In the course of the development of the P.1 into the anticipated fighter, WG760 was re-designated P.1A, the fighter project becoming P.1B. WG763 was armed with a pair of 30mm Aden canon fitted in the upper nose decking and flew with her heading edge flaps fixed in place, as they had been found to be superfluous.3,4,5

A decision was taken in 1954 to order three P.1B prototypes: XA847, XA853 and XA856. They would be powered by 200-Series Rolls-Royce Avons with four-stage reheat, and have provision for a Ferranti AI (Airborne Intercept) 23 (Airpass) radar and two de Havilland Blue Jay (later Firestreak) infra-red homing missiles. This brought about a virtually complete redesign of the aircraft, although the

general aerodynamic layout and concept were retained. The oval intake at the nose was changed to an annular design with a central shock cone; the airbrakes were modified; plain instead of area-increasing flaps appeared on the wing; and the cockpit canopy was raised. Handling trials

revealed that a larger fin area was desirable for better stability and this was increased later by thirty per cent. The change to 200-series Avons with re-heat nearly doubled the thrust available. An order for a pre-production batch of twenty P.1Bs, XG307–313 and XG325–337, plus three test airframes, came soon after, and was followed, in November 1956, by an order for nineteen production aircraft, designated F.1, and a non-flying specimen. RAF plans for an all-weather heavy interceptor (OR.329) capable of carrying two large radar-homing missiles (originally called Red Dean, later Red Hebe) never reached fruition and the RAF had to settle for the lightweight Lightning armed with clear-weather IR-homing missiles.

XA847, the first prototype P.1B, exceeded Mach 1 without re-heat on its maiden flight on 4 April 1957 from Warton, with 'Bee' Beamont at the controls. Ironically, that same day, Duncan Sandys, the Minister of Defence, published the now infamous White Paper forecasting the end of manned combat aircraft (including a supersonic manned bomber) and their replacement by missiles! In part it said:

In view of the good progress already made [with surface-to-air missiles], the Government has come to the conclusion that the RAF is

Air-to-air view of WG760 in the hands of Roland Beamont, taken by Charles E. Brown from a Gloster Meteor. The P.1A's leading edge chord-wise slot is very visible. *Aeroplane*

unlikely to have a requirement for fighter aircraft of types more advanced than the supersonic P.1, and work on such projects will stop.

Fortunately, the P.1 remained in being, for the simple reason that supersonic interceptors were needed to protect the V-bomber force based in the United Kingdom. From now on, the role of Fighter Command was to be purely defensive.

In April 1958 the first deliveries of the pre-production P.1Bs began. The first (XG307) flew on 3 April 1958. On 23 October, the name 'Lightning' was bestowed on the P.1B at Farnborough. During the year the idea of installing a Napier Double-Scorpion rocket pack, as had been fitted to a Canberra to create a new world altitude record in 1957, was dropped. On 25 November 1958 XA847 became the first British aircraft ever to fly at Mach 2, bettering this achievement on 6 January 1959. The first F.1 production example flew on 30 October 1959. It had two Rolls-Royce Avon RA.24R 210 engines, each giving 11,250lb (5,100kg) static thrust at maximum cold power and 14,430lb (6,600kg) static thrust in full re-heat. With an all-up weight of 34,000lb, (15,500kg) the 28,000lb (12,700kg) thrust of the engines provided a very good

This head-on shot of WG760 shows the pedigree of Petter's clean, aerodynamic design. *Aeroplane*

power/weight ratio. It had two 30mm Aden cannon in the upper front fuselage and could have two more fitted in the lower fuselage in lieu of the missile pack. It had the Ferranti AI 23 Airpass radar in the nose shock cone and carried two Firestreak infra-red missiles, one on each side of the fuselage.

There were no dramatic problems during the development flying stage with the P.1 series. However, on 1 October 1959, test pilot John W.C. Squier was fortunate to escape death after ejecting from XL628, the prototype T.4 two-seat variant, which 'Bee' Beamont had first flown from Warton on 6 May. At 11.15am on the morning of 1 October, Squier took off from Warton and climbed to 35,000ft (11,500m) before accelerating to Mach 1.7 over the Irish Sea. His brief was to note engine data at every 0.1 Mach above Mach 1.0 to Mach 1.7, when he was to climb to 40,000ft (13,000m), stabilize, and make a 360 degree roll to starboard using maximum aileron with his feet off the rudder pedals. This manoeuvre had previously been accomplished in single-seat Lightnings but it had never before been tried in the two-seat version. Squier reached Mach 1.7 and, 20m (32km) due west of St. Bees Head, and carried out the aileron turn. A high-speed roll immediately developed and when Squier centralized the controls to halt it, XL628 yawed violently to starboard in a manoeuvre far fiercer than had previously been encountered during maximum aileron rolls in the single-seat Lightning.

Squier knew that a structural failure had occurred and the aircraft was now totally uncontrollable, yawing violently right and left, and pitching. He had to get out, fast.

XA853, the second of three P.1B prototypes, was used for gun trials and is seen here at the firing-in butts. Pilots in the AFDS discovered that gun firing in a Lightning was not as successful as missile firing and they proved that the pilot attack gunsight was very basic and not so good under g conditions using lots of angle. However, guns were a very useful weapon to have and almost all pilots mourned their passing in the F.3 which was introduced in 1962. Guns were only reinstated in 1970 when it was decided to fit two Aden cannon into the front of the ventral tank of the F.6s. via Pete Nash

NS853, the second of the three P.1B prototypes, which was flown for the first time by D. de Villiers on 5 September 1957. Mostly it was used on gun trials and gas-concentration tests. It lost its fin during an accidental canopy ejection and on its fifty-first flight test pilot Jimmy Dell suffered an in-flight fire. via Ray Biddle

He reached up, noticing as he did so that the pitot tube was bent right across the air intake, and grabbed the seat blind; and the seemingly slow-motion ejection sequence was put in motion. The canopy was whisked away into the void and the Martin-Baker seat fired him out of the doomed Lightning. As he exited Squier took a blow to his right elbow as he hit the SARAH (search and rescue homing) battery, and both his legs from his knees downwards were badly bruised by the ascent. He tried to hold the blind to his face in the full force of the blast, which blew away his oxygen mask, but his arms were painfully wrenched away, almost out of their sockets. (Two compressed vertebrae were also diagnosed later.) Then the seat fell away, but the parachute failed to deploy. Squier only became aware of this when he passed through cloud and could see that the sea was getting ominously close! Instantly, he pulled the manual over-ride and at last the parachute deployed.

Squier plunged into the water and sank beneath the waves. He managed to inflate his life preserver and, as he soared to the surface, he became entangled in the shroud lines until he was able to disentangle himself and release the parachute. Fortunately, the dinghy in the PSP (Personal Survival Pack) had inflated and it now floated invitingly nearby. He

managed to clamber aboard but it was full of sea water, and in the absence of the bailer he had to use a shoe to scoop out the water. Then he rigged the SARAH homing beacon and its aerial, but to his dismay, the apparatus failed to work – the high-tension battery, which was one week beyond its inspection date, was flat.

For two hours Squier bobbed around on the sea before an amphibian approached. Squier managed to pull the pin on the two

star signal rocket, but it refused to fire and the aircraft failed to spot the tiny dinghy. Another hour passed and the aircraft returned, but again the signal rocket failed to work. Ironically, the third and final rocket worked perfectly, but by now the amphibian had departed.

Squier spent the rest of the day adrift on the sea and he must have begun to despair when darkness settled. He had still not been found the next morning when rain and bad visibility cloaked the horizon. However, he could make out what he thought must be the east coast of Ireland. (It was actually Wigtown Bay in western Scotland.) He tried paddling but all he succeeded in doing was to go around in circles. A piece of driftwood helped and he eventually reached a point about 200yd (180m) from the shore. Finally, after passing ships hour after endless hour had seemingly ignored his whistles for help, Squier berthed alongside a tower in a small inlet, and eventually he managed to reach the shore from where he was able to stumble to the safety of a house. In the garden was a matron from an adjoining school who told Squier that she had seen the story concerning his disappearance in the newspapers. He had spent thirty-six hours on the surface of the sea.

Squier was rushed to Stranraer Cottage Hospital where, the next day, he was examined by four doctors from the Institute of Aviation Medicine at Farnborough, who diagnosed the two compressed vertebrae. His eyes and middle

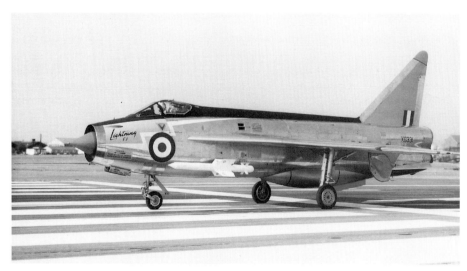

XG331, one of the twenty P.1B pre-production batch, which was first flown on 14 May 1959 by Jimmy Squier at Samlesbury. This aircraft was rebuilt following damage sustained after the No.1 engine starter exploded. It was later used for tropical trials in Aden in 1960. Ron Clarke

XA847, first of the three P.1B prototypes, which first flew on 4 April 1957 in the hands of 'Bee' Beamont. On 25 November 1958 it became the first British aircraft to fly at Mach 2. The Lightning, when it came into service in 1960, doubled the performance of the then-best RAF fighter (The Hunter) in front-line service. It was lightly armed, with only two Firestreak air-to-air infra-red guided weapons and two Aden cannon, but its ability to manoeuvre with the best and out-climb all of them gave its pilots an advantage which set them apart from others. The F-104 Starfighter had, eventually, the same straight-line top speeds but could never match the Lightning's rate of turn at any speed. It was not until the F-15 came along fifteen years later that the Lightning had any real competitor. *Aeroplane*

ears had also haemorrhaged and he became deaf after a week, fortunately only temporarily. Two weeks later, he was airlifted from West Freugh to Warton and was admitted to Preston Royal Infirmary, where he spent another month. The outcome of the investigation into the cause of the disaster found that the thickening of the forward part of the fuselage to accommodate the second seat had reduced the Lightning's stability, particularly with two Firestreaks attached. It would be eight months later before John Squier was able to fly again.

The F.1 Into Service

The Lightning entered service in December 1959 with the delivery to the AFDS (Air Fighting Development Squadron) at Coltishall of three pre-

production P.1Bs. These were followed, in July 1960, by the first production F.1s for 74 'Tiger' Squadron, also at Coltishall. Sqn Ldr John F.G. Howe, an assured, thirty year-old South African, (the 'Tigers' second South African CO, A.G. 'Sailor' Malan having been the first – August 1940–March 1941), who took command in February 1960, said at the time:

We know that we can catch the bombers and, going on past experience, we know we can outfight any fighter equivalent to the USAF Century series. The performance of the aircraft, coupled with the ease with which it is flown, gives the pilots confidence, and the fact that it is felt to be the best fighter in operational service in the world today gives our Lightning pilots the highest possible morale.

Born in East London, John Howe went on to attend the Military College at

Squadron Leader John Howe, CO 74 Squadron at RAF Coltishall in 1960. AVM John Howe Collection

Lightning Specifications

P.1A: Two non-afterburning Armstrong Siddeley Sapphire 5 engines rated at 7,500lb (3,400kg) (later rated at 9,200lb (4,200kg) in re-heated version). VHF radio (later replaced by UHF). Martin-Baker 4BS ejection seat. First flown (WG760), 4 August 1954 at Boscombe Down. Became first British aircraft to exceed Mach 1 in level flight on 11 August 1954.

P.1B. Two Rolls-Royce RA.24 Avon engines rated at 11,250lb (5,100kg) dry, later increased to 13,300lb (6,000kg) with installation of a four-stage afterburner (Avon 200R). Martin-Baker 4BS ejection seat. XG307 became the first aircraft built at Samlesbury, and first of the Development Batch (twenty aircraft) to fly, on 3 April 1958.

F.1: Two Rolls-Royce Avon 210R engines rated at 14,430lb (6,500kg). First production version. Flew for the first time on 29 October 1959. First aircraft (XM135) released to the CFE on 29 June 1960. First Squadron delivery (XM165 to 74 Squadron). Ferranti Airpass AI 23 radar and fire-control system, VHF radio (later replaced by UHF). Martin-Baker 4BS ejection seat. Four 30mm Aden cannon with 130 rounds each in nose, or two Firestreak missiles, plus two 30mm Aden cannon with 130 rounds each.

F.1A: Two Rolls-Royce Avon 210R engines with revised, four-position re-heat throttle control. First flown (XM169) on 15 August 1960. F.1A first entered service (XM172) with 56 Squadron on 4 December 1960. First version with detachable in-flight refuelling capability, probe being fitted beneath port wing. UHF radio, external cable ducts to missile pylon positions. Martin-Baker 4BSA Mks 1 and 2 ejection seat. Airpass AI 23 radar and fire-control system. Four 30mm Aden cannon with 130 rounds each in nose or two Firestreak missiles, plus two 30mm Aden cannon.

F.2: Two Rolls-Royce Avon 210R engines with revised tailpipes. First flown (XN723) on 11 July 1961. First F.2 (XN771) delivered to the CFE on 4 November 1962. Entered service (XN775) with 19 Squadron on 17 December 1962. Revised cockpit including partial OR.946 Flight Control System specification, liquid

oxygen breathing system, standby turbo generator for DC electric supply (identified by small cooling scoop on dorsal spine). Steerable nose-wheel in place of the earlier fixed nose-wheel. Airpass AI 23 radar and fire-control system. Martin-Baker 4BSA Mks 1 and 2 ejection seat. Four 30mm Aden cannon with 130 rounds each in nose or two Firestreak missiles, plus two 30mm Aden cannon with 130 rounds each.

F.2A: Two Rolls-Royce Avon 211R engines. F.2 rebuilt to incorporate some F.6 features, including kinked and cambered wing, square-cut tail fin, enlarged ventral fuel tank. Airpass AI 23 radar and fire-control system. F.2A released, 1 January 1968. Martin-Baker 4BSA Mks 1 and 2 ejection seat. Four 30mm Aden cannon with 130 rounds each in nose or two Firestreak missiles plus two/four 30mm Aden cannon with 130 rounds each. Last F.2A (XN788) delivered to RAF Germany on 22 July 1970.

F.3: Two Rolls-Royce Avon 301R engines, 12,690lb (5,800kg) dry thrust and 16,360lb (7,400kg) re-heat. First flown (XP693) on 16 June 1962. First delivery (XP695), to the CFE on 1 January 1964. First entered service (XP700) with 74 Squadron on 14 April 1964. (First flight of F.3 to F.6 standard (XP697), 17.4.64.) Square-cut fin of fifteen per cent greater area, built-in cannon armament deleted, more advanced AI 23B radar and fire-control system which allowed equipment with either two Red Top collision-course missiles or two Firestreaks. Full OR.946 Integrated Flight Control System instrumentation. Martin-Baker 4BSB Mks 1 and 2 ejection seat. Last F.3 (XR751) delivered to the RAF on 16 January 1968.

F.3A: Two Rolls-Royce Avon 301R engines. Kinked and cambered wing of greater area, and enlarged ventral fuel tank. Airpass AI 23 radar and fire-control system. Martin-Baker 4BSB Mks 1 and 2 ejection seat. Two Firestreak or Red Top missiles.

T.4: Two Rolls-Royce Avon 210R engines. Two-seat, dual-controlled trainer version of the F.1A. Aden cannon deleted. Airpass AI 23 radar and fire-control system. Two Martin-Baker 4BST Mks 1 and 2 ejection seats. Two Firestreak missiles normally carried.

T.5: Two Rolls-Royce Avon 301R engines. Two-

seat, dual-controlled trainer version of the F.3, able to carry two Firestreak or Red Top missiles. Airpass AI 23 radar and fire-control system. Two Martin-Baker 4BST Mks 1 and 2 ejection seats.

F.6: Two Rolls-Royce Avon 301R engines. First production F.6 (XR752) flown on 16 June 1965. Released to the CFE (XR753) on 16 November 1965. Entered service with 5 Squadron on 10 December 1965. Full production version of the F.3A with provision to carry overwing fuel tanks. Some small improvements to equipment, such as Airpass AI 23 radar and fire-control system. Martin-Baker 4BSB Mks 1 and 2 ejection seat. Two 30mm Aden cannon with 130 rounds each in ventral pod; plus two Firestreak or Red Top missiles, or forty-eight 2in (25mm) rockets in place of the missile pack. Last F.6 (XS938), delivered to RAF on 25 August 1967.

F.53: Two Rolls-Royce Avon 302C engines, 11,100lb (5,000kg) static thrust, 16,300lb (7,400kg) with re-heat. Export version of the F.6 with capability to carry a wide range of ordnance from overwing or underwing pylon hard points: two Firestreak or Red Top: Two 30mm Aden cannon with 130 rounds each in ventral pod; forty-four 2in (25mm) rockets in place of missile pack; two 1,000lb (450kg) HE bombs; thirty-six 68mm (2.7in) SNEB rockets in two Matra Type 155 launchers; or five Vinten Type 360 70mm cameras (1x6in f2.8 lens; 2x3in f2.0 lens; 2x1.75in f2.8 lens or 2x12in f2.0 lens) in reconnaissance pack. Ferranti Type AI 23S radar (export version of the AI 23B; approach and attack computers; search and attack display unit (CRT); radar control and mode selector switch; and visual display cine recorder. Light fighter sight). Martin-Baker 4BSB ejection seat.

T.55: Two Rolls-Royce Avon 302C engines. Export version of the T.5, with enlarged ventral fuel tank, kinked and cambered wing, and Type AI 23S radar. Martin-Baker BS4C ejection seat. Two Firestreak or Red Top missiles.

Jet fuel for the Lightning was AVTUR 50 (NATO AVTAG) with FSII (fuel systems icing inhibitor).

Robert's Heights, now Voortrekkerhoogte, and in 1950 he joined the South African Air Force. In 1951 he flew as an F-51 pilot in 2 'Cheetah' Squadron SAAF in Korea, later becoming a flying instructor before coming to Britain and joining the RAF in 1954. His first job was instructing on Vampires and in 1956 he moved over to the Hunter with 222 Squadron. That same year he did a four-month detachment for the Suez crisis, landing on the beach with Royal Marine Commandos to direct air strikes on the port. In 1959 he went on the day fighter combat leader course. A short spell of instructing followed before he took over the Tigers.

F.1s, though, were slow to arrive and Lightning spares were almost non-existent. Although seven Lightnings had arrived by August only one was operational. Then it was announced that the Tigers were to fly four Lightnings each day during Farnborough week in September! However, this helped speed deliveries and these enabled the squadron to begin work-up at Boscombe Down late that summer. Then the aircraft were back in the hangars at Coltishall again for much needed maintenance so that they could take part in Battle of Britain commemorations. Ground crews worked right around the clock, dealing with constant electrical failures and myriad other complex teething troubles to keep six to twelve Lightnings on the line at one time. 74 Squadron would not become fully operational until the following year. Progress was one step forward, two steps back. A few days after a three-day 'meet the press' event in February 1962, a serious Lightning fire hazard was discovered in the area between the ventral tanks and the No.1 engine and jet-pipe. As a temporary measure, the ventral tanks were removed for flight until the problem was solved by a manufacturer's modification. Finally, by the end of April, all 'Tiger' pilots had completed their conversion to fly the aircraft by both day and night.

Production of the twenty-eight improved F.1A version and twenty-one of its T.4 two-seat equivalent continued under the auspices of a new organization – In 1960, English Electric Aviation were merged with Bristol Aircraft, Vickers Armstrong (Aircraft) and Hunting Aircraft to create the British Aircraft Corporation (BAC). The F.1A had provision for a detachable in-flight refuelling probe under the port wing and improved

XG336, one of the twenty-strong P.1B pre-production batch, with Stage 2 fin and four Aden cannon, is towed out of the hangar at Samlesbury. This aircraft was first flown on 25 August 1959 by J.W.C. Squier and was delivered to the AFDS at RAF Coltishall in December 1959 where it was coded 'C', seen here with a Javelin and Hunter of the AFDS. BAe via Hugh Trevor/via Bruce Hopkins

windscreen rain dispersal. The other main difference was a UHF radio in place of the F.1's VHF. It also benefitted from a general cleaning-up of the electrics and layout (strakes were added). Later, all F.1s were modified to F.1A standard. The T.4 was basically a side-by-side two-seat version of the F.1A. It looked awkward and bulbous, but its performance was only very marginally down on that of the single-seaters. On

the squadrons it was classed as a front-line aircraft. All squadrons had one T.4 and the LTF (Lightning Training Flight), soon to become 226 Operational Conversion Unit (OCU), had eight initially. The first F.1A (XM169) flew on 16 August 1960 (the first production T.4 having flown on 15 July) and the first examples were issued to the Wattisham wing. 56 Squadron began receiving the first ones late in 1960, and

'Treble One' Squadron began receiving theirs in early 1961.

In 1962 another Lightning test pilot, George P. Aird, cheated death when he was forced to eject from P.1B XG332 near Hatfield on 13 September after an engine fire. Aird had just completed a re-heat test up to Mach 1.7 off the south coast of England at 36,000ft. All had gone well until during the return flight the test engine twice refused to relight. Aird's third attempt succeeded but fuel which should have been vented was retained in the rear fuselage by a blocked drain and eventually ignited via a small crack in the tailpipe.

As Aird descended at 400kt through 15,000ft, some 15–20 miles north-east of Hatfield, a 'double re-heat' engine fire warning glowed on the instrument panel. He weaved from side to side but was unable to confirm the extent of the problem. With the Hatfield runway in sight he decided to attempt a landing, hoping that it was only

F.1A XM216/P which was delivered to 111 Squadron on 29 August 1961. The engine starter exploded at Coltishall on 24 June 1965 and the aircraft was returned to 226 OCU in September 1966 after repair at Warton. Mick Cartwright

P.1B XG332 was first flown on 29 May 1959 by Jimmy Squier and was used by de Havilland for Firestreak and Red Top trials. This aircraft was lost on 13 September 1962 when George P. Aird was forced to eject from XG332 just short of the Hatfield runway after an engine fire. Aird had just completed a re-heat test up to Mach 1.7 off the south coast of England at 36,000ft (16,000m). via Peter Winning

Lightnings on the production line at Samlesbury. via Hugh Trevor

the fire warning light that had malfunctioned. He decided not to jettison the large ventral fuel tank as it could seriously injure anyone on the ground. Unfortunately, Runway 24, which was nearer, was not in use and Aird had to make for Runway 06, which proved a shade too far for the Lightning to remain airborne. Just ten seconds from touchdown, the tailplane actuator anchorage, weakened by the fire, failed completely and XG332 pitched violently upward. Aird instinctively pushed the stick forward and was horribly surprised to find that, when he waggled it around between his legs, it appeared to be disconnected. Aird pulled the ejection seat face blind and was blasted out of the doomed Lightning. He landed in the middle of a large greenhouse by the St. Albans Road at Smallford. Although he suffered no lasting back injuries, both his legs were smashed.

New Variants

The next stage of the Lightning's development was the introduction of the F.2,

Prototype T.4 XL628, the first two-seat trainer, which was first flown on 6 May 1959 by 'Bee' Beamont, seen here in formation with P.1B XG331 during a test flight from Warton. XL628 was lost over the Irish Sea on 1 October 1959. The pilot, Jimmy Squier, ejected safely, although he had a very uncomfortable time in a dinghy before coming ashore in Scotland. *Aeroplane*

DAILY MIRROR, Tuesday, October 9, 1962 PAGE 17

A JET FIGHTER NOSE-DIVES TO DESTRUCTION AS THE PILOT IS CATAPULTED OUT

George Aird drops in on the tomatoes ..

150 FT TO GO—AND A MIRROR READER'S CAMERA CATCHES THE ASTONISHING MOMENT

GEORGE AIRD is a test pilot who was flying a faster-than-sound Lightning jet fighter that suddenly started to roll out of control.

Jim Meads is a Mirror reader who was trying to amuse his two children, Paul, 4, and Barry, 3, by taking a picture of them as the Lightning was coming in to land at the De Havilland airfield near their home at Hatfield, Herts.

The idea was to picture the children against the airfield background.

But at 300ft. the jet was roaring nose-first to destruction at 200 miles an hour.

Pilot George Aird, 34,

pressed the button of his ejector-seat . . . an explosive capsule shot him out—and up. The cockpit canopy flew away to his right.

Then he began the headlong dive for earth, the seat trailing behind him with its half-opened parachute.

Captured

One hundred and fifty feet to go . . .

And reader Meads pressed his button releasing the shutter of his camera at 1,000th of a second at an exposure of f.8.

He captured the astonishing moment of life or death for George Aird as a farm-worker on a tractor jerked his head round to watch.

It was life . . .

George crashed through a green house roof—into tomato plants. He broke his legs, got a black eye and a full share of cuts.

Now he is recovering in hospital at St. Albans, and he says: "Thank God for those tomatoes. . ."

Thanks

Reader Meads took his pictures to the Ministry of Aviation for use in an inquiry into the accident.

Yesterday they released them, thanked him for the "excellent photographs" and for his eye-witness story of the accident. It was on September 13.

Test pilot George will never forget it.

Nor will reader Jim. . . .

THE INFERNO
HE ESCAPED

The end of George Aird's Lightning jet fighter. An explosion, a mountain of swirling smoke. Aird crashed into a greenhouse to the left of the wreckage, landing among tomato plants.

The man on a tractor watches helplessly . . . George Aird, ejector-seat trailing, falls to earth alongside his doomed plane. Zooming away on extreme left: His cockpit canopy.

Centre spread from the *Daily Mirror* of Tuesday 9 October 1962, showing George Aird's dramatic ejection at Hatfield on 13 September 1962.

Five F.1s, XM135/D, XM136/E, XM137/F, XM138/G and XM165, were delivered to the AFDS at Leconfield in June 1960 and on 11 July (pictured) were flown to Coltishall. XM165, piloted by Flt Lt Bruce Hopkins, has no markings or unit insignia as it was earmarked for 74 Squadron. via Bruce Hopkins

Specifications

Model	Span	Length	Height	Wing Area (sq ft)	Power Plant	Empty (Loaded) Weight	Max Speed	Service Ceiling	Armament
P.1A	34ft 10in	49ft 8in	17ft 3in	458.5	Arm-Siddeley Sapphire 5	22,221lb (27,077lb)	Mach 1.53 (1011mph) @ 36,000 ft	55,000ft	2 × 30mm Aden cannon
P.1B	"	55ft 3in	19ft 5in	"	RR Avon 200R	24,816lb (31,831lb)	Mach 2.1 (1390mph) @ 40,000ft	55,000ft	2 × 30mm Aden cannon
F.1	"	"	19ft 7in	"	RR Avon 200R	25,753lb	Mach 2.3 (1500mph) @ 36,000ft	60,000ft	4 × 30mm Aden cannon or 2 × Firestreak AAM +2 × 30mm
F.1A	"	"	"	"	RR Avon 210R	25,757lb	Mach 2.3 (1500mph) @ 36,000ft	60,000ft	4 × 30mm Aden cannon or 2 × Firestreak AAM +2 × 30mm
F.2	"	"	"	"	RR Avon 210R	27,000lb	Mach 2.3 (1500mph) @ 36,000ft	60,000ft	4 × 30mm Aden cannon or 2 × Firestreak AAM +2 × 30mm
F.2A	"	"	"	474.5	RR Avon 211R	27,500lb	Mach 2.3 (1500mph) @ 36,000ft	60,000ft+	4 × 30mm Aden cannon or 2mm Aden cannon
F.3	"	"	"	458.5	RR Avon 301R	26,905lb	Mach 2.3 (1500mph) @ 36,000ft	60,000ft+	2 × Firestreak AAm or 2 × Red Top AAM
F.3A	"	"	"	474.5	RR Avon 301R	28,041lb (41,700lb)	Mach 2.3 (1500mph) @ 36,000ft	60,000ft	2 × Firestreak AAM or 2 ×
T.4	"	"	"	458.5	RR Avon 210R	27,000	Mach 2.3 (1500mph) @ 36,000ft	60,000ft+	2 × Firestreak AAM
T.5	"	"	"	458.5	RR Avon 301R	27,000lb	Mach 2.3 (1500mph) @ 36,000ft	60,000ft+	2 × Firestreak AAM or 2 × Red Top AAM
F.6	"	"	"	474.5	RR Avon 301R	28,041lb	Mach 2.3 (1500mph) @ 40,000ft	60,000ft+	2 × Firestreak or 2 × Red Top + 2 × 30mm Aden cannon in ventral tank, 48 × 2" rockets in place of missile pack.
F.53	"	"	"	474	RR Avon 301	28,041lb	Mach 2.3 (1500mph) @ 36,000ft	60,000ft+	As F.6 + 2 × 1,000lb bombs, 4 SNEB Matra rocket packs & Vinten camera recce pack.
T.55	"	"	"	474	RR Avon 301	28,041lb	Mach 2.3 (1500mph) @ 36,000ft	60,000ft+	2 × Firestreak AAM or 2 × Red Top AAM

F.2 XN725 was one of a batch of forty-four built, the first to have a cambered wing, and was first flown on 31 March 1962 by Jimmy Dell. Seen here fitted with test overwing tanks, it was converted to the F.3 prototype and fitted with Avon 301 engines. It operated for a time at RAE Bedford for Concorde 'noise' and high-speed trials. BAe

F.2s XN774/775/776 and 777 on the production line at Samlesbury. XN774 first flew on 27 September 1962 and joined 19 Squadron in February 1963. XN776 first flew on 18 October 1962 and also joined 19 Squadron. XN775 first flew on 1 October 1962 and joined 19 Squadron on 17 December 1962. XN777 was first flown on 13 July 1962 and was assigned to the AFDS. It was later converted to F.2A standard and joined 19 Squadron in 1968. *Aeroplane*

F.2s nearing completion on the production line at Samlesbury. *Aeroplane*

F.1 XM165, one of twenty production models for the RAF. This aircraft was first flown on 30 May 1960 by 'Bee' Beamont and became the first Lightning to enter RAF squadron service, when it joined 74 'Tiger' Squadron at RAF Coltishall on 11 July 1960. It was subsequently operated by 226 OCU from October 1963 until October 1966, when it was scrapped. *Aeroplane*

On 16 August 1960 Coltishall celebrated '20 Years of Fighter Aircraft' with a uniquely special formation of aircraft ranging from Hurricane LF363, flown by Sqn Ldr Jack Ives; Spitfire XIX PM631, flown by Sqn Ldr F.J.F. 'Dickie' Dickinson; F.8 Meteor (target tug), flown by Flt Lt P.F. Hart; 74 Squadron Hunter 6, flown by Flg Off Martin Bee; 23 Squadron Javelin FAW.8, crewed by Flt Lt Barry Holmes and Flg Off John Wheeler; while Flt Lt Bruce Hopkins flew Lightning XM137. *via Bruce Hopkins*

Squadron Leader Dave Seward, CO 56 Squadron. Dave Seward Collection

F.3 XP697 was flown for the first time on 18 July 1963 by D.M. Knight from Samlesbury and was converted to F.6 configuration in August 1963, It is shown here with overwing tanks, which it tested during a support programme. It was also used on the programme to test 2in (50mm) rockets and large ventral tanks.
Aeroplane

Lightning Production Totals

Model	Registrations	Number	Manufacturer
P.1A	WG760,WG763	2	English Electric Co. Ltd.
P.1A	test airframe (WG765)	(1)	English Electric Co. Ltd.
P.1B	XA847,XA853,XA856	3	English Electric Co. Ltd.
P.1B	XG307/XG337	20*	English Electric Co. Ltd.
P.1B	test airframes	(3)	English Electric Co. Ltd.
F.1	XM134–XM147		English Electric Co. Ltd.
	XM163–XM168	20	English Electric Co. Ltd.
F.1A	XM169–XM192	24	English Electric Co. Ltd.
	XM213–XM216	4	English Electric Co. Ltd.
F.1A	XM217–218	Not built	English Electric Co. Ltd.
F.1A	test airframe	(1)	English Electric Co. Ltd.
T.4/P.11	XL628–XL629 (prototype)	2	English Electric Co. Ltd.
T.4	XM966–XM974	9	English Electric Co. Ltd.
F.2A	XM987–XM997	11	English Electric Co. Ltd.
F.2	XN723–XN735	13	English Electric Co. Ltd.
	XN767–XN797	31	English Electric Co. Ltd.
F.3	XP693–XP708	16	British Aircraft Corp. Ltd.
	XP735–XP751	17	British Aircraft Corp. Ltd.
F.3 ER/6int	XR752–XR767	16	British Aircraft Corp. Ltd.
F.6	XR768–XR773	6	British Aircraft Corp. Ltd.
	XS893–XS938	45	British Aircraft Corp. Ltd.
	XS918–XS938	21	British Aircraft Corp. Ltd.
T.5	XS416–XS423	8	British Aircraft Corp. Ltd.
	XS449–XS460	12	British Aircraft Corp. Ltd.
	XV328–XV329	2	British Aircraft Corp. Ltd.
T.55	55–711–716	6	British Aircraft Corp. Ltd.
	55–410–411	2	British Aircraft Corp. Ltd.
F.53	53–667–699	33	British Aircraft Corp. Ltd.
	53–700	1	British Aircraft Corp. Ltd.
	53–412–423	12	British Aircraft Corp. Ltd.

Total 334 (5)

*Pre-production batch

P.1A	2 prototypes
P.1B	3 prototypes
	20 development batch aircraft
F.1	19
F.1A	28
F.2	13 (5 converted to F.52)
F.2A	31
F.3	63
T.4	21
T.5	23
F.6	62
F.53	46
T.55	8

which externally resembled the F.1A and had the same radar and Avon 210 engines, but the latter with fully-variable after-burning in place of the earlier four-stage system. It also embodied a number of other refinements: a much improved cockpit layout, slightly better automatic flight control system and all-weather navigational aids, and liquid oxygen (LOX). XN723, the F.2 prototype, first flew on 11 July 1961 and was delivered to AFDS at Binbrook in November 1962. A month later, 19 Squadron at Leconfield became the first operational squadron in the RAF to equip with the F.2. It was joined, late in 1962, by 92 Squadron, which received its first Lightnings in April 1963, the Leconfield Wing becoming fully operational that summer. At the end of 1965 both squadrons became part of 2nd Tactical Air Force in RAF Germany, later becoming the Gütersloh wing. Altogether, forty-four Lightnings were built as F.2s, some thirty-one of them later being modified to F.2A standard with cranked and cambered wing leading edges; a large angular vertical tail; and a 610-gallon ventral tank which was part of the fuselage, and thus could not be jettisoned, in place of the earlier 250-gallon jettisonable tank.

What was the performance like on these early aircraft? Dave Seward makes the point that,

> If you look at the air intake of a Lightning, the radome forms a centre body which offsets the effects of compressibility over the engines as the speed is increased into the supersonic range, and theoretically, the Lightning could achieve Mach 2.4, or two-and-a-half times the speed of sound, before the supersonic shock wave angles back into the air intake, which would cause the engines to stall, and possibly flame out. This rarely occurred, however, because to achieve Mach 2.4 you would use an enormous amount of fuel and with the pointed fins, the Mks.1, 1a, 2, and T.4, could lose directional control at very high Mach numbers if harsh control movements were attempted, so these early aircraft were restricted to Mach 1.7.

To overcome the limitations of these early models, the F.3 was introduced in 1962. It had a larger, squared-off fin, and bigger Avon 301 engines, each giving 12,690lb dry thrust, and 16,360lb in reheat. These aircraft were cleared to Mach 2. The F.3 had the upgraded AI 23b fire control system with greater range and better definition, together with a visual identification mode for interrogating targets

XM967, the first T.4 to fly when Jimmy Dell took it aloft from Bristol on 30 March 1962. This aircraft was later used at Farnborough and it became 8433M. BAe

[OR.946 with Mk.2 master reference gyro]. But of course, you do not get anything for nothing, and the extra circuitry for the radar, plus a liquid oxygen system, meant that the guns had to be dispensed with – an unfortunate move which was to be felt later.

The F.3 made provision for two jetti-sonable overwing tanks but these were never fitted. It also introduced the Red Top (originally Blue Jay Mk4) missile, which was a development of Firestreak, but which allowed a head-on attack to be made on supersonic targets. XP693, the first prototype F.3, flew on 16 June 1962, and production models entered service with the RAF when XP695 was delivered to the Central Fighter Establishment at Binbrook in January 1964. 74 Squadron at Leuchars became the first front line squadron to so equip, in April, when it began replacing its F.1s, while 23 Squadron at the same base began replacing its Javelins with the F.3. Towards the end of the year both 56 and 111 Squadrons at Wattisham also began re-equipping with the F.3. Soon to join the F.3 in service was the T.5, a two-seat version of the F.3A. The T.5 prototype was produced by converting XM967, a T.4, from which it differed externally in having a squared-top fin. Internally, longer cable ducting was used. Jimmy Dell first flew XM967 in its new, T.5, configuration on

XR754 on test near Blackpool with 'Bee' Beamont at the controls. This aircraft first flew on 8 July 1965 and in March 1966 was assigned to the AFDS at Coltishall. In January 1967 it was modified to F.6 configuration before being issued to 23 Squadron. BAe

29 March 1962, at Filton, Bristol. XS417, the first production T.5, flew on 17 July 1964. Some twenty-two production T.5 aircraft were built, the first entering service with 226 OCU at Coltishall in April 1965.

Lightnings have always been very tight on fuel, especially the F.3 and T.5, which had the more powerful engines and the small ventral tank. To overcome this the F.6, essentially an F.3 but with modifications for extra range, was introduced. (Originally the F.6 was referred to as the F.3* or F.3A, or the 'interim Mk.6'.) In addition to the 600-gallon (2,700l) ventral tank, provision was made for overwing 260-gallon (1,200l) ferry tanks, and it had an extra crank in the leading edge to give better control throughout the speed range.

XP697, the F.6 prototype, which flew for the first time on 17 April 1964, was, like the first production series F.6s, an early build F.3 in F.6 configuration. All had the

flying characteristics of the new mark, but initially these were not fitted with the arrester hook for runway cable engagements. (This modification, which entailed re-designing and strengthening the rear fuselage, was introduced later, in 1967, after it was found that the conventional arrester barriers tended to ride over the Lightning cockpit and rupture the spine, often setting fire to the AVPIN starter fuel.) The first of the sixty-two F.6 production models went to AFDS in November 1965, and shortly afterwards entered front line service with 5 Squadron at Binbrook. In September 1966 74 Squadron at Leuchars began converting from the F.3 to the F.6, and in 1967, 23 Squadron, also at Leuchars, followed suit. On 1 April 1967 11 Squadron at Leuchars began to equip with the F.6 and on 1 May, 29 Squadron at Wattisham became the last Lightning squadron to form, when it equipped with the F.3. In August 1967 the final Lightning

F.6 for the RAF came off the production line.*

By now, all UK front line squadrons had either F.3s or F.6s, and the F.1As and T.4s were used in the OCU at Coltishall, together with F.3s and T.5s. It was then decided to convert all F.3s to F.6 standard, although in the end only enough aircraft were modified or produced to equip four squadrons (5, 11, 23 and 74). The remaining F.3s were eventually passed to the OCU as they were an embarrassment

---

* Inter-squadron rivalry being what it is, out of earshot 74 'Tiger' Squadron were referred to as the 'Ginger Toms', while it was said that 'when things get hot, 56 chicken out' – a reference to its badge of the phoenix rising from the ashes! Treble One were universally known as the 'Tremblers', the 'Trembling First', or, if you really wanted to upset them, 'One, double-one'. 92 Squadron were simply known as 'Ninety-Blue', a reference to their aircraft colour scheme.

F.3 XR760, which first flew on 20 September 1965 before being assigned to 5 Squadron in February 1966. In January 1968 this aircraft was modified to F.6 configuration and reallocated to 23 Squadron in 1967 (in whose colours it is seen here). In later years XR760 served with 56 Squadron and finally with the LTF at Binbrook. On 15 July 1986 XR760 was abandoned near Whitby after a rear fuselage fire. Bob Bees of 11 Squadron ejected safely. *Aeroplane*

to the squadrons due to their poor range/endurance compared to the F.6. So the F.3, with its very short range, remained in service. It was decided, however, to rebuild 31 of the RAF Germany F.2s and give them the larger, 600-gallon ventral tank, large fin and cranked leading edge, but retaining the smaller Avon engines and the upper guns. They were re-designated the F.2a. They were very popular with the pilots and many reckoned they were the most versatile of them all.

Dave Seward concludes:

In 1970, it was decided to fit two Aden cannon into the front of the ventral tank of the F.6s, reducing its fuel volume [by only 640lb] to 535 gallons [because some fuel was carried in a compartment formed in the gun pack]. The F.3, however, remained without the guns. [For peacetime policing sorties, guns can be used to fire warning shots to deter intruders and, in war, the gun is the only weapon which is unaffected by electronic or decoy jamming. It is also a very useful thing to have in close combat.] We also fitted drop tanks to the Mk.6s to extend the range, but because the long undercarriage retracted outwards, putting them

under the wing was impossible, so overwing tanks were installed. Only we British could defy the laws of gravity and prevent fuel from flowing downwards, and the cases of non-feeding tanks were legion. Essentially, they were a ferry tank, and with them fitted, the aircraft was limited to subsonic speeds; but some squadrons put them on more less permanently in the quest for more flying hours.

The aeroplane was superb to fly, a bitch to maintain and always short of fuel. In hindsight we probably wouldn't have wanted it any other way.'

Final preparations and testing of Firestreak missile prior to firing at the missile practice camp, RAF Valley, in March 1964. The aircraft is Lighting F.1A XM184 'A'. George Black

CHAPTER TWO

Flying Tigers and the Firebirds

Christmas came early for the Central Fighter Establishment in 1959. At the morning briefing at Warton on the 23rd, Sqn Ldr John Nicholls, an RAF liaison pilot and a member of the test flying team, had been told that XG334, the first of the twenty development batch aircraft for delivery to the RAF, would be ready to fly to the AFDS at RAF Coltishall, Norfolk, where it would be used for service handling trials. Aware that his Christmas present would perhaps be better delivered with him wearing a Father Christmas outfit, John Nicholls rang around to get one.

A Santa suit was duly found and he took off with it for Coltishall. As he taxied in at the famous old Battle of Britain station, all and sundry who had gathered to welcome the momentous arrival could not fail to notice that the pilot was wearing a red hood round his shoulders, a huge white beard and a broad grin! John Nicholls then got a shock, as he recalls:

I expected that the station commander, Gp Capt Bird-Wilson, and a few others would be there, but as I taxied past I noticed this 'area' of gold braid! Where had *they* all come from?! I quickly stuffed all the Father Christmas gear into my very early post-war flight suit, which I was wearing, and climbed out. All the top brass were there, from the AOC and his SASO, to 'Birdie' and others. Thankfully, nobody mentioned the Father Christmas outfit. I had a cup of coffee and waited for the Meteor 7 that was coming to take me back to Warton.

However, one of them asked me how long I had been at Warton. I said, 'About a year, Sir.'

'Where were you before that?' he enquired.

I said, Fighter Command HQ, Bentley Priory (where I had been Project Officer for the Lightning Simulator).

He winked and said, 'Oh, you're a serving officer then?' Obviously, he had not noticed

F.1 XM165, the first Lightning to enter RAF squadron service, was first flown at Coltishall by John Howe, CO of 74 'Tiger' Squadron, on 14 July 1960. AVM John Howe Collection

my rank tapes on the shoulder of my flying suit, which perhaps looked more like a rubber mac!

I'd done quite a lot of Lightning flying by that date – I'd been at Warton since May 1959 – and had done about forty flights by then. I quickly discovered that flying the Lightning was hugely exhilarating. It was comparable to the F-104 which, as well as the F-100 and the F-86L, I had flown in the USA in 1958. The Lightning was a real kick up the behind, a terribly impressive aircraft for its day. There was never anything quite like it in that respect, as far as I was concerned, until I got a chance to fly the F-15.

Later that month XG336 became the second P.1B delivered to the AFDS at Coltishall, and on 4 January 1960 the LCS (Lightning Conversion School) was formed at the station. Its job was to train Lightning pilots for the front line squadrons in Fighter Command. At first, only the more experienced jet pilots with 1,000 flying hours or more were selected to fly the new aircraft, and some of these were retained as instructors, before the qualifications were relaxed to include younger pilots on their first squadron tour. The initial training was accomplished with various systems aids and a flight simulator, and because the LCU had no Lightnings of its own, these were borrowed from AFDS and later 74 Squadron.

Flt Lt Bruce Hopkins was the last of the original group to join the AFDS at

F.1 XM137 which was assigned to the CFE at Coltishall on 28 June 1960. It went on to serve with 74 Squadron, 1962–64, before being used by 226 OCU for two years and seeing final duty with 23 Squadron and then the Leuchars and Wattisham TTFs. Mick Cartwright

Coltishall, at the beginning of February 1960. He recalls:

The CO was Wg Cdr David Simmonds and Major Al Moore, an American on exchange, was the A Flight commander. The group also included Flt Lt Peter Collins, an ex-Javelin pilot, and Flt Lt Ken Goodwin and Flt Lt Ron Harding, ex-Hunter men like myself. There were only three Development Batch Lightnings [XG334, XG335 and XG336] at

this time. [On 5 March Harding was forced to abandon XG334, which John Nicholls had delivered on 23 December, off the Norfolk coast near Wells-Next-The-Sea after hydraulic failure. This was only the second Lightning loss so far recorded. Harding ejected safely but suffered spinal injuries, and was picked up by helicopter from the sea.] Our role was to carry out trials to develop tactics and procedures for the aircraft and its weapon systems. We had Hunter 6s for target and chase work and a Meteor 7 for OR.946 instrumentation (later fitted to the Lightning F.2), which AFDS was trialling for the CFE. We also had two Javelin FAW.Mk.6 aircraft for target work.

My first Lightning solo was in XG336 at Leconfield (the runway at Coltishall was being re-surfaced), on 16 May 1960. The Lightning was an awesome aircraft, totally different to the Hunter. For a Hunter pilot like me it was a long climb to the cockpit. On my first two trips I had difficulty in keeping the nose up high enough to get the right climb angle to climb at Mach 0.9 (400 knots to begin with). The performance was out of this world.

On the early sorties we were chased by the Hunter, whose pilot would get airborne, then orbit at 10,000ft waiting for the Lightning to take off. It took the Lightning just 3½ minutes (with reheat, under 2½ minutes) to reach 36,000ft, easily passing the Hunter in the climb! At height the Lightning pilot would watch the Hunter still climbing underneath. (The Lightning climb angle was twenty-two degrees without reheat, or forty degrees with

Sqn Ldr John Howe climbs out of the XM135 after his flight. AVM John Howe Collection

Squadron Leader Ken Goodwin, one of the greatest Lightning aerobatic pilots of all time, had joined the AFDS in July 1960 and that summer flew the No.9 spot in the *Tigers* team and as the solo man at the 1961 Paris Air Show. Mick Cartwright

The tail of 'Finless Jim' Burn's aircraft, XM142, after he successfully landed it following the loss of its rudder and a considerable proportion of the fin. via Mike Harris

reheat.) Once in position the Hunter, who was there to observe and to help out in any emergency, would chase the Lightning. As the Lightning accelerated to Mach 1.6 (our maximum cleared speed at that time because of the problems of directional stability) the Hunter got left behind of course, and we would pick him up on the way back. We would then recover and land.

We developed intercept techniques. Don't forget, the Lightning was the first RAF single-seat aircraft with intercept radar. We would film the radar scope pictures and the navigators on the AFDS Javelins would advise us on the radar techniques. The radar hand grip controller had fourteen controls on it so it took some time getting used to it. Radar profiles were practised in the simulator. Another important consideration at this time was fuel. Every time we fired off into the blue in this aircraft which had so little fuel we became so fuel-conscious. How could we minimize the fuel use? As far as possible we did not use reheat.

Then we got five F.1s – XM135, XM136, XM137, XM138, and XM165 for 74 Squadron – delivered to us at Leconfield. I flew XM135 on 13 June 1960. On 11 July I flew XM165 to Coltishall where it became the first 74 Squadron aircraft, with the four other AFDS F.1s. When I arrived I was directed to the 74 Squadron flight line in this shiny, brand new, aircraft. After I had climbed down the ladder

there was no 'Thank You'. Their only comment was, 'Is it serviceable then?' [Sqn Ldr John Howe who, after a short spell of instructing, had taken over 74 Squadron in February 1960, first flew this aircraft on 14 July.] There was little difference between the DBs [Development Batch aircraft] and the F.1s, they just cleaned up the cockpit a little. The first reheat take-off was quite an experience. The performance was incredible. Reheat though, was not necessary. The take-off performance was perfectly adequate, so we didn't use it as a rule.

Enter The *Tigers*

Early that July, the conversion team at Coltishall had the task of converting 74 'Tiger' Squadron, the first front-line Lightning squadron. 'At this point', recalls Ken Goodwin,

I had nearly thirty hours on type; Sqn Ldr John Robertson [who now commanded the team] had one or two, and the remainder almost nil. However, we did have a set of those multi-coloured display boards, pilots' notes from English Electric and the confidence of the blind leading the blind. The conversion process consisted of lectures for a month, followed by a first solo (there were no two-

seaters), which included a good brief before the instructor got airborne in a Hunter chase and, having wound on about 500kt, and timed a pass over the field nicely with the student's brakes off, kept the two aircraft in near proximity up to about 25,000ft. Thereafter, with much corner-cutting and help from Neatishead radar, we could join company again for the descent.

I suppose the main objectives of the chase were firstly to tell the convertee if his nosewheel was still down after selecting gear up – a fairly commonplace occurrence with new pilots being a little behind the rapid acceleration after take-off, thus allowing aerodynamic pressure to out-do the hydraulics. Secondly, to advise generally from close proximity (better psychologically than a remote ground station) on the unexpected or unfamiliar and, lastly, to offer an opinion on fire warnings – we had frequent spurious and spurious/real warnings. Having done a good job with 74 – they flew a Diamond nine with yours truly as No.9, and the solo aeros spot at the 1961 Paris Air Show

– our little team and its boards went to Wattisham to convert 56 and 111 Squadrons.

The Lightning first appeared on the aerobatic stage in 1960, when the *Tigers* of 74 Squadron, led by the CO, Sqn Ldr John F.G. Howe, introduced their routine of formation aerobatics. As from July, only four aircraft were available, but the 'Tigers' were soon training hard for their new role, as John Howe recalls:

We started flying high-speed, low level runs (just subsonic, at about 200ft) in formation, but this put the Lightning airframe under more than normal pressures. One day during that summer 'Lefty' Wright was leading a box formation at Coltishall when the fin came off Jim Burns' aircraft. I watched from the tower as bits sprinkled to the ground. Jim now had no fin, and no radio either, so I told Lefty to close in and try to tell Jim of the problem. Should Jim now eject or land? The weather was perfect and the wind straight down the runway, so he was cleared to land. He did, and without any problems. Thereafter he was always known as 'Finless Jim'. [On 26 April 1963 Burns was forced to abandon XM142/B, after hydraulic power loss, off the Norfolk coast whilst on an air test following a 400-hour servicing. He ejected safely, just missing 33,000-volt electricity cables by 30 yd as he landed.]

Unfortunately, the C-in-C now ruled out high-speed, low-level runs in formation so we flew high-speed, low-level in battle formation (spread out).

74 'Tiger' Squadron pilots step out for the camera. Left to right: Sqn Ldr John Howe (CO), Jerry Cohu, 'Lefty' Wright, Ted Nance, Mike Cooke. AVM John Howe Collection

The *Tigers* performed before the public for the first time at Duxford on 14 August, at Little Rissington on the 28th and at Stradishall on the 31st. By the end of August John Howe, for instance, had just eight hours on Lightnings in his log book! Beginning on 5 September he led his formation of four in flypasts at the Farnborough Air Show each day, and the team finished the month with a Battle of Britain display at Coltishall on the 16th.

Before each display or rehearsal, the CO would brief the pilots who were to fly in the formation and explain the programme. For example, when the four-aircraft display was given:

Tiger Black, four aircraft to do formation aerobatics over the airfield. R/T checks will be on Four Romeo, India and Four Quebec, followed

Tigers on the prowl during a sortie from RAF Coltishall. XM165/F was the first Lightning to enter RAF service and was originally coded 'A'. XM164/K joined 74 Squadron in August 1960. *Aeroplane*

74 'Tiger' Squadron pilots in pressure jerkins at Coltishall, 23 February 1961. Left to right: Flg Off Ted Nance, Flg Off Martin Bee, Sqn Ldr John Howe (CO), Flg Off Laurie Jones, Flg Off Pete Phillips, Flg Off Mike Cooke, Flg Off Jacques Kleynhans. AVM John Howe Collection

by a drill start-up. Taxi at 100yd intervals, and line up in the runway in echelon. We'll use eighty per cent rpm holding on the brakes, and roll at three-second intervals for maximum reheat take-off. Aim to use the same pull-up point for an 80° climb. I'll call cancelling reheat and use eighty-two per cent rpm to give us 300 knots at 6,000ft, join up in box. The display will start with the fly-past in 'Swan' with wheels and flaps down. We shall clean-up the aircraft in front of the crowd to move into the rest of the display. No.4 remember to call 'Clear!' for the change into line astern, and Nos. 2 and 3 guard against dropping low in the very steep turn. Rejoin in box for the run in and two-way break; we shall fly synchronised circuits leading to the ten-second stream landing. Any questions?

With such a radically new and complex aircraft as the Lightning, there was a corresponding change in the technique of formation flying: the physical and metal strains imposed on pilots flying high-speed aircraft in close formation are intense.

Line up of 'Tiger' Squadron F.1s at RAF Coltishall, 1961. XM143/A joined the squadron on 15 September 1960 and was reassigned to 226 OCU in September 1963. XM142/B joined the squadron on 30 August 1960 and crashed into the sea off Cromer on 26 April 1963 after a control failure. Flt Lt Jim Burns ejected safely. XM139/C joined the squadron on 2 August 1960 and was assigned to the OCU in 1964. XM141/D was assigned to the squadron on 29 August 1960 and reassigned to the OCU in September 1963. EDP

Sqn Ldr John Howe, CO, 74 Squadron, puts XM147 into a dive near the Great Yarmouth racecourse near the coast of Norfolk with Scroby Sands in the distance. AVM John Howe Collection

With a power/weight ratio of roughly 1:1 there was an immense reserve of power, and the team leader had to use it with discretion, bearing in mind that the rest of the formation must from time to time use more power to maintain their position. Although the Lightning was a Mach 2 aircraft, aerobatics in close formation, only five or six feet apart, could be flown at 450mph (720kph) – about one-third of the speed which the Lightning would achieve in level flight on an operational mission. Like the Hunter, the Lightning was an extremely manoeuvrable aircraft and despite its great size and weight was capable of astonishing low-speed turns, even when the reheat of the two Avon

turbojets was not being used. The tight turning qualities of the Lightning permitted a display to be given in a small area of sky, so that the public could have no difficulty in keeping the formation in view.

The two engines of the Lightning caused greater jet wash than the single engine of the Hunter, and in formations the aircraft had to be stepped down to a slightly greater extent to avoid interference. The rapid rate of rotation in a turn meant that the pilot at the rear had to fly a slightly longer flight-path to avoid the jet wash and still hold his place. In a tight turn the Lightning was put onto its side, the power stepped up and the nose pulled back to increase lift; and the aircraft would go round smoothly.

At higher speeds an aircraft like the Lightning is surrounded by an envelope of disturbance which must be avoided by other aircraft in the formation. The sixty-degree swept wing of the Lightning made it a little more difficult for the pilot to maintain accurate formation than with the Hunter, because he could not see his own wingtips. Accordingly, when flying in echelon, he lined up on the trailing edge of the aileron of the adjacent aircraft. Judgement of lateral separation comes only from experience, and constant practice is necessary before pilots can hold their aircraft in a tight and accurate formation. Each man lines up a point on his wing leading edge with a point on the fuselage of the next aircraft, and after lengthy practice can accurately estimate his distance. The leader has no fixed point on which to fly. He concentrates on placing his aircraft in the best possible position to let the crowd see the show, timing to a split second each stage of the flight, and the rest of the team watch him constantly and are alert for his radio instructions ('Pulling up for wing-over starboard. Pulling more g. Taking off bank and relaxing back-pressure. Pulling up for roll to port, and rolling – NOW!').

1960 proved an auspicious year for 74 Squadron in more ways than one. When John Howe discovered that an old friend from the Korean War, Lt Col Ed Rackham, was commanding the 79th Tactical Fighter Squadron – 'the Tigers' – at Woodbridge, they got together to form the first of the now famous 'Tiger meets'. The *Tigers* finished their first year as the Lightning aerobatic display team with a fly-by over all the fighter stations in East Anglia on 23 December. In the New Year, 1961, the *Tigers* received more Lightnings – enough for a diamond nine formation, a solo aerobatic display pilot and spares – and work-up began in earnest for the Paris Air Show scheduled for 3 and 4 June.

John Howe's team of *Tigers* was a mixture of youth and experience. Flt Lt Maurice J. Williams (30) and Flt Lt Alan W.A. 'Lefty' Wright (30) were the two flight commanders. The two deputy flight commanders were Flt Lt 'Finless Jim' Burns (26) and Flt Lt Jeremy J.R. Cohu (24). The son of an air vice-marshal, Cohu had converted to Lightnings in 1960 after flying Hunters in 74 Squadron at Horsham St. Faith. The rest of the team comprised Flight Lieutenants Tim Nelson (25) (the adjutant), George P. Black (29), Edward J. Nance (25), Jeremy E. Brown (25), Martin Bee (23), and Michael J. Dodd (26). The Flying Officers were David Maxwell Jones (27), Jacques W. Kleynhans (33) – like his CO, a native of South Africa – Peter J. Phillips (24), T. Vaughan Radford (23), an admirer of Picasso, Graham Sutherland – whose ability to paint abstracts in oils was put to good use between flights, painting the squadron crest on the main hangar – and Mike S. Cooke, who had converted to the Lightning in June 1960.

The solo slot was flown by Flt Lt Ken Goodwin of the LCU, whom John Howe rated as one of the most fantastic low-level aerobatic pilots he'd ever seen. The *Tigers* performed wingovers with nine F.1As, the largest number ever seen publicly together, and rolls with four. Between times Ken Goodwin, having detached himself at the end of the nine-man demonstration, put in solo aerobatics which included Derry turns and low inversions. It was all a stunning success. Back home again, the *Tigers* displayed at Farnborough in September. *Flight* reported:

Nothing in the show exuded more sheer power than the three second interval stream take-off by the nine Lightnings of 74 Squadron, beating down the runway in a sustained blast of brown dust and stomach-shaking noise. As the rear machines were taking off, the leaders were climbing an invisible, vertical wall over Laffan's Plain. All were airborne in thirty-five seconds. [After the sixteen blue Hunters of 92 Squadron] the Lightnings were on stage,

111 Squadron began equipping with the Lightning F.1A on 6 March 1961, when it took delivery of XM185. XM215/C, the nearest aircraft, was delivered on 2 August 1961 and XM216, the last F.1A built, was delivered later that month. XM190/G later joined 226 OCU and crashed into the sea off Cromer, Norfolk, on 15 March 1966. Captain Al Peterson USAF ejected safely. XM188/F later served with 226 OCU also, and was written-off after crashing into the No.1 Hangar at Coltishall. *Aeroplane*

Squadron Leader John Howe in the cockpit of XM143/A together with the rest of his squadron at Coltishall. *Aeroplane*

74 Squadron lined up at Coltishall on 22 February 1961 for the world's press. 23 Squadron's Javelins can be seen in the background. EDP

smoking in towards the airfield in arrowhead formation, changing to Diamond nine and including wingovers and [in the first public demonstration of nine Lightnings rolling in tight formation] a roll in their programme. A split into three echelons preceded the final run-in and break for landing.

More displays followed, on Battle of Britain day at Biggin Hill and Coltishall, and at Cranwell on 21 October. Two days later, at Leconfield, they performed for the Queen Mother, and on the 24th John Howe brought his team back to Coltishall to bring the curtain down on a highly successful season. Persuaded to land first he was surprised, then delighted, to see the other eleven Lightnings fly over him in 'H–Howe' formation! In December Howe left to take up a new post at Fighter Command HQ at Bentley Priory and on the 12th, Sqn Ldr Peter G. Botterill assumed command of the squadron. In 1962, 92 Squadron's Hunters began converting to the Lightning, and the *Tigers* became the only official Fighter Command aerobatic team. At Farnborough they brought down the curtain with an unforgettable diamond flypast of seven Lightnings and sixteen Hunters.

Firebirds

Meanwhile, a new Lightning aerobatic team, from 56 Squadron, had been selected for the 1963 season. Sqn Ldr David Seward, the 32-year-old CO, had first got wind of his squadron's new role in mid-October 1962, as their second detachment in Cyprus (see Chapter 5) came to a close.

We began to pick up rumours that 74

56 Squadron began conversion to the Lightning F.1 in December 1960, to become only the second Lightning squadron in the RAF, and the first to receive the F.1A (XM172 being the first to arrive, on 14 December 1960). Work-up to operational status took place at Wattisham, then, when the runways were resurfaced, this continued at Coltishall. Their full complement of F.1As was received by March 1961.

19 Squadron began conversion from the Hunter F.6 to the Lightning F.2 at Leconfield in October 1962, the first RAF unit so to do. T.4 XM988 was the first aircraft to arrive, on 29 October 1962. The first F.2, XN755/D, was received on 17 December 1962. 19 Squadron became operational as an all-weather unit in March 1963 with 12 F.2s and one T.4. *Aeroplane*

Squadron were starting air-to-air refuelling and 56 Squadron were to become the next RAF formation aerobatic team. This was indeed confirmed a week later. The first thing was to get ourselves a name. We chose *Firebirds* because of the 56 Squadron badge, the 'Phoenix rising from the ashes', and we devised a paint scheme. We painted the spine and fin red, and we rounded this off with the leading edges of the wings and tailplanes red also.

We started the leaders doing individual aerobatics, and in choosing the leaders and deputy leaders, I went purely on seniority in the squadron. In other words, I was the formation leader; the 'A' Flight Commander, 27-year-old Flt Lt John M. Curry, led the rear formation, the 'B' Flight Commander, Flt Lt Jeremy Cohu, was my deputy leader, and the deputy 'B' Flight Commander was the deputy

rear formation leader. Four of us had experience in formation aerobatics. [Curry had flown in the 229 OCU aerobatic team before March 1960 saw him with Treble One Squadron at Wattisham, flying with the 'Black Arrows', while Cohu (and Mike Cooke) had of course flown with the 'Tigers' aerobatic team before joining 56 Squadron in October 1962.] I had dabbled in the 1950s in Meteors, and on T-33s, Sabres, F-102s and F-106s whilst on an exchange tour in America, but not really seriously. As luck happened, all the leadership choices fitted in.

We also had one or two queens who fancied themselves, but who really had no experience. We had fifteen pilots on the Squadron, so that was ten in the team plus an airborne reserve, the solo man ['Noddy' MacEwen], which made twelve, the commentator/manager [Flt Lt Robert E. 'Bob' Offord, a QFI who had

flown Meteors and Sabres with 66 Squadron, before converting to the Lightning], which only left two on the squadron as spares.

Apart from those already mentioned, the other pilots were all equally first-rate Lightning men. Flt Lt Henry R. Ploszek (27), the No.3, had flown Hunters before converting to the Lightning and had been with 56 Squadron since September 1960. His father had been a major in the Polish Air Force and joined the RAF in the UK in 1940, serving as an engineer officer during the war. After the war he joined the RAF, retiring as a Wing Commander. Ploszek and his mother came to Britain in 1946. (In the 1980s, Henry, now a Squadron Leader in his early fifties, managed the world famous *Red Arrows* team for several seasons, and he also flew the team's spare aircraft, Red 10.) The rest of the squadron comprised Flight Lieutenants, Robert J. Manning (26), Timothy F.H. Mermagen (25), Terry R. Thompson RCAF (31), Ernie E. Jones (30), Malcolm J. 'Mo' Moore (30), Peter M. 'Jimmy' Jewell (29), and Richard Cloke (24). Wg Cdr Bernard H. Howard (39) was team manager, and Flt Lt Brian J. Cheater (25) was the Adjutant.

The real work of building up the team began on 1 March 1963. Dave Seward continues:

The only guidance we were given was that the main formation was to be a nine-ship, and for the display, we were to provide continuous aerobatics so that something was going on in front of the crowd all the time. There were to be no gaps. We decided, therefore, that we would start the show with a stream take-off and the very steep climb and as we joined up in formation, a solo Lightning would perform solo aerobatics, clearing as we came round in a Diamond nine to do the odd roll and loop before splitting into two formations of five. We had a tenth man airborne to link up with the rear formation after the first bomb-burst away from the 'nine'. We then would do manoeuvres in two separate fives, with the solo man interspersing with bomb bursts and join ups when a gap appeared. [In a bomb burst the aircraft break formation sharply and fan outwards.]

We also devised a means of making smoke. The Lightning had fuel in the flaps, and we isolated the port flap tank, ran a copper pipe from the tank along the inside port spar strake on the fuselage (the starboard strake carried all the electrical wiring looms and the left-hand one was a dummy strake to balance it up), to a small nozzle above the bottom jet pipe, and connected an electric pump to the gun trigger. We filled the flap tank with diesel fuel, selected 'guns', pulled the tiger, and we had instant smoke! Now, we did all this ourselves, by self help, at very little cost, but I got a telling off from Fighter Command engineers for being too 'enthusiastic'.

In 1963 56 Squadron, commanded by Sqn Ldr Dave Seward, became the official Fighter Command aerobatic team, and were named the *Firebirds*.

Late in 1962, the Leconfield Wing began equipping with the Lightning F.2, the first, XN783/A, arriving at 92 Squadron on 17 April 1963. Declared fully operational that summer, a team of blue-finned F.2s displayed at Farnborough that September. via Alex Reed/Tony Aldridge

74 Squadron's Lightnings were joined at Coltishall on 7 August 1962 by sixteen Hawker Hunters of 92 Squadron – the *Blue Diamonds* – to practise formation manoeuvres for a display, involving the Hunters and ten Lightning F.1s at Farnborough, 1962. Norfolk & Norwich Aviation Museum

So there we were: a name, a paint job, smoke on demand, and four of us reasonably proficient in aerobatics. We then worked up in pairs doing steep turns and wingovers, then loops and rolls, progressing to five-ship formations doing all the various aerobatic manoeuvres and formation changes. This was 'arrow formation', and we called this 'Fork'. We used to do these various changes during a roll, loop, or wing-over. We then worked up into the full nine doing rolls, loops and wingovers. Unfortunately, we then hit a snag. The tail fin tips started to work loose. The aerobatics were blamed and we were banned from doing rolls or loops in the 'big nine' formation so we had to step our line astern position down lower. I was suspicious from the start as my aircraft, which had always been the lead ship, was one of the ones to have a loose fin tip. By coincidence, it was the one which had done the most flight refuelling in the Valiants' jet efflux, but despite our protestations, the powers that were would not lift the ban on aerobating the nine ship, so we were restricted to level turns and formation changes with the nine formation before splitting into the two five-ship formations. We

The *Firebirds* team at Wattisham, 1963. Left to right, Flt Lt Ernie Jones, Flt Lt Mike Cooke, Flt Lt Jerry Cohu, Sqn Ldr Dave Seward, Bob Offord, Tim Mermagen, Pete Jewell, ???, Brian Cheater, 'Mo' Moore, Brian Allchin, John Curry, Terry Thompson RCAF, Robert Manning, Henry Ploszek. Dave Seward Collection

then did semi-synchronized manoeuvres with the two fives and the solo man, ending up with the lead five bomb bursting down and the other five bomb bursting up through the smoke. We then joined up in a big 'vic' formation with the airborne reserve and the solo man in as well for a simultaneous 'vic' peel off and rapid landing, followed by a formation taxi in.

At first all practice had been carried out at an altitude which would have given pilots enough time for recovery if any snags were encountered. After the 'threes' had achieved a reasonable degree of skill Sqn Ldr Seward had added two other aircraft to fly 'fives'. Soon after this he was confident enough of his pilots' ability to ask for clearance to operate down to 1,500ft (450m). This was granted and, a short while later, was followed by another clearance down to 500ft (150m), and finally clearance was approved down to just 200ft (60m), one of the lowest clearances ever given to an RAF aerobatic team.

On the morning of 13 May 1963, Geoffrey Norris of the RAF *Flying Review* was privileged to fly a forty-minute sortie with the *Firebirds* in T.4 XM989, as the team began their work-up to show standard. He wrote:

> With Flt Lt Bob Offord at the controls, we took off as number six behind a section of five. This may have been only a practice sortie, but all the excitement of a real show was there. The six aircraft taxied along the perimeter track, staggered with alternate aircraft left and right. At the end of the runway we lined up in position, our aircraft almost struggling to go as the brakes held it against full throttle.
>
> The Section Leader was Flt Lt John Curry. When we were all set he announced that he was rolling and his aircraft accelerated rapidly down the runway at Wattisham. At three-second intervals the others followed. By the time it was our turn to go, the runway had almost disappeared in a haze of swirling fumes and, just before Offord released our brakes, Curry's Lightning suddenly leaped skywards like a runaway rocket at the other end of the runway. This steep, afterburner take-off had become an accepted part of Lightning aerobatics and the *Firebirds* have proved they can do it as well as any others. It certainly is most exciting to watch; it is breath-taking to actually do it.
>
> As soon as we had started rolling the acceleration was patently obvious. Then Offord cut in the afterburners and – there is only one

Flg Off (later Flt Lt) Mike Cooke pictured in the cockpit of a Hunter of 74 Squadron. Mike was an accomplished Hunter and Lightning aerobatic pilot and following his tour in the *Tigers*, was posted to 56 Squadron in 1961. Mike Cooke Collection

On 6 June 1963 tragedy struck the *Firebirds* team when Flg Off Mike Cooke, flying XM179 (pictured here, right, with XM178), collided with XM171, flown by Flt Lt Mo Moore, during a practice bomb burst over Wattisham. Cooke ejected but suffered a broken spine in the process and was permanently paralysed. Mo Moore managed to nurse XM171 back to Wattisham with nothing more than a few dents in the fuselage and minus both Firestreaks. *Aeroplane*

The *Firebirds* of 56 Squadron perform a break. XM171/A, the nearest F.1A, was being flown by Flt Lt Mo Moore on 6 June 1963 when it was hit by XM179 flown by Flt Lt Mike Cooke. via Mike Cooke

word for it – we simply belted down the runway. Glued firmly to the back of my ejection seat, I watched the ground flash past and, at regular intervals, the aircraft ahead of us shot upwards. Then we were airborne with our wheels up. For a few seconds Offord held the aircraft level at about thirty feet to let the speed build up.

By roughly three-quarters of the way down the runway we had 250kt showing. Then Offord pulled the stick back smartly into his stomach. The ground disappeared as if by magic and I sank into my seat as the sudden upwards turn gave us some 3½-g – not much by modern standards, but quite something at such an early and critical part of the take-off. But perhaps the biggest sensation of this dramatic take-off technique is the almost frightening loss of apparent speed. One second you are roaring down the runway with trees and hangars blurring in the distance, and the next you are almost on your back in the cockpit, looking straight up at the clouds with seemingly no speed whatsoever. A reassuring glance at the air speed indicator showed,

Sqn Ldr Dave Seward goes through the finer points of the *Firebirds* display routine. Watching are, left to right, Henry Ploszek, Mike Cooke, Dick Cloke, Jerry Cohu and Terry Thompson RCAF. Dave Seward Collection

Sqn Ldr (later ACM Sir Patrick) 'Paddy' Hine, CO 92 Squadron, with some of his team at RAF Leconfield in 1963. Behind him (clockwise) are Flt Lts Tony Aldridge, Dave Kuun, John Vickery, Tim Elworthy and Ernie Jones. via Tony Aldridge

Sir James Martin, ejection seat pioneer, whose company's ejection seats have been responsible for saving the lives of thousands of pilots. Martin-Baker

however, that we still had 230 knots and the Lightning, which, with full afterburner, has almost as much thrust as its weight, could maintain this attitude and speed for a long time.

Still with the afterburners on, we trailed the five aircraft ahead which were already forming up. As we broke through the clouds, Curry, in the leading Lightning, eased off the climb and announced that he was coming out of afterburner. There was a short breathing space while we looked for a clear area in which to practice, and then, over a large break in the clouds below, we started. Curry calmly announced rolls, wingovers and loops and the formation changes while the team followed.

As we brought up the rear in the T.4,

making all the manoeuvres with the team, the sky and the ground ceased to mean up or down. Our reference point became the five aircraft ahead and the Suffolk countryside and the horizon whirled over and around us unceasingly as the section of five flew smoothly through their practice. At no point were we straight and level for more than a second. The accelerometer showed peaks of up to 4g and most of the time we were between 2 and 3g. Our speed remained fairly constant at 350 knots.

Keeping station with the *Firebirds* as we were, one could appreciate their faultless station-keeping and the smoothness of their manoeuvres. It was almost like putting a work of art under a microscope and still finding it

flawless. Watching the team in action like this it was difficult to realize that, only a few months previously, hardly any of the pilots had experience of formation aerobatics. That they have achieved a standard of perfection is a tribute not only to the general calibre of the average RAF pilot today, but to the work of Sqn Ldr David Seward.

Although the *Firebirds* display is, in every way, a team effort, right through from pilots to the equally essential and highly skilled ground crew, there is little doubt that Dave Seward is the man who can make or break a show. One of the great assets of the Lightning for formation aerobatics – apart, of course, from its excellent handling characteristics – is the great amount of power which pilots can call on

F.2s of 92 Squadron in very close formation. XN789, the nearest aircraft, arrived on the squadron on 26 April 1963. via Tony Aldridge

if necessary. This means that the pilot on the outside of a turn should have no difficulty in keeping his station. This excess power does, however, pose problems for Seward. He must concentrate on flying a course which pilots in all parts of the large formation behind him can follow. If he allows too much power to build up in a turn he could well cause embarrassment to a pilot on the outside of the formation.

We stayed with Curry's section at practice for some twenty minutes. Although Offord had not flown as close to the formation as the other aircraft were close to each other (the view from the T.4 is a little restricted for close-formation aerobatics) he had to concentrate closely on the movements of the aircraft ahead of us. Obviously, the pilots who were literally flying only a few feet apart were concentrating even harder. Back on the ground I asked several of them whether they found this concentration tiring. They did not seem to take their task as anything particularly out of the ordinary. 'You have to concentrate pretty hard, anyway, when you are flying a Lightning,' one said. This applies whether you are flying formation aeros or making a radar interception.

But one thing is certain. Although the pilots might say that their job is 'not particu-

larly out of the ordinary', by the end of this summer many people in various parts of Europe will have had an opportunity to judge for themselves how 'out of the ordinary' their show is. My guess is that the *Firebirds* will be ajudged one of the best yet.

'However', continues Dave Seward, 'before we really got going, 'Noddy' MacEwen, the solo man, was posted and promoted, so Fg Off Alan Garside, the 111

Squadron solo aeros man, joined us. [In April 1963, Flt Lt Brian C. Allchin (25) joined 56 Squadron. 'Alch' had flown Hunters in 92 Squadron, and in the 'Blue Diamonds' aerobatic team in 1961 and 1962.] Everyone then became involved after we had a mid-air collision.'

The collision occurred during a formation horizontal bomb burst over Wattisham airfield on 6 June. 'The day before', recalls Mike Cooke, the No.3, (left

92 Squadron F.2s XN789/G, XN786/D, XN783, XN732 and XN735 getting airborne on full re-heat at Leconfield in 1963. via Tony Aldridge

43

The *Firebirds* begin their display. The immaculate white overalled ground crew would march smartly forward in line abreast as the aircraft prepared to move off. This move was not just 'bull'. Each airman was there to marshal one of the Lightnings from its line-up position and to give it a last-minute visual check. via Edwin Carter

of centre in the five-vic formation, in F.1A XM179, behind Gerry Cohu),

Sqn Ldr Seward had given us a 'pleasant ear bashing' to smarten up the horizontal bomb burst because of the 'slack' bomb burst at the

end of the sequence. We did a practice. On one roll I must have been low because I saw rather a lot of trees near the airfield at Wattisham. We were then coming in, each Lightning 6–7ft apart as usual, and Gerry Cohu ordered: 'Bomb Burst, Bomb Burst . . .

GO!' 'Mo' Moore, the No.5, and No.4, went straight away. One second later it was my turn and that of the No.2. I made a very sharp turn, and at the same time, I pulled the stick to make it 'slicker'. You then didn't normally look too far over to the left. We were about to reassemble and I looked ahead for the leader, took off the left bank, coming out of the left turn to go right.

Suddenly, I felt a 'bump'. [His port wing had touched the under fuselage of XM171, 'Mo' Moore's Lightning, knocking the starboard Firestreak missile off. Moore managed to land safely at Wattisham.] Immediately the aircraft carried on rolling to the right despite full left aileron and full left rudder. I couldn't stop it. I remember that the height was 500–700ft AGL. In a few milliseconds I realized I'd have to eject. At that height I could eject into the ground, so I had reflex – 'go for the handle'. I used my left hand to pull it. Glancing at the ASI I saw that it was around 450–500kt, and rising. I pulled. It seemed an age before anything happened. The canopy went. I waited for the 'nip' in the back of the neck (previously I had done two training ejections in a static ramp), but it did not happen.

The next thing I remember was that I was coming down in the parachute and into a green field. I could not move my arms or my legs. I couldn't breathe either. Because of the whiplash effect caused by a malfunction in the ejection seat sequence, the parachute had opened at too high a speed (called a

Mike Cooke (far left) pictured with fellow patients at Stoke Mandeville Hospital, Cambridge in 1963 following his terrible accident on 6 June 1963. Mike Cooke Collection

56 Squadron air- and ground-crews pose for the camera at Wattisham. Sqn Ldr 'Hank' Martin, the CO, stands in the Lightning cockpit. via Edwin Carter

'hangman's deployment'), and the whiplash effect had broken my neck (actually, my fifth and sixth vertebrae had been severed), although I did not know this until a few days later. (A 'hangman's deployment' is so-called because we breathe through the diaphragm and when someone is hanged on the scaffold the noose breaks the neck and breathing stops. This is what had happened to me when the parachute had deployed.)

I came to on the ground. I still had my face mask on. I could not breathe too well. I thought this was because I was laying on my breathing apparatus. Two labourers came over. I said: 'Mask off, Mask off!'. They said: 'He's still alive', and moved back. Overhead, another Lightning circled, pin-pointing my position presumably. A crash crew arrived with an ambulance and a very uncomfortable ride ensued. I was taken to hospital in Ipswich and later that day was helicoptered to Stoke Mandeville.

Dr Goodman oversaw my treatment. He was a German Jew who had fled to Britain in 1937 and had become world renowned in the treatment of spinal injuries at Stoke Mandeville. His technique was to permit the

patient good, basic nursing to avoid potentially dangerous bladder and kidney failures later and so prolong the patient's lifespan. (At one time, the normal prognosis for spinal injury patients was only ten years.) I had a

tracheotomy to improve my breathing and my head was put in traction for three months after a harness was bolted to my skull. The first night, I couldn't move, and I was more occupied with coping with the present effects of my

The _Firebirds_ taxi in after a display. At the end of each performance the Firebirds made a simultaneous 'vic' peel off and rapid landing, followed by a formation taxi in. via Dave Seward

Underside view of thirteen Lightnings of 111 Squadron in June 1965. *Aeroplane*

accident than thinking about what the future now held. Stoke Mandeville was something of a culture shock after RAF station quarters. The wooden huts had nicotine stained ceilings and it was so cramped, you could touch the patient's bed next to you on both sides. The food wasn't at all good. Everyone though, was in the same boat.

Recovery, if you do recover, comes after six weeks. At the time of my accident my wife Patsy was five months pregnant, and she was understandably very upset. All told, I spent seventeen weeks in bed. Gradually, my arms got a little movement. My first day's outing on 23 October, coincided with the birth, at RAF Bicester, of our son, Simon.

Mike Cooke's RAF career was finished; he was just twenty-six years old at the time. Incredibly, he did not qualify for compensation (under Section 10 of the Crown Proceedings Act of 1947, he could not sue the MoD), nor a pension; he had not been in the RAF long enough. Without a trace of bitterness, he says: 'The RAF is there to

fight wars, not look after the injured.' The RAF Benevolent Fund also was unable to help the pilot, who was now a paraplegic. However, Sir James Martin at Martin Baker had told Patsy Cooke that if there was anything Mike needed he could have it. In 1968 Martin Baker provided money to enable the Cookes to buy a Citroen Safari and to have it specially adapted for his use. Mike used it for twelve years and Martin Baker then provided another £10,000 for him to replace it with a Nissan Prairie.

Dave Seward, who had been filming the formation from the ground, now had tough decisions to make:

Sad though it was, I had a job to do and suddenly, you have to fight back the tears, harden it, and get on with the job. Not a pleasant thing. You've got to tell the relatives. The station commander asked me what I was going to do. I said, 'We carry on.' It was the only way. This was one of the times when you had to make a hard decision. You're not the

most popular guy. Then again. you're not running a popularity poll. We had a Queen's Birthday flypast the next day and not only that but we were scheduled to lead it. I'll give Mo Moore his due. I said, 'This accident has shaken you up boy. What are you going to do?' (I counselled him and told him he had done nothing wrong). He said, 'I'll carry on'. We needed all the aircraft so Edwin Carter and his engineers changed the missile pack on Mo Moore's aircraft and hammered the dents out and put it in the air.

Although the *Firebirds* gave most of their displays with synchronized aerobatics from two sections of four or five aircraft, each show that summer of 1963 was opened by the full formation of nine with, sometimes, an extra solo performance thrown in. On 18 July 1963 Fg Off Alan Garside was killed when he became disorientated in cloud during an aerobatic presentation at RAF Wittering and so Sam Lucas, the 111 Squadron solo aerobatic pilot, took Garside's place in the *Firebirds* for the rest of the season. Seward recalls that, 'Lucas was an 'ad libber' who would get 'bored' with his show and throw in some unannounced routines. On one occasion I saw him enter the fog at Biggin Hill inverted and I never expected him to come out alive, but he did!'

On 12 June The *Firebirds* flew to France to perform at the Paris Air Show at Le Bourget. The *Flight* correspondent wrote:

The programme at Le Bourget proved that Dave Seward was fully aware of the showmanship part of his job as he was of his airmanship. The French crowd were treated to a dazzling display of colour and spectacle, but above all, one of precision, which began as soon as the pilots strapped themselves into their cockpits. If there was to be a full take-off of ten Lightnings the onlooker would be treated to the sight of ten canopies closing as one on Sqn Ldr Seward's orders. Next, the immaculately white overalled ground crew would march smartly forward in line abreast as the aircraft prepared to move off. This move was not just 'bull'. Each airman was there to marshal one of the Lightnings from its line-up position and to give it a last-minute visual check. The aircraft moved off in two sections of five and, again on their Sqn Leader's command, each aircraft in each section of five would check its brakes at precisely the same instant after it had rolled a few feet. The effect was almost that of a gracious bow towards the crowd. 56 Squadron's pre-take-off manoeuvres were, certainly, a fitting prelude to the precision which was to follow in the air.

Unbeknown to the *Flight* correspondent, things did not go as smoothly as hoped, as Dave Seward explains: 'We were pushed for time (the Greek Air Force had already been diverted for overstepping their slot). We only had something like twelve minutes from take-off to landing. (Normally, we timed ourselves from the time the first aircraft (mine) started to roll.) The French said that our start time was as soon as I taxied out.'

Dave Seward was also the man who faced the last-minute decision on what type of show was to be given:

Despite met reports it is sometimes impossible to know exactly what flying conditions are like until you are in the air. Basically, we planned for three different types of show to meet all eventualities. If the clouds were above 4,000ft we would give the complete show. We had another display which we could use if the ceiling was lower and a final bad weather show with which we operated within a radius of two miles with a 500ft ceiling.

For Paris we would do a loop in a 5,000ft cloud base. However, it was a murky day and so I had sent Bob Manning, the spare, up to see

'Treble One's Lightnings in diamond nine formation in June 1965 being led by the squadron's T.4. *Aeroplane*

what the cloud base was. He said, 'No clouds below 6,000ft'. I told John Curry, 'OK, we'll do a full show.' Up we went – straight into cloud at 2,500ft! We did the whole loop in cloud using the altitude indicator (a nasty little instrument with no 'aircraft' mounted on the artificial horizon) and came out at 2,500ft. It was a 'dodgy' time but we all stuck together – I'll say that for the team. So then the rest of the display was the flat show. Afterwards, I asked Manning why the hell he had told me there was no cloud below 6,000ft and he said, 'Well Boss, you've been practising the loop for so long now, that I thought you wouldn't want to miss it!'

After we came down we went into the BAC tent. [AM Sir Desmond] 'Zulu' Morris, the C-in-C Fighter Command, had a face as black as thunder. I could see him looking at me and saying, 'What about that loop?'. He was not that happy anyway that a front-line squadron had been taken out of the line for aerobatting. (It did not make economic sense using a front-line squadron like us when you're trying to maintain a watching brief in a Cold War situation.) I explained to him that we'd been given the wrong weather forecast and that was it. He was just starting to get to the awkward question when Bill Bedford suddenly dropped the P.1127 Kestrel right outside the judges' tent! The crash took me off the hook and with other things now on his mind, Zulu Morris never mentioned it again!

Geoffrey Norris' prediction that the *Firebirds* would be adjudged one of the best yet was proved true, and they became the last squadron formation aerobatic team to display: the following September, a team of five yellow-painted Gnat T.1 trainers from 4 Flying Training School, led by Flt Lt Lee Jones, performed at Farnborough 1964. The *Yellowjacks'* success led, in 1965, to the world-renowned *Red Arrows*, whose first public performance was at Biggin Hill in May that year. The rest, of course, is history.

Mixed formation, old and new, on 5 August 1964 over Suffolk, the Lightnings being led by a Hurricane and two Spitfires of the RAF flight from Wattisham. F.1 XM165 from 226 OCU at Coltishall is flanked by two Wattisham-based F.1As from 56 Squadron, the lower aircraft being XM172/B. Sqn Ldr Dave Seward is flying Mk. 19 Spitfire PM631, between the upper two Lightnings. Spitfire PS853 is between the lower two Lightnings and Hurricane LF363 is leading the formation. Peter M. Warren via *Aeroplane*

CHAPTER THREE

T-Birds and the Ten Tonners

The LCU had moved to Middleton St. George in August 1961 and become the Lightning Conversion Squadron (LCS). Gp Capt Freddie Rothwell was Station Commander, Wg Cdr Charles Laughton OC Ops, and Sqn Ldr Ken J. Goodwin, Commander of the LCS. The LCS were without aircraft until December 1961 when their first T.4 came, only to leave almost as quickly as it had arrived. It returned six months later after a major rework of the hydraulic pipes in No.1 engine bay. The LCS continued to borrow Lightnings, now mainly from 56 and 'Treble One' Squadrons. Usually, only a single aircraft for a few days at a time could be spared, but nevertheless the LCS was responsible for the successful conversion of

several squadrons to Lightnings. Not until 27 June 1962 did the LCS receive its own aircraft when T.4 XM970 was delivered to Middleton St. George, and was soon coded 'G'. By the end of July the number of T.4s had risen to four. One of the LCS's first students was AVM 'Tubby' Clayton, AOC 12 Group, who was sent solo after only five dual rides. By the end of October the LCS had eight T.4s on strength. On 12 December 1962 XM993 ran off the runway at Middleton St. George after landing while returning from Chivenor, and turned over. Fortunately, Al Turley of the LCS and his student, Wg Cdr C.M. Gibbs, escaped before the aircraft caught fire and burned out.

On 1 June 1963 the LCS was re-titled

226 OCU (Operational Conversion Unit) and shortly afterwards it received seven ex-74 Squadron F.1s, via 60 MU (Maintenance Unit), where they had been overhauled. In August, the OCU introduced a red and white livery which was based on the St. George's Cross and reflected the unit's 'shadow' identity which was adopted during the many Fighter Command exercises that would follow, and in time of crisis.

Ken Goodwin was posted to Bangkok in October 1963. That same month, Sqn Ldr Dave Seward arrived from 56 Squadron to be the Chief Ground Instructor in the ground school. 'Already', he recalls,

a very effective organization had been devel-

Members of the Lightning Conversion Squadron at Middleton St. George, where it was established in August 1961 under the command of Sqn Ldr Ken J. Goodwin. Left to right: Flt Lts 'Roly' Jackson, Instructor; Reg Phillips, Andy Greenhalgh, Engineering; and Donald 'D D' Donaldson-Davidson, Radar Instructor. Air Cdre Ken Goodwin

Grp Capt Mike Hobson, the Coltishall Station Commander, 1966–1968, pictured here with the outgoing station commander, Roger Topp. Mike Hobson Collection

226 OCU Instructors. Back Row, left to right: Ed Scott, Terry Bond, Brian Johnson and Dave Jones. Front Row left to right: Brian Voller, Flt Lt Alex Reed, Sqn Ldr Terry Carlton, OC No 2 Squadron, and Paul Holmes. Flt Lt Terry Bond ejected safely from F.1 XM134 on 11 September 1964 after the starboard undercarriage leg had failed to fully lower. Alex Reed Collection

Wg Cdr Mick Swiney (far right), who took over as Chief Instructor, and OC Flying Wing in mid-1965. To his right is Flt Lt Mike Graydon. These two instructor crews were visiting Gütersloh to check out squadron pilots to see if they were still using the skills taught them at OCU, and were not 'trappers', which descended on bases to test squadron readiness for action. Air Cdre Mick Swiney Collection

oped by Geoff Steggall and Roly Jackson from the LCS. I was sent to Coltishall in February 1964 to set up the OCU there prior to their move in April. [Middleton St. George had been sold, for just £340,000, to become Teeside Airport and on 13 April, 226 OCU and its fourteen Lightnings flew to their new home at Coltishall.] 74 Squadron had moved to Leuchars and we had Coltishall to ourselves, save for the Search and Rescue helicopters. Setting up the OCU at Coltishall went very smoothly and the station personnel, from the CO, Gp Capt Roger Topp, down, were all very enthusiastic to receive the new unit. [Topp continued in the post until 3 June 1966, when Gp Capt Mike Hobson took over.]

The plan was to provide the OCU with three squadrons. No.1 would be responsible for *ab initio* conversion to the Lightning, the course length being around seventy hours, split between the T.4, with solo hours on the F.1A. No.2 would give basic radar training on the AI 23 (and AI 23B for pilots going to F.2 and F.2A squadrons in RAF Germany), while No.3 would provide advanced radar training on the AI 23B for students joining UK F.3 and F.6 squadrons and Cyprus. Occasionally, it would operate Interceptor Weapons Instructor (IWI) courses for the RAF Germany Lightning squadrons, and be responsible for advanced weapons training, including the AI 23B/Red Top missile system. (Later, No.3 Squadron operated only T.5s, and what little solo flying there was on this final part of the course was completed in the two-seat aircraft.) During 1964, Les Davis, OC 3 Squadron, was away with the front-line squadrons, and OC 2 Squadron had not yet converted, so the OCU operated essentially a two squadron organization. Students were a mixture of ex-Hunter and Javelin pilots including Flg Off (later ACM Sir) Bill Wratten, Paul 'Humpty' Holmes, Al Morgan and Gerry Crumbie, and various staff officers.

The OCU was not without incident, as Dave Seward recalls:

An accident on 11 September 1964 involved a bale out by Sqn Ldr Terry Bond, the Unit Test Pilot. He was flying a F.1 on a post minor air test when he could not get the starboard undercarriage leg fully down, having suffered a serious hydraulic failure. The secondary system also failed and after a series of low, slow flypasts, it was obvious that there had been a sequence valve malfunction and the gear was

In 1965, 226 OCU at RAF Coltishall began to expand to its full strength and during this period received the first *ab initio* students straight from Training Command. This line up of T.4s was taken at the station in June 1965. EDP

stuck partially (almost half way) down on both sides. It was therefore decided that he would eject. A runway landing was considered, but advice was that the aircraft could cartwheel. Terry Bond ejected as near to the coast as possible to ensure the aircraft went into the sea, but he hoped to keep his feet dry. In the event, he landed about twenty yards off the shore just south of Bacton with the helicopter virtually waiting for him. I had worked out his ejection area using Met winds to 10,000ft and he was quite annoyed that I'd played it just too close. He was unhurt and quickly returned to flying status.

There was one other accident, which was really an incident, very well handled by the student, Ian MacFadyen. He had a nose wheel stuck in the 'up' position and landed on the runway keeping the nose up until the last moment, causing only minimal damage to the aircraft.

In 1965, the OCU began to expand to its full strength and during this period we received the first *ab initio* students straight

XS419 was 226 OCU's first T.5 to arrive, on 20 April 1965. It was damaged shortly afterwards, when it hit a landing light. It was repaired and later served with the LTF at Binbrook. *via Mick Jennings*

F.1A XM184 and T.4 XM971 taking off from RAF Coltishall. XM971 was lost on a dual radar sortie on 2 January 1967. Both Sqn Ldr Terry Carlton, OC No.2 Squadron, and his student, Flt Lt Lloyd Gross, ejected safely after the aircraft suffered an immediate loss of power caused by the radome coming loose and the debris being ingested by the engines. Gross ejected first, Carlton going at about 800ft, the aircraft crashing at Tunstead. Both pilots, each of whom suffered spinal injuries, were recovered by a Whirlwind from the SAR Flight of 202 Squadron on the base. While being flown by Flt Lt Gerry Crumbie, XM184 caught fire on landing on 17 April 1967 and had to be written-off. Crumbie was unhurt. Simon Parry

from Training Command. On the first of these courses were John Ward, Dickie Duckett (who would later lead the *Red Arrows*) and Doug Aylward, who all did exceptionally well on the Lightning.

In mid-1965, Wg Cdr Mick Swiney took over as Chief Instructor and OC Flying Wing. On 20 April XS419, the OCU's first T.5, arrived. By now the F.1s were being replaced with F.1As from 56 and 111 Squadrons. By the late 1960s the OCU had forty-two Lightnings on its inventory, divided fairly evenly between the three versions, to which eight F.3s were added as of from June 1970. Some of the F.1As were now periodically operated as targets, in much the same way as the Target Facility Flight (TFF) Lightnings, with the AI 23 radar replaced with a Luneberg Lens to create a larger radar 'signature'.

Lightnings and the *Magic Carpet*

T.5 XS454 comes in to land at RAF Coltishall. On 7 March 1967 Flt Lt Mike Graydon and his instructor, Flt Lt Bob Offord, alighted on runway 22 in this aircraft at the end of a Rad-ex when suddenly the main undercarriage collapsed. The engine was shut down before the T.5 veered off to the right of the runway and stopped. Both pilots escaped injury. Ronald Johnson

Saudi Arabia ordered thirty-four of the F.53 export variant (twelve were also ordered by Kuwait) and aircraft 53-666, the first Lightning for the Royal Saudi Air Force, flew on 1 December 1966, the first delivery taking place in December 1967.

The first Saudi pilot to convert to the Lightning was Lt A. Thunneyan, whom Mick Swiney checked out on a standardization sortie at the conclusion of his conversion phase on 9 June 1967. In an effort to stop Yemeni incursions, the delivery of the Saudi Lightnings was preceded, in June 1966, by the arrival in that country of five ex-RAF F.2s (designated F.52), two ex-RAF T.4s and ex-RAF pilots to fly them, under a programme, codenamed *Magic Carpet*, which also included Hunters and Thunderbird surface to air missiles (SAMs).

Bumps Along the Way

Along the way there were a few accidents at 226 OCU at Coltishall. In 1966 three Lightnings were lost. On 15 March Capt Al Peterson USAF safely ejected from XM190 after an ECU fire and the F.1A crashed into the North Sea off Cromer. On 1 June Flg Off Geoff Fish, who was on his first T.5 solo in XS453, suffered an undercarriage failure on the down-wind leg in the circuit. At the end of runway zero-five Wg Cdr Mick Swiney was waiting to start his instrument rating test with Don Oakden in a T.4. Swiney recalls:

Fish flew by the tower at 500ft [150m] and we could all see that the young South African was in trouble. He was told by Pete VanGucci, the DOCFW [Deputy Officer Commanding Flying Wing], to re-cycle the undercarriage. I decided we could go up and see what was what. We formated close behind his tail and could see quite clearly that there was a 'buggers muddle'. The sequencing of the oleos and the undercarriage doors had gone wrong – a 'D' door had closed prior to the undercarriage leg being retracted. It was quite clear that he was not going to get that aircraft down on the ground. Fish would have to eject. We stayed with him the whole time, SAR were alerted and positioned over the sea off Happisburgh. Fish seemed very calm, although his fuel was now running out. Flt Lt Jimmy Jewell in the tower had the presence of mind to tell Fish to check that his straps were done up tightly – they weren't as it happened. He had failed to insert one of the harness 'lugs' properly during strapping in prior to start up. Coolly, Fish undid and then reconnected them. By now his No.1 engine had flamed out and he had to go now while he still had a modicum of control provided by the No.2 engine. At about 3,000ft he ejected perfectly. His 'chute opened as it

On 6 April 1967 the Freedom of Norwich flypast was held to mark twenty-seven years of RAF association with that fine city. The intention was for Wg Cdr Mick Swiney to lead twenty-seven aircraft (made up of twenty-four Lightnings and three Spitfires from the Battle of Britain Memorial Flight) but the weather intervened and he took just a token box across the city to coincide with the parade outside City Hall, together with three Spitfires. EDP via Air Cdre Mick Swiney

should have. From my cockpit it all seemed to happen in slow motion. Then, to our great alarm, the Lightning started to head back towards land! Eventually though, it nosed into the sea. Fish was picked up so quickly he hardly got his feet wet.

A few weeks earlier, on 6 May, XM213 had crashed on take off from Coltishall. The F.1A was being flown by Sqn Ldr Paul Hobley, CGI, who was unhurt. 'As CGI', recalls Flt Lt Alex Reed, his flight commander, who authorized the flight,

T.5s of 226 OCU break. XS449 later joined 23 Squadron and, later still, became 8533M at Binbrook, while XS420, which had joined 226 OCU on 29 April 1965, finished its career with the LTF at Binbrook. XS423 was damaged in a landing accident on 17 January 1968 and in 1968 became 8532M at Binbrook. via Peter Haywood

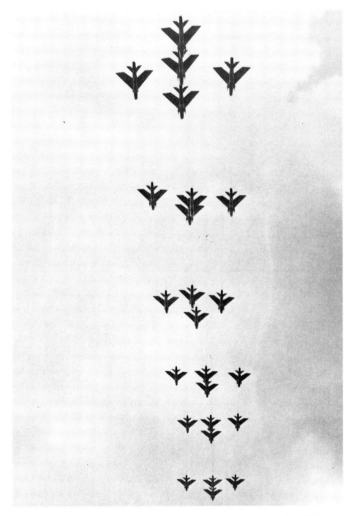

On 23 May 1967 the mass flypast over Norwich finally went ahead and Wng Cdr Mick Swiney led twenty-five Lightnings in six boxes behind two Spitfires of the BBMF.

Wg Cdr George Black, Chief Flying Instructor 226 (Lightning) OCU, RAF Coltishall, in T.5 XS420 in the summer of 1968.

Paul could only fly on a grace and favour basis. SCT (Staff Conversion Training), though, was required. I was coming back from lunch through the hangar. By then I knew there had been an accident. Paul had done a normal take-off, but he took the gear up too quickly and sat it down on its ventral tank. Guys who saw it said they saw a great stream of flame going down the runway and off onto the grass, thirty yards short of a brick building. He was very lucky to walk away. Paul just looked at me. 'Sorry Alex, I just f—ed it!' was all he said!

'Don't worry', I said, 'but for the grace of God . . .'

On another occasion [on 2 January 1967] when I was coming back from lunch (these things always seemed to happen after lunch!), I bumped into Sqn Ldr Terry Carlton, OC No.2 Squadron. I was surprised because I knew

he should be airborne. He said, looking across the airfield at a plume of smoke, 'that's my aircraft!'

Carleton had been on a dual radar sortie in XM971 with his student, Flt Lt Tony Gross, when, on the climb-out shortly after take off, there was a very expensive noise internally and an immediate loss of power. (The radome had come loose and the debris had been ingested by the engines.) Assuming control, Carlton throttled back and commenced a recovery to Coltishall. On a high down-wind leg, he applied throttle to check his descent, but found that he had no power. Gross ejected first, Carlton going at about 800ft (240m), the aircraft crashing at Tunstead. Both pilots, each of whom suffered minor spinal

injuries, were recovered by a Whirlwind helicopter from the SAR Flight of 202 Squadron on the base.

Carlton was involved in another incident, on 12 September, returning from working up on Red Section in a four-ship formation. Alex Reed was flying No.3:

We carried out an echleon starboard break into the circuit, and Terry called 'Downward for the formation'. As he came round on finals at the far end there was a 'twinkle, twinkle, boom'! Obviously, an aircraft had crashed! Terry saw this as well and as we had all broken and fanned out he thought his No.4 must have crashed. Terry called, 'Check In!' and we all did. I was just coming off the runway as the crash vehicles were heading for the column of smoke, 200 yards off the runway. Well, we

T.4 XM997 taking off from RAF Coltishall on 28 February 1968. This aircraft first flew on 22 May 1962 and was delivered to the OCU at Middleton St. George on 14 January 1963. EDP

were all here. Puzzled, we wondered, 'Where did that come from!'

Flt Lt Jock Sneddon, a Wattisham TFF pilot, had experienced a cockpit fire in XM136. Sneddon ejected safely and he landed at Scottow, close to RAF Coltishall. The F.1, which had begun its career with 74 Squadron at Coltishall, seemed to know its way home because the wreckage landed on the airfield boundary!

During the afternoon of 7 March 1967 there occurred another incident at Coltishall, the first in a series to plague the T.5. Flt Lt Mike Graydon (later ACM Sir Michael Graydon GCB CBE ADC FRAeS, Chief of Air Staff), and his instructor, Flt Lt Bob Offord, who were at the end of a Rad-ex in XS454, alighted on runway 22 when suddenly, despite three greens showing on the instrument panel, the main undercarriage collapsed! The nose wheel, however, stayed down. Bob Offord recalls:

The drag chute bit, then the wheels went. Because the levers were on his side, I told Mike Graydon to shut down the engine and open

Being the main operator of two-seat Lightnings, 226 OCU's T.4s and T.5s were in great demand to qualify people to be members of the 'Ten Ton Club', complete with scroll and special tie. Diana Barnato-Walker, a famous flyer and wartime ATA pilot, became the first British woman to achieve the distinction, on 26 August 1963, when she was accompanied by Sqn Ldr Ken Goodwin, the CO, in XM996. Another member is TV personality David Jacobs, an anxious passenger in November 1968, his debonair look returning once the champagne cork popped as he celebrated the flight with pilot, Sqn Ldr Terry Madden, Gp Capt Mike Hobson (left) and Wg Cdr George Black (right), standing in as temporary waiter. Gp Capt Mike Hobson Collection

the canopy. We had no control. It just went straight and then veered off to the right and stopped. I said, 'Get Out!' and I went over the side. I didn't know at this stage what had happened. You can imagine the looks we got!

Peter Hayward, a technician at 226 OCU, explains:

The landing gear failures affected only the T.5. The leg(s) would fold towards the end of the landing run when the aircraft was rolling relatively slowly, and so, apart from the pilots' injured pride, and a somewhat scraped wingtip, little damage was done. Many investigations were carried out and many theories put forward. One theory was that the pilots were inadvertently operating the 'gear up' lever instead of the brake chute lever (on the T.5 the two levers were quite close to each other). This was immediately rejected by the pilots, who pointed out that with the aircraft on the ground with weight on the landing gear, the gear select lever is locked in the 'down' position and a positive override action is

On 21 June 1968 Sqn Ldr Arthur Tilsley taxied in with no brakes and buried F.1A XM188 in the side of No.1 Hangar. Both engines jammed at about eighty per cent power and a Rolls-Royce technician scrambled underneath to the engine bay and eventually managed to stop the engine. Arthur Tilsley (being led away, left of the picture) climbed out of the cockpit onto the roof of the hangar offices. via Jean Stangroom

required before it can be selected 'up'.

The theory that pilots were inadvertently operating the landing gear lever led to an unexpected bonus for the ground crews. 'Joy trips' for technicians in the right hand seat of a Lightning were highly desirable, but because of the training commitment at Coltishall were rare occurrences. When the above theory was first mooted the decision was taken that whenever a T.5 had to be flown solo (test flight, conversion pilot's first solo etc.), the right hand seat would be occupied by a ground tech-

On 29 February 1968 19-year old Plt Off Vivian Whyer WAAF, a flight control officer at Coltishall, became the 1,000th member of the Ten Ton Club when the station commander, Gp Capt Mike Hobson, flew her at 1,000mph plus in T.4 XM970 although, because only one engine would go to re-heat, Mike had to put the nose down over the North Sea to reach the magic 1,000mph! Gp Capt Hobson Collection

F.1A XM188 in happier times coming in to land at RAF Coltishall. Ronald Johnson

Wings Appeal! Battle of Britain Week 1968, the year of the 50th anniversary of the RAF, opened in Norwich on 9 September with an ear-splitting roar as a formation of sixteen Lightnings from RAF Coltishall flew low over the City Hall on the first stroke of twelve noon. The Lightnings passed the cathedral (right) and swooped down from behind the castle (left). The Lord Mayor, Mr E.A. Gambling, declared BoB Week open from the steps of the City Hall; his speech was transmitted by radio to Wg Cdr George Black, the leader of the formation and, just as it ended, the Lightnings came over for the second time. Gp Capt Mike Hobson Collection

Sixteen Lightnings from Coltishall led by Wg Cdr George Black fly over Norwich and the parade outside City Hall on 9 September 1968 to officially open Battle of Britain week. via Gp Capt Mike Hobson

nician so that the brake chute could be deployed by him from the lever in the right hand side of the cockpit. There was no shortage of volunteers.

On some flights the opportunity arose for a number of those technicians to join the 1,000 mph Club. I achieved it during a flight with Flt Lt Henry Ploszek. Two other flights I had as a passenger are indelibly recorded in my mind. One of these was a low level PI with Flt Lt 'Oscar' Wild. Low level PIs consisted of flying at 50 to 250ft above the sea and intercepting 'enemy' aircraft (usually another Lightning). Interceptions were carried out under instructions from ground control and using the information supplied by the aircraft's AI 23B radar. This meant that the pilot had his eyes glued inside the radar visor and the aircraft was flying on autopilot in the altitude hold mode. Now this may sound perfectly normal, but if you are a passenger sitting in the right hand seat and have got nothing to look at other than the white caps of waves or North Sea gas rigs and shipping flashing past below you at close range, and perhaps if you do not share the pilot's blind faith in the technology that is supposed to prevent you flying into the sea, then a feeling of being in the wrong place can overcome you.

Similarly, a formation let-down with a USAF exchange pilot at the controls led to a feeling of wishing I was back in the crew room enjoying a cup of coffee and a cigarette. There were perhaps four aircraft in the let-down. Above the clouds in the bright sunlight everything looked easy and was most enjoyable, but then we entered cloud and remained in formation. The separation from the other aircraft was maybe ten or fifteen feet and the only visual contact I had with them was the flash of the anti-collision lights on the wingtips. Then the lights would disappear again in the gloom. It was like driving in thick fog with candles for headlights. The relief, when we finally broke cloud, was immense. It was after this flight that I realized why pilots are called, 'steely-eyed'.

BAC sent a team of specialists to assist the

Getting Lightnings of 226 OCU ready for formation practice and flypasts put a great strain on the ground crews at Coltishall but they always managed to have enough aircraft airworthy for ceremonial occasions. Simon Parry

F.1As and T-birds line up at Coltishall on 14th September 1968 on the occasion of the Battle of Britain Air Show. F.1A XM215 originally served with 111 Squadron before joining the OCU, and later served with Binbrook TFF. XM183 arrived at the OCU from 56 Squadron and later became 8416M at Binbrook. XM172, the first F.1A in RAF service, was first used by 56 Squadron and in 1974 became the Coltishall gate guardian. Gp Capt Mike Hobson Collection

RAF. Test equipment was installed on a sample T.5 and even a movie camera was mounted in the airframe to take a film of the behaviour of the landing gear during the landing. However, as is often the case, when you want something to happen, it never does, and no incidents occurred on the test aircraft. So nothing was proved conclusively and it was decided that stray voltages induced into the wiring to the landing gear control unit

Line-up of 226 OCU F.1As and T.4s at Coltishall early in 1968. F.1A XM174, which arrived at the OCU after serving with 56 Squadron, was later used by the TFF at Leuchars, where it crashed into a quarry at Bulmullo on approach on 29 November 1968. The pilot ejected safely. Simon Parry

Three Lightnings – T.5 XS458, F.1A XM215 and T.4 XM969 – flying close formation with a Spitfire of the BBMF from RAF Coltishall in the late 1960s. Simon Parry

were the most likely cause of the problem and that the routing of the wiring would be modified. This involved approximately two days' work on each aircraft and the Coltishall T.5 fleet (which included four T.55s belonging to the RSAF) was completed in the record time of three weeks.

Flypasts and Ten Ton T-Birds

Coltishall's association with Norwich stretches back to the Battle of Britain in 1940, the days of Douglas Bader and Bob Stanford-Tuck. A most notable event in the station's calendar in 1967 therefore was the Freedom of Norwich flypast on 6 April, held to mark twenty-seven years of RAF association with the fine city. Gp Capt Mike Hobson selected Wg Cdr Mick Swiney to lead the formation flypast, which would comprise no fewer that twenty-seven aircraft (made up of twenty-four Lightnings and three Spitfires from the Battle of Britain Memorial Flight), the largest Lightning formation ever to take off from and recover to its parent station, as Mick Swiney recalls:

No other station could produce so many Lightnings from their own resources. I had forty-two. Also, I had enough instructors to fly them in boxes without turning a hair, so I decided we would fly in boxes of four, all in line astern, behind the three Spitfires.

Flt Lt Gil Pink (37), a Canberra PR7 navigator and an old acquaintance from my Laarbruch days, was on a ground tour at Coltishall, and he helped plan the route and calculate the precise timings needed. A brilliant navigator, he also loved flying. He flew two 'recces' with me in the T.4. Our first

During the 1960s at the start of every Battle of Britain Week the good citizens of Norwich were treated to some spectacular flypasts over their city by aircraft from RAF Coltishall, not least by a Hurricane, Spitfire and four Lightnings. Simon Parry

Sixteen Lightnings overfly Coltishall on Battle of Britain Day, September 1969. Dick Jeeves

practice was with twenty-four Lightnings on 3 April, and on the auspicious day, the weather intervened and I took just a token box across the city to coincide with the parade outside City Hall, together with three Spitfires.

On 27 April I led sixteen Lightnings in formation for the AOC's parade. In the mean-time, 23 May was chosen to re-stage the mass flypast over Norwich and this time I was able to mount the whole show. We could not get twenty-seven aircraft onto the runway at once so I led twelve Lightnings off in three boxes, and Sqn Ldr Brian Farrer, OC 3 Squadron, with twelve in the second lot, would fall in behind. I led Red, Blue and Green Boxes off, did a wide, right handed circuit, turned in over the coast, and ran up the runway at 1,000ft [300m]. Brian Farrer's formation took off and pulled in behind. I did not want our entire formation to 'snake', so to avoid any changes in direction, we had a long run in point. (I got one of the SAR Whirlwinds to drop a smoke float at a precise point in the sea.) Ahead of us were two Spitfires (a third developed engine trouble after take off and had to return so Flt Lt Alex Reed, the 'whipper-in', replaced it to make up the magic twenty-seven). We lined up and I led all twenty-five Lightnings straight to Norwich, aiming for the Cathedral spire. The Spitfires flew at 180 knots, the Lightnings at 360 knots. I am happy to say that it was a DCO [Duty Carried Out] exercise. I sent Brian Farrer's lot in to land first as they were slightly thirstier aircraft.

Sadly, Gil Pink, who had got me to the right place at the right time, was killed on 22 June when the SAR Whirlwind he was riding in on an training exercise lost a rotor blade and crashed into the sea, killing everyone on board.

On 19 September 1970, Battle of Britain Air Show day at Coltishall, the Lightning diamond sixteen had to divert to Wattisham nearby after the runway was blocked by Sqn Ldr Eric Hopkins' Lightning with a locked brake. Pete Nash took this photo of T.4 XM990 on the Wattisham flight line that evening before the aircraft took off again for RAF Coltishall, where XM990 lost aileron control when a bolt dropped out, and Flt Lt John Sims and Flt Lt Brian Fuller of 226 OCU ejected safely before the aircraft crashed into a small wood near the station. Pete Nash

In October 1967 Wg Cdr George P. Black AFC arrived at Coltishall to take over command of 226 OCU/145

Four of 226 OCU's T-birds on a sortie from RAF Coltishall in the late 1960s. Peter Hayward

Squadron, and the added responsibilities of CFI/Wg Cdr Flying. Having already accumulated 1,000 hours on the Lightning, he was given a brief conversion course consisting of one dual and three solo sorties to initiate him in his new post! Being the main operator of two-seat Lightnings, 226 OCU's T.4s and T.5s were in great demand in 1963–74 to fly VIPs and other notables at speeds greater than 1,000 mph and so qualify them to be members of the Thousand Miles Per Hour Club, otherwise known as the 'Ten Ton Club', complete with scroll and special tie. 226 OCU had made it possible for Diana Barnato-Walker, a famous flyer and wartime Air Transport Auxiliary pilot, to become the first British woman to achieve the distinction, on 26 August 1963, when she was accompanied by Sqn Ldr Ken Goodwin, the CO, in XM996. Diana clocked Mach 1.65 – 1,262mph (2,000km) – which, for a short time, was an unofficial women's speed record, beating that of Jacqueline Cochrane of America and Jacqueline Auriol of France.

It was also around this time that a Guinness Toucan bird, stolen from a pub in Newcastle, was flown to 1,000 mph membership and became a jealously guarded trophy held for short periods variously by 19 and 92 Squadrons, and the LCS. Amid all the publicity, Guinness threw a celebration party at the Park Royal Hotel in London but the festivities were brought to an abrupt end after the Park Royal tower clock disappeared.

By 1968, appropriately the RAF's 50th Anniversary year, the club's membership now included well over 900 members, from royal personages such as King Hussein of Jordan and the Shah of Iran, to people of more humble origins. On 27 February David Hastings, a member of the Norwich Observer Corps, became the 999th member of the club when he was flown by Gp Capt Mike Hobson at 1,066 mph! 1968 being a leap year, the station commander considered it appropriate that a woman should be the 1,000th member to achieve the distinction of membership to the Ten Ton Club and 19-year old Plt Off Vivian Whyer WAAF, a flight control officer at Coltishall, was the lucky candidate, on 29 February. (The three safety equipment workers responsible for packing their parachutes were all women.) 'However', recalls Mike Hobson,

the weather was appalling and all flying was cancelled, but the press and the TV were there in force so we couldn't really back down. It was all right to take off and I could always land elsewhere if necessary, so off we went in the T.4. (XM970). Only problem was, once Neatishead said that the high speed run could begin, I could only get one engine to re-heat, so to reach the magic 1,000mph, I had to put the nose down over the North Sea!

Early in 1968 four T.55s of the Royal Saudi Air Force arrived at RAF Coltishall for training Saudi pilots. On this formation sortie along the Norfolk coast are 55-711/A and 55-713/C, which arrived at Coltishall on 2 February, and 55-714/D, which arrived on 22 March. The last aircraft was flown to Saudi Arabia via Akrotiri, Cyprus on 27 August 1969 by Al Love. Prior to the first course of Saudi pilots, Lt A. Thunneyan was the first RSAF pilot to convert to the Lightning, on 9 June 1967. via Tony Aldridge

Col. Akbar Khan, Chief of Staff to the C-in-C of the Royal Afghan Air Force, who had just presented the RAF with a Hawker Hind as a 50th Anniversary

55-711/A, 55-713/C, 55-714/D and 55-712/B, which arrived at Coltishall for Saudi pilot training on 15 February 1968, in formation over Norfolk. 55-712, which was flown to Saudi Arabia together with 55-714, 55-416 and 53-418 on 11 July 1969, crashed into Half Moon Bay on 21 May 1974 after an inverted low pass over sand dunes, killing Col Ainousa and Lt Otaibi. via Peter Hayward

present, became a member of the Ten Ton Club on 12 June 1968 when he flew in XM974 with Mike Hobson. (The Hind is now displayed at the RAF Museum, Hendon.) 226 OCU also flew Colonel Cesar Rohon, the Ecuadorian Chief of Staff, as Mike Hobson recalls:

> He duly received his tie, but he did not receive his certificate. An opportunity to correct this came late in 1969. I was now DD Ops at MoD

Photos of Saudi pilots at Coltishall are rare. This one, taken by EDP staff photographer Dick Jeeves, shows three of them, Captain 'Mo' Algehani, Prince Turki Nasser (later Chief of Defence, Saudi Air Force) and Ahmed Sudari. On the right is Princess Laura Say, wife of Prince Turki. To the left of the photo are Jan Jeeves and her children, Bob and Mark, and Erica Sobers, MoD press relations officer. Dick Jeeves and was one of the team sent to Ecuador with BAC when it looked like the Ecuadorians were going to buy Lightnings. I sent Rohon's certificate to the Air Attaché in Quito, only to be told that he had been kidnapped! About five days later he was found dumped by the side of the road, and a few days after that, he was placed under arrest. He never did get his certificate!

Meanwhile, in 1968 Fighter Command had made way for Strike Command and at Coltishall twenty Lightnings (in four boxes of four, plus reserves) were required for the 50th Anniversary flypast at Abingdon on 1 April. Fuel requirements for the flypast dictated flying from RAF Wyton so most of the Coltishall Wing was deployed there for almost two weeks. Wg Cdr George Black recalls:

I led the formation in a T.5 and behind the Lightnings were four boxes of four Hunters led by Wg Cdr Nigel Price, 229 OCU. The exciting bit was the join up and on one of the rehearsals the Hunter Wing overcooked the join-up and came in at a very interesting angle – I graciously let them have the lead! On the very last day we could not get all the way around the route safely and chose to come back to Coltishall; we really had to land at Wyton. But we had tremendous confidence in

F.3 XP696 of 226 OCU in the white-finned scheme adopted by display pilot Pete Chapman taking off in characteristically spectacular fashion. This aircraft joined the OCU in August 1972 after being used by the CFE at Binbrook, 1964–1967, and on Red Top trials at Boscombe Down from 16 February 1966 to 5 June 1967 before modification to full F.3 standard at Warton. Simon Parry

the aircraft and the systems so we devised a somewhat unusual plan for the recovery. Once we had completed the flypast a codeword was given and we all shut down one engine! Once overhead Coltishall every single engine was relit without a problem and we did two flypasts at Coltishall before landing.

It was shortly after this that we had to produce twelve aircraft for the demise of Fighter Command. [At the disbandment parade at Bentley Priory on 25 April, the flypast was by Lightnings of 5, 23, 29 and 111 Squadrons, and 226 OCU.] The Flypast was not so spectacular as we were involved in Abingdon, and we also had aircraft in the Queen's Birthday Flypast.

Another significant incident during my reign was [on 21 June 1968] when Sqn Ldr Arthur Tilsley taxied in with no brakes and buried the aircraft in the side of No.1 Hangar. Both engines jammed at about eighty per cent and the Rolls-Royce rep did a splendid job going underneath to the engine bay and eventually managing to stop the engine. It was a horrific sight as the intake sucked in the bricks and mortar (and much of Bob Lightfoot's and Nick Galpin's desks), chewed them up and then hurled stones and gravel at ATC: there was a brown column of dust about 200ft (60m) high. Arthur Tilsley climbed out of the cockpit onto the roof of the hangar offices and was an amusing sight running around as though his hair was on fire.

Our recent formation flying proficiency was remembered and I was persuaded to put up a Diamond Sixteen, which had never been

Instructors in 65(F) Squadron at Coltishall, 1973, face the camera in a variety of guises dating back to World War One! Left to right: Pete Howarth, John Baggott, Sqn Ldr John Bryant, Jack Brown, Sqn Ldr Dickie Duckett (seated), ???, SENGO, Paul Holmes, Wg Cdr Murdo MacDermid (seated), Sandy Davis, Brian Carroll (in white with monocle), Bob Turbin (seated), Rick Peacock-Edwards, ???, Furry Lloyd and John Brady with Union Jack. Wg Cdr John Bryant Collection

Sqn Ldr Dickie Duckett, one of the first *ab initio* students straight from Training Command to complete the OCU course in 1965, and who did exceptionally well on the Lightning, is pictured at Coltishall in front of a 65 Squadron aircraft in 1972 when he was an instructor at the OCU and also an RAF aerobatic pilot. Duckett later led the *Red Arrows*. Simon Parry

brakes!' The pilot somehow 'threaded the needle' beautifully, took the lead from me and went straight into the barrier in front of me. An unfortunate end to what had been a great occasion. It was a year of interesting flypasts that interrupted the OCU training but ensured everyone on the OCU worked extremely hard, and as a result, we even managed to get the courses out on time.

On 19 September 1970, the Battle of Britain airshow ended in disaster at RAF Coltishall with the loss of XM990. The T.4, crewed by Flt Lts John Sims and Brian Fuller of 226 OCU, was being used as a reserve for the diamond sixteen formation display and was called into the centre of the box. However, the Coltishall runway was blocked by Sqn Ldr Eric Hopkins' Lightning with a locked brake and the formation had to be diverted to Wattisham.

On the return, later that evening, XM990 lost aileron control when a bolt dropped out, and the aircraft began corkscrewing and losing height with every revolution. To people on the airfield it seemed that they were being treated to an impromptu air display by the single Lightning! Both pilots were able to hold

the wing up, but landing was not possible and they were forced to eject. Sims went first, at 1,500ft (450m) and 220 knots. Fuller, who had to time his ejection on the next upward corkscrew, followed at 1,000ft (300m).

The aircraft had time to complete only one-and-a-half more turns before it crashed into a small wood bordering the A1140 Norwich–South Walsham road near the village of Little Plumstead. Part of the tail unit was hurled across the road, inches in front of a car driven by 28-year old Michael Howard who, with two friends, were returning from an unsuccessful fishing trip. Standing by his car a few minutes after the crash, Mr Howard recounted:

Suddenly there was a hell of a screech and a shrieking noise. I glanced up to the trees on the right-hand side of the road – they were almost overhanging the road – when I saw a white flash going into the top of the trees. The plane hit a big oak tree and burst into a mass of flames right in front of my eyes. The tail piece crashed right across the road a few feet in front of me and the next thing I knew I was right in a mass of flames from the trees where the rest of the plane was burning. It was all over in a

flown by Lightnings before, in the September Battle of Britain Open Day at Coltishall.

First, a rehearsal was flown, and then, at the beginning of Battle of Britain Week, Monday 9 September, the formation flew over the city hall. All this activity placed a great strain on the ground crews, as Peter Hayward recalls: 'Preparations were pretty hectic. This was always a joint effort between the two flights of 226 OCU. (One flight alone did not possess sixteen aircraft.) It was often said that to get one Lightning serviceable for a flight was a pretty remarkable achievement, but to get thirty-two Avons started in quick succession (the most infernal noise imaginable) and see sixteen aircraft off without any major problems bordered on a miracle!'

Problems, however, did arise on the Saturday during the Battle of Britain Day show, but it had nothing to do with the Lightnings, as George Black explains:

We had 12–14 aircraft landing, following the convention of the time landing left–right–left etc., when a Hunter landed and called, 'No

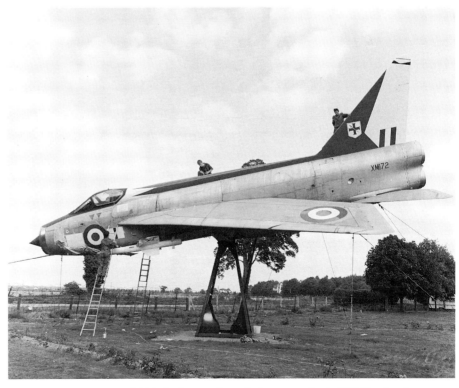

XM172 is put out to grass at Coltishall to become the station's gate guardian in 1970. The aircraft, now owned by Haydon-Baille, is under the threat of being moved to another location. Adrian Savage

flash. Then we were OK. I thought that the whole road was a ball of flames as we drove through it. We were all in one piece and the car was all right.

Sims, who landed in the wood, had a scuffed neck, while Fuller had just harness bruising. Both pilots were helicoptered to Coltishall aboard the station's SAR Whirlwind.

Blinding Lightnings

Meanwhile, the Royal Saudi Air Force had contracted to buy newer marks of Lightning to replace their earlier marks and in 1969 226 OCU was given the Saudi training commitment, with four Saudi T.55s (two more were purchased by Kuwait) being attached to No.3 Squadron. *Magic Palm*, the second phase of the Saudi delivery programme, had begun in 1968, the year that Kuwait also took delivery of the Lightning. The F.53 was first used in action by the RSAF on ground strikes against border positions in Yemen late in 1969. Kuwait operated the Lightning for seven years, before replacing them with the French Mirage.

At Coltishall, the RSAF course was almost double the RAF course. To quote the Koran, 'The lightning all but blinds them'. George Black recalls one memorable incident which involved a Saudi student who somehow managed to align his compass 180 degrees out and instead of heading out over the North Sea, ended up over London at 36,000ft (11,000m) much to the consternation of Air Traffic Control. Another aircraft had to be sent up to get him back.

Flt Lt Bob Offord, who completed three years as an instructor on 3 Squadron, 226 OCU in 1969, the year he retired from the RAF, recalls the Saudi pilots:

During my time, 1968–69, I flew Capt [later General and Commander of the RSAF] Ahmed Behery, Capt Bakry, Prince Turki bin Nasser [later Brigadier General, Deputy Defence Minister], Major Essa Ghimlas [killed in an F.52 whilst practising single engine approaches to Khamis Mushayt, on 28 November 1968], Major Hamdullah, Capt Aziz, and Prince Bandar Faisal, one of the King's sons. Bandar arrived at Coltishall in a Lamborghini, crashed it, and bought another. Not to replace it mind, for when the first one was repaired, he kept both. The Saudis were loaded, and well paid, but to them, flying was a hobby rather than a career. Some of them

65 Squadron instructors pose for the camera at Coltishall in 1972. Left to right: John Brady, Jack Brown, Sqn Ldr John Bryant and Sqn Ldr Bob Turbin. Simon Parry

came from Cranwell, some had flown F-86s. Most of them were quite good, some very good, three we would like to have had in our squadron. I went out to Saudi Arabia in 1969 and continued training for Airwork Services. The runways there were longer. Dhahran for instance, was a former USAF SAC base.

'For a young Air Traffic Controller in the early 1970s', recalls Flt Lt Dick Doleman,

there was no finer place to be than the Lightning OCU at Coltishall. You did not have to be a pilot to enjoy the aura or potency of this magnificent beast and I never tired of watching it. The Lightning seemed to attract or develop pilots of a certain character. For me this character was epitomized by the leadership team that came together about a third of the way through my tour. A finer bunch of larger than life characters you couldn't wish to meet: Gp Capt Joe Gilbert (station commander); Wg Cdr Dave Seward (OC OPs Wing); Wg Cdr Paul Hobley (OC 2(T) Squadron), an ex-junior 'Mr Midlands'; and Wg Cdr Murdo MacDermid (OC 65(F) Squadron) – the 'gang of four'! They were all immensely likeable people with totally different but complimentary characters and a great pleasure to work for and with.

The instructors on the OCU were an

T.5 XS455 which was abandoned on 6 September 1972, after hydraulic failure caused a loss of control. Sqn Ldr T.J.L. Gauvain of 226 OCU and Lt R. Verbist of the Belgian Air Force both ejected before the aircraft crashed north of Spurn Head of Withensea. The T.5 had joined 226 OCU on 20 December 1965. via Mick Jennings

Lightning T.5 cockpit. Simon Parry

Dicky Duckett, Trevor 'McDoogle-Boogle' McDonald-Bennett and Rory Downes, to name just a few.

Coltishall was a very busy OCU and, like all OCUs, each conversion course was a mixed bag of both experience and rank. The description of a Lightning as 'an aluminium tube with a frightened teenager strapped inside' was not altogether strictly correct as it could sometimes contain a frightened Group Captain! From a controller's viewpoint, work at Coltishall was always interesting and very often demanding. Student inexperience, weather, aircraft speed and shortage of fuel often combined to make for some very 'interesting' moments; adrenalin was never in short supply. Considering the prodigious fuel consumption of the Lightning and the limits to which it was operated, it has always surprised me that we never lost an aircraft due to lack of fuel. However, it was mighty close on many occasions and flame-outs on the ground were not unheard of. As Captain Ed Crump, a USAF exchange officer and Vietnam veteran succinctly summarised: 'With that kind of endurance, I don't call 'take-off', I call PAN!' (Ed was killed flying his own home-built aircraft in 1975, aged 34, when he hit a tree at Seeley lake, Montana.) Another tribute to the OCU at Coltishall is that, as far as I am aware, there was never a fatality and the aircraft attrition rate was surprisingly low compared

equally impressive and unforgettable bunch of personalities. These included 'Furz' Lloyd, Pete 'Chappie' Chapman, whose spectacular solo display was never bettered, and 'Oscar' Wild, whose premise that a fighter circuit meant no levelling the wings before the threshold resulted in some spectacular approaches and one wheel touchdowns. Sometimes, it was rumoured, that to achieve

the objective, required the judicious use of burner in the finals turn! Others were 'Taff' Butcher, Rick Peacock-Edwards, 'Thumbs' Gosling; 'Duk' Webb, 'Jimmy' Jewell, Dave 'Quingle' Hampton (killed after spinning in Cyprus), 'Jonx' Kendrick, Ian Sanford (later killed in mid-air between Gnats while instructing at Valley), Rick Groombridge, John Spencer, Bob Turbin, 'Jack' Frost,

On the night of 31 January 1973 instructor Capt Gary Catren, a USAF exchange officer, with student Flt Lt George Smith took off on an SCT sortie in T.5 XS420 from Runway 04 at RAF Coltishall, but the lower re-heat failed to ignite and, with flaps down, the resultant force of the upper re-heat did not allow the nosewheel to be raised. XS420 took the barrier with it into the overshoot. Both pilots walked away unhurt. Simon Parry

T.4 XM988, pictured at Coltishall in September 1968, was lost in the North Sea on 5 June 1973 when Wg Cdr Christopher Bruce of 74 Squadron entered a spin from a Mach 1.1 spiral descent and was forced to abandon the aircraft after losing control. He ejected safely and was quickly picked up by an ASR Whirlwind. Ron Clarke

overhead, necessitating landing in the opposite direction. Calls of 'land over me' from the pilot in the barrier went unheeded as the various elements diverted off to Marham, including one aircraft having declared 'Mayday'. I'm not sure whether the AOC was impressed or not!

Organizational Changes

In November 1971 Wg Cdr McLeod left for HQ 11 Group and was succeeded by Wg Cdr Dave Seward, who filled the posts of Chief Instructor and OC Ops. For operational reasons it was decided to declare the Lightning F.1A element of the OCU to SACEUR (NATO) as an operational squadron. No.1, with F.1A and T.4 aircraft, now became a front-line squadron, taking the 'number plate' of 65 Squadron, while No.3 was absorbed by 2(T) to become a full training squadron and postgraduate course using F.3s (and F.6 systems) and T.5s. Wg Cdr MacDermid became OC 65 Squadron, which was declared to NATO as such, with its war base at Coltishall. OC 2 Squadron, Wg Cdr Paul Hobley, became known as OC 2(T) Squadren, and in war either would operate from Coltishall, or disperse its aircraft and personnel to support other front-line squadrons.

'We therefore had,' recalls Wg Cdr Dave Seward,

> an OCU with a wing commander Chief Instructor, who was also OC Ops Wing RAF Coltishall, and two wing commander squadron commanders, one of which had a front line number plate. Personally, I have always thought this to be distinctly unfortunate as it really split the wing into two. Before this, we were one identifiable unit with a single Reserve Squadron number, which engendered a true unit spirit. If it were imperative that No.1 Squadron should become 65 Squadron I felt that 2(T) Squadron should have retained the reserve number plate of 145 Squadron, and at least we would have had parity in squadron identification, but just one squadron number plate for the whole OCU would have been preferable.
>
> In the event, the running of the unit required careful handling and demanded the utmost co-operation of the three wing commanders in carrying out the OCU training task as well as maintaining operational efficiency to front-line squadron standards.

to my experience at other fighter bases operating more modern types of aircraft.

There were so many memorable controlling incidents that it is very hard to pick out the outstanding moments. Some memories, however, seem more vivid. Rory Downes (2(T) Squadron) launched on a very foggy Friday. It was his last day in RAF service and he needed the flight to achieve the coveted 1,000 hours on type. No pressure to fly of course! Unfortunately, his exodus spurred the otherwise dormant opposition (65(F) Squadron) into instant action and a mass launch. Unfortunately, Rory's minimum fuel instrument recovery was baulked by a pair on the runway. With only fuel for a visual circuit, he completed this in the fog using only vertical visibility to position himself onto finals. An ambition only just achieved in more sense than one.

A further incident occurred around one of the AOC's [AM Sir Ivor Broom] inspections early in my tour. As part of the occasion, it had been decided to fly a Diamond Nine [led by Wg Cdr John McLeod, who had taken over as

OC OPs Wing and Chief Instructor (although not a QFI) in October 1969] and a solo aerobatic display. Unfortunately, the weather once again had its part to play. Before the planned take-off, we had been tracking a truly large thunderstorm on radar which was heading directly for the airfield. Despite our best advice, it was decided to launch. The arrival of the formation and the thunderstorm coincided perfectly and chaos soon ensured.

The radar was now completely weather cluttered and unable to help. The frequency became frenetic with all kinds of join up calls being made as the broken formation tried to re-establish contact with each other. In the middle of this chaos, the solo display pilot ran in fast at low level, hotly pursued by one of the formation, who assumed he had found part of his section. The subsequent manoeuvre seemed to take him completely by surprise! The first landing, on the by now flooded runway, resulted in aquaplaning and the aircraft overrunning and entering the barrier (safety net at the end of the runway). The wind had now changed direction as the storm passed

I started my refresher conversion on No.67 Course in January 1972 and had hoped to refresh on the full long course with both squadrons, but in the event it was decided that I should be in post bt the end of April 1972 when Coltishall's runway was to be complete [which involved digging out the existing runway to 12ft and replacing it]. For me the course was reduced to three months, half with each squadron. Thus, for four months the OCU was dispersed. 65 Squadron went to Honington, Suffolk, and then back to Norfolk, to Marham, and No.2(T) to Binbrook. The Battle of Britain Flight went to Wattisham. Due to an attempted takeover bid by Ken Goodwin to retain the historic aircraft at Wattisham I was dispatched there for most of the detachment to ensure that it returned to Coltishall. I therefore managed to get some hours hours on the Lightning in those four months, but had a veritable feast on the Hurricanes and Spitfires.

226 OCU returned to Coltishall on 1 September 1972, much to the surprise of some new house owners in the area who had purchased their property believing that all flying had ceased. We had a few months of complaints and visits to local councils and organizations plus several parties visiting the station to see for themselves, but by Christmas all was relatively serene. [Before the move, on 6 September, 226 OCU lost a T.5 flying from Binbrook when Sqn Ldr Tim Gauvain took Lt. R. Verbist of the Belgian Air Force on a familiarization trip in XS455. Fifteen minutes after take off, near Spurn Head, Gauvain was alerted by both hydraulic captions illuminating on his instrument panel. The T.5 had suffered a double hydraulic failure! Four minutes later, Gauvain sent a 'Mayday' and said he and his Belgian passenger were both ejecting. Gauvain landed in a cornfield, suffering four crush fractures, while Verbist landed hard near houses and twisted his right knee. The aircraft crashed in the North Sea off Withensea.]

1973 was an exceptionally busy year. We had a very vigorous TACEVAL, and incidentally won the TACEVAL Trophy. [Despite all the problems, RAF Coltishall also won the 1973 Stainforth Trophy for the 'most efficient station, and flting efficiency'] On 27 July we had a Royal visit by His Royal Highness the Prince Philip, Duke of Edinburgh, which was very successful, and training continued at an intensive rate. In addition to the long and short Lightning conversions and refreshers, we ran the Interceptor Weapons Instructor (IWI) courses.

During my period of office, we had three accidents. Two were bale outs and one an aborted take-off. The first bale out [14 December 1972] was due to the break up of an engine when [T.4 XM974] the target aircraft was acting as a high speed, low level target for the IWI (Intercept Weapons Instructors) course. In order to maintain 650kt, re-heat was engaged and shortly afterwards the engines rapidly exited the rear end of the aircraft in a

T.5 XS418 beautifully captured on camera by Dick Jeeves on 25 September 1974 during a sortie from RAF Coltishall. This aircraft had joined the OCU on 7 May 1965 and on 23 August 1968 had crashed at Stradishall when the undercarriage retracted on landing. Flt Lt Henry Ploszek and SAC Lewis were unhurt. Dick Jeeves/EDP

plume of black smoke. The crew, an instructor and a student who had finished his course and was awaiting posting [Sqn Ldr John Spencer and Flg Off Geoff Evans respectively], both ejected.

At 1,000ft (300m) near Happisburgh, and flying at 600 knots, XM974 developed a ECU/re-heat fire. Spencer pulled up to 9–10,000ft (2,700–3,000m) and put out distress calls. At 270 knots and one minute after the critical emergency, Evans ejected first, followed by Spencer. Both men were picked up after eighty-five minutes (thirty of them in the dinghy), by helicopter. By then Spencer, who was wearing too small a girth of immersion suit and totally inadequate insulation, was hypothermic. Evans, on the other hand, in his Bunny suit and Mk.10 coverall, was reported to be warm and dry.

'It is possible', continues Seward,

that somehow medical records may have been inexplicably switched, because the student, looking exceedingly healthy, was kept in hospital and the instructor, with his head sagging to one side, was returned to duty. I seem to recall that shortly afterwards he was posted to RAF Germany as a Flight Commander and was very rapidly sorted out in Wegberg [RAF hospital in Germany]. He also went on to complete a very distinguished career and achieved air rank.

The aborted take-off was a singularly unfortunate occurrence. The F.6 used flap for take-off in order to give more positive lift off during the take-off roll. It is interesting that due to not having inter-connected flaps the F.2A did flapless take-offs without any difficulty. It was decided by higher authority that all re-heat take-offs by F.3s and T.5s would also be with flaps down. This was a very uncomfortable manoeuvre and was considered by the OCU to be unnecessary. We were overruled. The case [31 January 1973] involved an instructor, [Capt Gary Catren] a USAF exchange officer, on an SCT [Staff Continuation Training] sortie in a T.5 [XS420] with a student [Flt Lt George Smith] as ballast. During the re-heat take-off at night the lower re-heat failed to ignite, and with flap down, the resultant force of the upper re-heat did not allow the nosewheel to be raised. The whole affair was settled when the instructor uttered an expletive which the student interpreted as 'chute George', and he promptly deployed the drag-chute. Although it rapidly burnt off, the deployed 'chute scuppered any chance of take-off and the aircraft took the barrier with it into the overshoot. Of course the instructor took the blame, and when I tried to take the matter up with the Wg Cdr Training at HQ 11 Group, he had already progressed to better fields, but I seem to recall that flaps were no longer used for re-heat take-offs in F.3s and T.5s.

The second bale out occurred [on 5 June 1973] when the student [Wg Cdr Chris Bruce of 74 Squadron, in a solo sortie in T.4 XM988] pitched up when carrying out a hard diving turn from supersonic to subsonic. He hit the transonic 'cobbles' and lost control, causing a violent pitch up, which became uncontrollable. [Bruce, who was just twenty-three minutes into his flight, called 'Mayday' during the descent, the Lightning spinning to the left, nose down, and out of control. At just above 10,000ft he ejected using the SPH and landed in the North Sea, suffering from a few cuts and bruises. After forty-five minutes in the water (which was 10°C) he became hypothermic, but after being picked up by helicopter and once back at Coltishall a hot bath restored matters. Bruce was unhurt and continued with his distinguished career as a senior officer.]

By the end of July 1974 the writing was on the wall for the Lightning OCU; the F.1s and T.4s were disposed of to various airfields as decoys, crash, rescue, etc, and I flew my last Lightning sortie on 29 August. Jaguars were now at Coltishall and those Lightnings to be retained were flown to Binbrook, where the LTF continued to serve the remaining Lightning squadrons.

I found the task of running 226 OCU during the period 1972–1974 to be challenging and extremely satisfying. I am sure that we had a first-class team at Coltishall, and produced for the squadrons a very high calibre pilot. Most of these young men went on to give excellent service and many distinguished themselves in their future careers.

In September 1974, 226 OCU was disbanded and many of its Lighting F.1As and T.4s were withdrawn from service and scrapped.

CHAPTER FOUR

Flying the 'Frightening'

Initially, before two-seat Lightnings became available, the trainee 'Frightening' pilot would begin his introduction to the aircraft by spending three days at ground school at Middleton St. George, followed by a week in a simulator at his front line squadron station, where he would make twelve 'flights'. It was therefore expected that on the student's momentous actual first flight he would be able to perform starting procedures and pre-take-off vital actions perfectly. Later, when two-seat Lightnings became available, the student was subjected to an intensive syllabus consisting of thirteen and a half hours' dual and six hours solo – plus one and a quarter hours, spare for dual or solo as required – on the Lightning T.4 or T.5.

The first conversion exercise would be a familiarization sortie and was given to the student on the very first day that he arrived at the OCU. He would be a passenger only,

Pre-take off vital actions would be performed in dispersal on the first sortie. When the student carried them out whilst taxying, such as here, in T.5 XS457 of the LTF, he was reminded not to commence until the aircraft was well clear of the dispersal area. Taxying the Lightning caused difficulty during the first sortie. The student would be unaccustomed to being high off the ground and the considerable force needed to operate the rudder pedals. Ron Clarke

The student's first conversion exercise would be a familiarization sortie and was given on the very first day that he arrived at the OCU. He would be a passenger only, the instructor flying the T.4, or the T.5, like XS459, from the left-hand seat and no attempt would be made to give any flying instruction. Ronald Johnson

the instructor flying the aircraft from the left-hand seat, and no attempt would be made to give any flying instruction. This sortie proved to be of great value in that it whetted the appetite and helped to make the ground instruction that much easier to absorb. However, if the weather was unfit for flying on the first day of the course, the sortie was normally lost and no provision was made to give this exercise at a later date.

First Flight

Pre-take-off vital actions would be performed in dispersal on the first sortie. When the student carried them out whilst taxying, he was reminded not to commence until the aircraft was well clear of the dispersal area. Taxying the Lightning caused difficulty during the first sortie. The student would be unaccustomed to being high off the ground and

F.1A XM182 of 56 Squadron using cold power for take-off from RAF Wattisham in July 1961. The Lightning's acceleration on take-off was spectacular, even without re-heat. The E-Type Jaguar, then the epitome of sports cars, was out-accelerated to 60mph by a factor of about three – and the Lightning could reach 500mph in just over forty seconds . . . its pilots were indeed privileged men. *Aeroplane*

to the considerable force needed to operate the rudder pedals. In the T.4, full rudder deflection was required to produce full differential braking, whereas in the single-seater, only half rudder was needed. With the throttles set at idle/fast idle, the Lightning would easily accelerate whilst taxying, and braking against the power was essential. This would result in a tendency to taxi too fast and towards poor directional control due to under-controlling of the rudder pedals. (At idle/fast idle, fuel

Once airborne with the undercarriage selected and locked up, and at a safe climbing attitude, a turn onto the climbing heading could begin. When the speed reached 420kt, the angle of climb was then increased to eighteen degrees to maintain 450kt. Ken Johnson

consumption would be 55lb (25kg) per minute and approximately 400–500lb (180–230kg) would be used to get to the take-off point. Students were therefore instructed not to delay on the ground!)

When clearance to take-off had been obtained from ATC (Air Traffic Control), and the intention to taxi signalled to the marshalling airman by flashing the taxi lights, the aircraft would taxi to the runway for a cold-power take-off (the re-heat take-off was practised to show to the students the full performance and capability of the aircraft).

First, the cold power take-off (ie. without re-heat). The aircraft would be lined up along the centreline of the runway in between the Bomber Command start markers with the nosewheel straight. From this starting position, a good acceleration check could be made during the roll. Throttles would be paralleled and power increased to 100 per cent. Acceleration would be rapid and, if the aircraft had not been lined up correctly, it could lead to difficulty during the early part of the take-off run. The rudder would be become effective at about 90kt. Once the nozzle position, JPTs (Jet Pipe Temperatures) and RPMs (Revolutions Per Minute) had been checked, the ASI (Airspeed Indicator) had to be monitored closely. Under normal take-off conditions, the control column would be moved back at 125kt to bring the nosewheel off the ground by 135kt. Once the nosewheel was raised, a forward movement of the control column would be made as required to hold the correct attitude. At 160kt, a further smooth, progressive, backward movement of the stick would lift the aircraft off the ground at 170kt. Violent backward movement of the control column at the unstick speed had to be avoided as the tail bumper could strike the runway.

Once airborne with the undercarriage selected and locked up and at a safe climbing attitude, a turn onto the climbing heading could begin. When the speed reached 420kt, the angle of climb was then increased to eighteen degrees to maintain 450kt. Once the aircraft had been trimmed, small adjustments only would be required to maintain the correct climbing speed. After settling down in the climb, the post take-off checks would begin.

Due to the high fuel consumption when re-heat was used and the consequent reduction in total endurance, only one dual and one solo re-heat take-off and

Due to the high fuel consumption when re-heat was used and the consequent reduction in total endurance, only one dual and one solo re-heat take-off and climb were carried out during OCU training. Fuel used on a re-heat climb only exceeded that used in a cold climb by a small margin. Distance to height was 28nm on cold power, and 16nm on re-heat; while time to height was 3¾ minutes on cold power and 2½ minutes on re-heat. via Bruce Hopkins/*Aeroplane*

climb were carried out during OCU training. Students had to be reminded that fuel used on a re-heat climb only exceeded that used in a cold climb by a small margin; time and range covered to height would be

markedly reduced, though overall range was hardly affected. (Distance to height on cold power was twenty-eight nautical miles, and sixteen nautical miles on reheat, while time to height was 3¾ mins on cold

power, and 2½mins on reheat.) In the Lightning T.4 when the throttles were pushed forward into the full re-heat position, the undercarriage 'up' selector button was difficult to reach. (During the left to right pre-start cockpit checks it was considered advisable to pause at the TTC (Top Temperature Control) light check and let the student sort out for himself how he could best select 'wheels up').

On take-off, re-heat ought to be selected as soon as the JPTs had stabilized at 100 per cent cold power. This allowed time to take the necessary action should one or both afterburners not light, and it was most important that this eventuality was covered during the briefing. If, after selecting re-heat, one or both nozzles went into pre-open only, and the re-heat did not light up, re-heat could be cancelled and re-selected again when the JPTs had once again stabilized. If No.1 re-heat failed, the 'piano-keys' on the runway would have to be used. Only two attempts at selecting re-heat could be made and, if unsuccessful, the take-off had to be continued in cold power. If a light up occurred normally but then failed with the nozzle in the fully open position, only fifty-seven per cent cold thrust was available and the JPT would be very low. In this case, re-heat had to be cancelled immediately and the take-off continued in cold power. If a re-heat malfunction resulted in a cold power

After lift-off, there was a gentle lurch forward as the main legs unlocked and retracted backwards and outwards into the sixty-degree swept wings. Their hinge axes were cleverly angled to achieve the desired orientation of the wheel. The nose leg, retracting against the airflow, took longer to lock up. The aircraft, climbing at about ten degrees, quickly accelerated to its normal climbing speed of 450kt IAS (not much has ever matched that!) by which time the pilot would have eased the nose up to about twenty-two degrees. Simon Parry

take-off, re-heat could be re-selected when safely airborne so that the exercise could be completed.

With re-heat lighting up normally after the first selection, the increased acceleration was marked and the ASI had to be watched closely. Speeds for raising the nosewheel and getting airborne were as for the cold take-off. There was even more danger of the tail-bumper striking the ground if harsh control was used during a re-heat take-off. If the wheels were not selected 'up' as soon as the aircraft was safely airborne, the acceleration was such that the nosewheel would not retract forward against the airflow. If this happened, in order to get the nosewheel undercarriage light out, re-heat would have to be cancelled and speed reduced, but reheat could be re-applied once the undercarriage was completely retracted. Once the undercarriage was locked up and a safe climb away initiated, a hard turn ought to be made onto the climbing heading. At 420 knots the angle of climb

At 20,000ft (6,000m) AGL the Mach number crept up to 0.9 and the trim had to be adjusted quite strongly backwards to hold that figure or the aircraft would, still in cold (un-reheated) power, slip through the 'sound barrier' in the climb. Quite a machine. Before then, the pilot would have checked out his radar and the rest of his cockpit information, with radios, oxygen and fuel flows taking a prominent place in his mind. Dick Bell Collection

Handling the aircraft at Mach 0.95 was practised during the first conversion exercise and would normally consist of the student getting the feel of the controls. A speed of Mach 0.95 was chosen as this was the best subsonic manoeuvring speed. Ronald Johnson

Recovery, through the dive circle, was a very efficient procedure. The circle was centred on a point 18nm out on the centreline of the duty runway, and its radius in nm equated to the altitude of the aircraft in thousands of feet. Dick Bell Collection

then ought to be increased to about thirty degrees on the attitude indicator and, as in the cold take-off, once the aircraft had been trimmed, small adjustments of the angle of climb maintained the climbing speed of 450kt. It was important to attain the correct climbing speed early, since, if the student's reaction was slow, the speed would rapidly accelerate beyond 450kt and, in order to get the correct speed, large alterations in the angle of climb would be necessary and he would probably not settle down at all.

Because of the increased performance and greater rate of climb, the post take-off checks would really be left until Mach 0.96 was reached. The student may have noticed the fuel gauges going down during the climb, but this was normal since the engine demand was more than could be supplied from the slipper tank alone. Four thousand feet (1,200m) would be allowed

for levelling out. As the aircraft passed through 30,000ft (9,000m), the angle of climb would be progressively reduced and re-heat cancelled.

On a cold-power take-off the transition from 450kt to Mach 0.9 occurred at approximately 16,000 ft (4,800m) and poor instrument scanning would usually cause it to be missed on early sorties. Above 30,000ft, the angle of climb would have to be reduced slightly in order to maintain the speed. During the climb to altitude, particular attention had to be paid to the rudder trim since the small slip indicator might get hidden behind the student's right knee. The level-out from the climb would ideally be commenced as the altimeter passed through 32,500ft (9,800m) to level out at 34,000ft (10,000m). There would be a considerable 'dead-band' in the throttle movement and they needed to be brought back a long way

in order to bring the nozzles into the cruise position. While the power was being reduced, the nose had to be eased down to maintain the speed and once flying level, the power could be adjusted to maintain the required cruising speed with the nozzles remaining at cruise and the aircraft trimmed.

Handling the aircraft at Mach 0.95 was practised during the first conversion exercise and would normally consist of the student getting the feel of the controls. A speed of Mach 0.95 was chosen as this was the best subsonic manoeuvering speed. (During normal handling, the aircraft was flown at Mach 0.9.)

During this short period of subsonic general handling the student would get used to the slow action of the tailplane trim, which was considerably slower than in other aircraft that the student may have flown previously. He could also practise

F.3 XP764 of 29 Squadron in flight. Before accelerating to supersonic speeds, clearance had to be obtained from the controlling authority. Clearance to fly supersonic is normally given on an easterly heading. It was essential, while flying at high speed, to constantly monitor the fuel gauges and TACAN position, since fuel consumption was so high. Dick Bell

turns, noting the apparent difference when turning left and right while sitting in the left-hand seat. Once settled down, turns to the buffet, maintaining the speed at Mach 0.95, would be practised. During these turns, the student would be asked to note the increase in power required to maintain the speed. As the bank was increased and the power increased to 100 per cent, the student would be asked to note the angle of bank (about 60–65 degrees) and the reading (about 2–2½g) at which buffet occurred, and be aware that the speed dropped, even though full cold power was being applied.

Before accelerating to supersonic speeds, clearance had to be obtained from the controlling authority. Clearance to fly supersonic speed was normally given on an easterly heading. It was essential, while flying at high speed, to constantly monitor the fuel gauges and TACAN position, since fuel consumption was so very high. (It was essential that the student be taught the use of TACAN at a very early stage in

his training, and made to use it at every available opportunity from then on in order to induce a flexible mental approach to the operation of the Lightning.)

The acceleration to supersonic height was termed 'precision acceleration' and this was stressed from the start since it would form part of the instrument rating test at a later date. During the acceleration the 'cobblestone' effect would be noticed at about Mach 0.97. This is caused by the breakaway of airflow from different parts of the aircraft and could be mistaken for slight clear air turbulence. As the aircraft further accelerated, at about Mach 0.99 the pressure instruments would become unreliable until the shock wave moved back past the static vents (at about 1.04 TMN (True Mach Number)). At this point the altimeter would 'jump up' approximately 1,800ft (550m), the RCDI (Rate of Climb & Descent Indicator) would show a high rate of climb, the ASI (Air Speed Indicator) would show an increase of about 30 knots, and the TMN

would settle at about Mach 1.04. For this reason, the aircraft would be eased into a gentle dive during the initial acceleration so that it lost 1,800ft in height and, when the 'jump up' of the altimeter occurred, the height would be back to 34,000ft (10,000m). During this transonic period when the altimeter and RCDI were giving false readings, attitude would normally have to be maintained by reference to the attitude indicator. Trim changes throughout the acceleration were only moderate. At Mach 1.3, power could be reduced to that stage of re-heat required to maintain the speed. The instructor would emphasize the need to check directional trim and possible over-pressurization.

The high rate of fuel consumption limited handling at Mach 1.3 to a turn each way, and the turns had to be completed before the aircraft was positioning towards land when within thirty-five miles of the coast. On the first turn it would be shown that the maximum angle of bank could be reached whilst maintaining Mach 1.3, and on the second turn, that the aircraft should be pulled to the judder with consequent speed reduction. It could then be pointed out that the first turn was the more efficient method. Approximately seventy degrees of bank and 4g could be obtained at the judder. Entry would be the same as for the Mach 0.95 turns, except that apparent increased sensitivity of the RCDI would be noticed at Mach 1.3.

The precision deceleration is the exact reverse of the acceleration, the intention being to decrease the height by approximately 1,800ft (550m) during the initial deceleration so that when the 'jump up' occurred at Mach 1.04, the altimeter again finished at 34,000ft (10,000m). To decelerate, the power would be reduced to idle/fast idle and a gentle climb commenced. The student would maintain the attitude obtained as the RCDI passed 1,500ft/min (450m/min). At the point of 'jump-down', the aircraft would have considerable climb inertia and the change in attitude required to maintain level flight at 34,000ft (10,000m) would be marked and

had to be anticipated. Air brakes were not used. As soon as the 'jump-down' occurred, power had to be increased to hold the required subsonic speed and the aircraft trimmed for straight and level flight.

Once subsonic speed was obtained, the recovery to the descent point could be commenced, either under GCI control or by pilot navigation using TACAN fixes. The ILS (Instrument Landing System) approach aid was new to many pilots converting onto the Lightning, and though the approach pattern may have been practised to a limited extent in the Lightning simulator, its use had to be thoroughly briefed and not taken for granted. Being essentially a pilot-interpreted aid, it would not involve a different scan pattern to that used for the more normal GCA approach, and in order to get this practice, ILS approaches had to be carried out whenever wind direction and serviceability allowed. The base QFE would be obtained and set on the altimeter before reaching the dive circle. After the deceleration, any out of balance fuel state would have to be corrected by using the wing-to-wing

transfer system during the cruise to the dive circle, and descent made by using differential throttle.

The return to the dive circle was carried out at 36,000ft (11,000m) and might be under GCI control, or by TACAN, during which period the student would practise fuel and time calculations. To save fuel, it was the instructor's job to make him aim directly for 'Point Alpha' (if on a direct approach), or 'Point Bravo' (if approaching to the opposite end of the runway), so long as the course did not take him outside the limits of the dive segment. It was important that the descent should be commenced as soon as the dive circle was reached, since a small error in the speed during the descent would make a considerable difference to the rate of descent. If the rate of descent was found to be insufficient, the power would have to be reduced to idle/idle maintaining the speed. If the rate of descent was subsequently still found to be insufficient, speed had to be increased. If, during the descent, the rate of descent was found to be excessive, then the air brakes had to be selected 'in'.

Circuit work commenced right at the beginning of the conversion. The flapless circuit was practised in order to demonstrate to the student the approach pattern in the event of a landing without the use of flaps or airbrakes. The systems failure was assumed from the over-shoot from a normal circuit and the student was required to perform the complete circuit with the flaps and airbrakes inoperative. It was strongly emphasized to the student that if he had to overshoot with a known failure of this nature, he must *not* raise the undercarriage. Dick Bell

Point Alpha (or Bravo) would ideally have been reached at 3,000ft (900m), at which height the aircraft could be levelled off and speed reduced to 240kt. The aircraft would be trimmed as the speed reduced and then descended to 1,500ft (450m) upon GCA permission being received. The talk-down controller should be asked to stop talking when the aircraft reached two miles from touch-down on the very first approach practised, so that the instructor could take over control and demonstrate the final stage of the approach and the overshoot, to demonstrate the approach angle, and engine handling technique and speed control.

The overshoot action could be taken just before the wheels touched, and the Lightning would climb away easily with ninety per cent power so full power was unnecessary. As the power increased, airbrakes could be selected 'in' with the same movement and the climb angle set. Wheels could then be selected 'up' followed by the flaps at 180kt. When the speed reached 240kt, power was then reduced to eighty-five per cent to maintain this speed during the climb to the downwind leg. If a further instrument approach was to be flown, the instrument overshoot procedure would be used. To overshoot into a visual circuit, a minimum of 50 degrees of bank would be used, commencing at a safe height. Power would be reduced progressively to roll out on the downwind leg at 240kt. Once straight and level, seventy-five per cent power would normally be sufficient to maintain the speed.

Circuits and Crabs

Circuit work commenced right at the beginning of the conversion course, each pre-solo dual sortie finishing with the different types of circuit being practised. The flapless circuit was practised in order to demonstrate to the student the approach pattern in the event of a landing without the use of flaps or airbrakes. (Although a flapless landing was never practised, the instructor had to brief fully on the flapless landing technique.) The systems failure was assumed from the overshoot from a normal circuit and the student was required to perform the complete circuit with the flaps and airbrakes inoperative. It was strongly emphasized to the student that if he had to

F.3 XP696 pictured in August 1970 performing a night take-off from RAF Coltishall. At 125kt IAS the nose-wheel could be eased off the ground, but it was prudent to induce a steady and gentle rotation to the take-off altitude at 175kt IAS as, whenever there was a cross-wind, too high a nose attack too early could induce weather-cocking and a consequent scrubbing of the very high-pressure main wheel tyres. Before flying his first solo, the student would be briefed on the crosswind technique for take-off and landing. Crosswind landings in a Lightning, with its slab-sided fuselage and enormous tail fin, could prove particularly terrifying for the unwary, and even the most experienced, pilot, especially on a wet and dark night! EDP

overshoot with a known failure of this nature, he must *not* raise the undercarriage. A flapless landing run would be about 200yd (180m) longer than for a normal landing.

The single-engined handling of the Lightning presented no difficulty and the circuit pattern, approach and landing were carried out at the normal speeds. However, when practising on No.1 Engine, this would be throttled to idle after touch-down along with No.2. Due to the poor engine response from this RPM an overshoot would be hazardous; therefore, all single-engined landings were treated as precautionary landings. The downwind R/T call would be, 'C/S Downwind Practice Single-Engine Precautionary Landing.'

To maintain the normal circuit pattern with one engine throttled back to idle, approximately 8–10 per cent extra in RPM was required on the other engine. The approach on one engine would present no problems if accurate speeds were maintained. The normal approach RPM was 90–92 per cent. If the speed was allowed to fall off, the increase in power required to regain it may well move the engine nozzle to the 'closed' position with a subsequent increase in thrust. If this occurred, it had

to be remembered to re-open the nozzle, otherwise speed control would be difficult during the final stages of the approach.

The final approach and landing would be exactly the same as for the normal circuit, but it was even more important on one engine that power was not reduced too much before touch-down, or the aircraft would sink rapidly and land short. This was particularly important in strong and gusty wind conditions. On the overshoot, 100 per cent cold power had to be applied initially and the airbrakes retracted immediately. The undercarriage must not be retracted until the aircraft was safely away, and the flaps would be raised at the normal speed of 180kt.

Before flying his first solo, the student would be briefed on the crosswind technique for take-off and landing in a Lightning (crosswind landings in a Lightning, with its slab-sided fuselage and enormous tail fin, could prove particularly terrifying for the unwary, and even for the most experienced pilot, especially on a wet and dark night!). Before starting-up in strong crosswind conditions, careful note had to made of the condition of the tyres, and the student had to be conversant with what was acceptable under these conditions.

The 'crab' technique was recommended for approach and landing. A sufficiently long final approach should be flown in order to assess the drift. Normal approach speeds were used and drift kicked off as the aircraft was rounded-out; aileron might have to be used to counteract roll if there was much drift to remove. The student had to be initially told to keep the ailerons neutral after touchdown; later, he might be shown the effect of using downwind aileron. Dick Bell Collection

As soon as the aircraft settled on the downwind leg, vital actions would be commenced. The sooner they were completed the more time there would be to concentrate on the circuit pattern. Dick Bell Collection

Initial take-off actions were normal, but as the aircraft started accelerating down the runway, it might be necessary to keep straight initially by differential braking, and then by use of the rudder when it became effective. The rotation method was then used. This involved keeping the nose-wheel on the runway until 150kt and then lifting it, and then the aircraft, off the runway at 170kt with one smooth, backward movement of the control column. The effect of maintaining the nose-wheel on the runway until the higher speed was to provide extra stability against the cross-wind and reduce main wheel tyre wear; however, care had to be exercised not to over-control when moving the control column as under these conditions the pilot ran a greater risk of scraping the tail. As the aircraft became airborne, the downwind wing might drop, and would have to be levelled.

The 'crab' technique was recommended for approach and landing. A sufficiently long final approach should be flown in order to assess the drift. Normal approach speeds were used and drift kicked off as the aircraft was rounded-out; aileron might have to be used to counteract roll if there was much drift to remove. The student had to be told initially to keep the ailerons neutral after touch-down; latterly, he might be shown the effect of using downwind aileron. As the brake parachute was deployed, he had to be prepared to use downwind rudder to prevent excessive weather-cocking, particularly at the moment of deployment. The tendency of the aircraft's nose to weather-cock would gradually become more pronounced as the aircraft speed reduced, when differential braking might have to be used; this in turn might lead to a longer landing roll. If the weather-cocking became excessive and directional control difficult, the brake parachute would have to be jettisoned, though use of downwind aileron would

effectively delay the point at which control could no longer be maintained. The student would be told that if he allowed the nose of the aircraft to yaw too far, there might not be sufficient rudder available to regain directional control.

It had to be borne in mind that gusty conditions are frequently associated with strong crosswinds. Therefore, care had to be exercised in throttle handling as the aircraft was landed and, if necessary, some power had to be left on until touch-down; the more drift to be removed, the more important did this point become. By the same token, large fluctuations in wind speed could also be encountered. It was therefore essential under these conditions to ensure that low speeds were never used on the approach, and in the severest turbulence it might be necessary to increase the approach speed slightly.

The student would also have been thoroughly briefed before his first solo on

The turn onto the final approach would start at about one runway's length from the end of the runway. If the wind was down the runway, approximately thirty-five degrees of bank would be sufficient, and a rate of descent of about 1,000ft (300m)/minute would be aimed for. Dick Bell Collection

the technique of carrying out a precautionary landing, where he was committed to stopping 'come what may', and all the circumstances under which he would perform it. As soon as possible after first solo, he would carry out a dual practice; subsequently, he would be made to decide whether or not such a landing should be made, and any disinclination to use the precautionary technique would be immediately curbed. The overriding factor as to the necessity for a precautionary landing was circumstances dictating that, even if the brake parachute failed, the pilot would not overshoot the aircraft; with this in mind, the student would more readily remember the technique involved.

The occasions when a precautionary landing was mandatory included: after overshooting following a brake parachute failure; or when the fuel remaining would be below 800/800lb (360/360kg) on touch-down; below any higher fuel minima as laid down by the DOCFW; when to overshoot would constitute a hazard to the aircraft; when weather conditions were 'Yellow Two' state or worse; and when practising a single-engined landing. (A fuel state of '800/800lb' means 800lb of fuel in each side of the aircraft.)

The intention to make a precautionary landing would be announced with the downwind R/T call, or when appropriate on an Instrument Approach. A normal touch-down would be made, engines throttled to idle/idle and the nose-wheel lowered. Maximum wheel braking was then to be applied at the same time as the brake parachute was deployed. If the brake parachute operated, a normal landing was to be completed and the aircraft returned to dispersal. If it failed, hard wheel braking was continued and one engine shut down. After the runway had been cleared, the aircraft would be turned into wind on the ORP and shut down, and a towing vehicle requested.

Most students found that good landings followed from good approaches. Landings had to be made with a minimum of 800/800lb (360/360kg) of fuel and a decision made before landing on the action to take in the event of a brake parachute failure. Final approach speeds altered according to all-up weight. Up to 1,500lb (680kg)/side fuel load required a final approach speed of 175 knots and a one knot increase for every additional 200lb (90kg)/side beyond this load. The overshoot into the circuit pattern was difficult at first, since the aircraft accelerated

quickly once power was applied and circuit height would soon be reached.

As soon as the aircraft settled on the downwind leg, vital actions (VAs) would be commenced. The sooner they were completed, the more time there would be to concentrate on the circuit pattern. There would be an attitude change, not experienced in the flight simulator, once the flaps were lowered, and unless it was anticipated it would result in a sudden gain in height of 200–300ft (60–90m). Once the vital actions were completed, speed would fall off quickly and at 200kt power would have to be increased to approximately eighty-three per cent in order to maintain 190kt.

The turn onto the final approach would start at about one runway's length from the end of the runway. If the wind was down the runway, approximately thirty-five degrees of bank would be sufficient, and a rate of descent of about 1,000ft (300m)/minute would be aimed for. The throttles were extremely sensitive over the range of RPM being used, and very small throttle movements would give comparatively large increases in percentage RPM, and equally large changes in thrust. The RPM gauges were obscurely positioned on the right-hand side of the cockpit in the

Touch-down speed would be about 155kt. A gentle flare – no 'snatch', as the tail end might scrape the runway and wear away the wires, routed around the tail-bumper to the brake parachute – and the Lightning would settle smoothly. Its main landing gear was reasonably resilient and would soak up moderate rates of descent easily. As soon as the aircraft was on the ground the pilot would ease the control forward to bring the nose-wheel firmly down on the ground. via Tony Aldridge

An idle/fast idle, 350kt IAS, descent with airbrakes out used only 100lb (45kg) of fuel from each wing, with another 300lb (135kg) per side being consumed on the final GCA or ILS approach to touchdown. The usual 'last-look' speed at the runway threshold was 165kt IAS, after an approach at 180kt. Dick Bell Collection

T.4, so most students had considerable difficulty in making accurate power adjustments; these would only improve with practice.

If a student tended to over-control the throttles, he would be advised to set No.2 throttle and adjust his power on No.1 only. During the finals turn the airbrakes would be selected 'out' when appropriate. As the bank was gradually taken off, speed would be reduced to 185kt, further reducing to 175kt when lined up with the runway. At this stage, a 2½ degree glide-path would be intercepted with a RED/PINK indication from the VGPIs (Visual Glide Path Indicators), but at half a mile the aircraft would be descended below this glide-path and the nose raised slightly. Approaching the lights, the speed would be reduced to 170kt, and from here on the speed would be reduced constantly to achieve 165kt at the runway threshold, which would be crossed at an approach angle of about half a degree. Under normal wind conditions, the power should at this stage be about eighty per cent.

As the aircraft approached the runway threshold, power could again be reduced slightly (but not taken completely off) and the nose-wheel raised still further. At the threshold, which was probably the last time that the airspeed would be checked, the speed should be 165kt. As the threshold was crossed, power could be progressively reduced and the control column brought back to what appeared at first to be quite a high nose-up position. Normally, power was still being used at touch-down and therefore, as the wheels touched, power ought to be reduced to idle/fast idle. If too much power was reduced too early, the aircraft could drop and even hit the ground before the threshold. At this stage, the overshoot could be initiated if required.

Touch-down speed would be about 155kt. As soon as the aircraft was on the ground the control column would be eased forward to bring the nose-wheel down, and at 150kt the brake parachute would be deployed. As soon as the deceleration was felt, and it was most marked, power would be reduced to idle/idle. Little or no braking would be required initially, but brakes needed to be checked and used as required to reduce the speed. When stabilized at about 100kt the aircraft would be moved to the turn-off side of the runway, and at

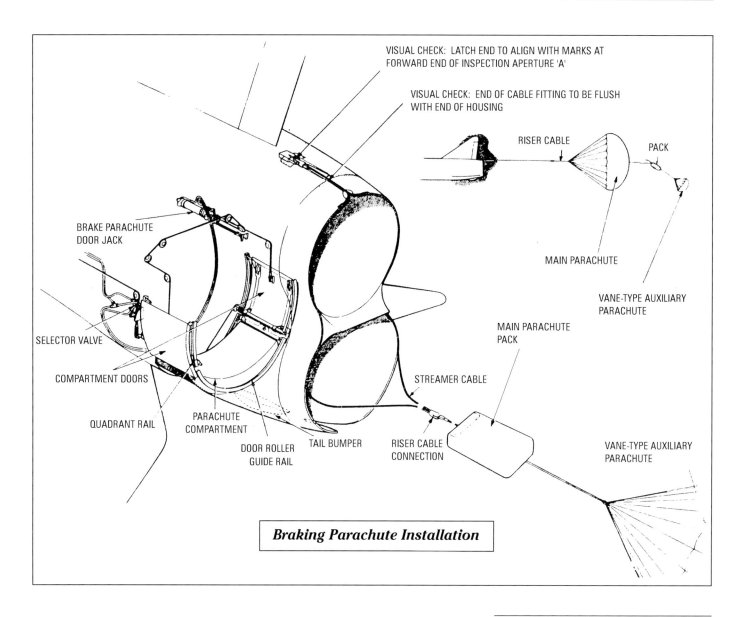

VISUAL CHECK: LATCH END TO ALIGN WITH MARKS AT
FORWARD END OF INSPECTION APERTURE 'A'

VISUAL CHECK: END OF CABLE FITTING TO BE FLUSH
WITH END OF HOUSING

RISER CABLE

PACK

MAIN PARACHUTE

VANE-TYPE AUXILIARY
PARACHUTE

MAIN PARACHUTE
PACK

BRAKE PARACHUTE
DOOR JACK

SELECTOR VALVE

COMPARTMENT DOORS

QUADRANT RAIL

PARACHUTE
COMPARTMENT

DOOR ROLLER
GUIDE RAIL

TAIL BUMPER

STREAMER CABLE

RISER CABLE
CONNECTION

VANE-TYPE AUXILIARY
PARACHUTE

Braking Parachute Installation

approximately ten knots the parachute could be released. Once released, the SWP (Standard Warning Panel) would be tested, and No.2 engine moved to the fast idle position. Hydraulic pressures could be checked and No.1 engine shut down when the aircraft had cleared the runway.

If the runway was wet, the braking effect could be greatly reduced and would depend directly upon the amount of water on the runway surface. Generally, under wet conditions, it was recommended that light braking action be commenced once the aircraft was firmly on the ground and the wheels had had time to spin up. The brake application could then be progressively increased and could be held continuously as the speed fell off. When maximum wheel braking was necessary, its effectiveness could be increased by

progressive backward movement of the control column as the speed reduced, thereby transferring more weight to the main wheels. Care had to be taken to ensure that this movement was not started at a speed high enough to raise the nosewheel from the runway. If a slip or skid was suspected, the pressure had to be released momentarily and re-applied gradually.

Once clear of the runway, and with No.1 engine below ten per cent power, flaps and airbrakes would be selected 'IN' and all the non-essential switches turned 'OFF'. It was important to check the recovery of the services hydraulic pressure, thus ensuring that both pumps had been checked.

Going Solo

All students would have covered the full dual syllabus before their first solo, whatever their previous experience. Few students failed to achieve the standard required on schedule, but it need hardly be said that the instructor had to be in no doubt as to the ability of the student to safely operate the aircraft before he was allowed to fly solo. Many factors would enter into this, some of them beyond the control of the student, and particularly close (personal) supervision by the instructor would be needed with regard to weather conditions, though this situation was to a certain extent relieved by the requirement for the student to complete a dual ride on the same day as his first solo.

At 150kt the pilot would deploy the brake parachute. This provided good retardation when the energy levels were high, and the brakes would handle the phase when the parachute became fairly ineffective, below about 100kt IAS. A 'chute failure was always a bit exciting, as the brakes could not really absorb all the landing energy and would often weld solid if they had to do all the work on their own. As soon as the deceleration was felt, and it was most marked, power would be reduced to idle/idle. When stabilized at about 100kt the aircraft would be moved to the turn-off side of the runway, and at approximately 10kt, the 'chute could be released. Adrian Savage

Apart from the straightforward sortie brief, the student had also to be thoroughly briefed on the crash diversion procedure, action in the event of a brake parachute failure and the precautionary landing technique, as well as the reasons for a precautionary landing. He also had to know the technique for flapless and single-engine landings (the circuits for these having been demonstrated and practised) and the crosswind technique for take-off and landing.

The start-up would be supervised by the instructor from the right-hand side of the T.4 or T.5, and the student would be told to carry out pre-take-off VAs in dispersal. The instructor would then be in the control tower for the duration of the student's sortie. Subsequent solo sorties would, wherever possible, be carried out in the F.1A.

As soon as possible after his first solo, the student would be introduced to variations to the dive circle recovery where it was required to conserve fuel. An important aspect was that the student was being encouraged to think all the while in terms of fuel economy, even though the amounts saved may not have been very large. The

first method was the one flown at Mach 0.9 (250kt). This had a 'height loss/range relationship' of two nautical miles/1,000ft (300m) compared with the SOP (Standard Operating Procedure) descent of one nautical mile/1,000ft, and consequently twice the range could be achieved for the same height loss. The fuel saved was only of the order of 75lb (34kg) but this might, nevertheless, prove valuable under certain circumstances. The increased time taken to descend must also be considered as to its desirability, along with the fact that the aircraft was at height for a longer period at a low speed, and so was vulnerable to strong winds. The descent was entered by throttling back to idle/idle and lowering the nose to maintain Mach 0.9 and full windscreen de-mist had to be used to obtain de-misting at the reduced power. A careful check had to be kept of height and range, and rate of descent altered if necessary either by increasing the speed or the power setting. The IAS could not be allowed to fall below 250kt, for the sharply increasing drag would increase the rate of descent. Due to the low windmilling RPM below 20,000ft (6,000m), gradually increasing throttle would be required on

one engine in order to keep the A/C power on line.

Should there be reasons why the slower descent was not practicable, a good method which lay between this and the SOP was to descend at Mach 0.9/375kt with airbrakes 'IN'. This configuration would give a descent rate of one and a half nautical miles/1,000ft, and height/range corrections could be made by increasing or decreasing the airspeed. A range of forty-five nautical miles from Point Alpha would be allowed for this, and although under ideal conditions the fuel saving would not be as much as for the slow rate of descent, there would be tactical advantages which might outweigh this consideration.

The student, having already flown up to Mach 1.3 in previous exercises, would fly the T.4 to its airspeed and Mach number limits of 650kt/Mach 1.6 (or 600kt/Mach 1.6 when Firestreaks or Red Tops were fitted) to investigate the handling at these maximum speeds. As the speed increased beyond Mach 0.9 there would be a slight nose-up change of trim and buffeting (the 'cobblestones') at about Mach 0.97. The nose-up change in trim increased during the transonic region

Once clear of the runway, and with No.1 engine below ten per cent power, flaps and airbrakes would be selected 'in' and all the non-essential switches turned 'off'. It was important to check the recovery of the services hydraulic pressure, thus ensuring that both pumps had been checked. Ronald Johnson

up to approximately Mach 1.1 and from Mach 1.2 to 1.6 there would be a nose-down change in trim. Between Mach 1.2 and 1.6, JPTs, cabin altitude, directional trim and position had to be constantly checked. Above Mach 1.2 the student had to remember that the airbrakes must not be selected. The acceleration was normally carried out on one heading, but should a change of heading be necessary which would result in g being applied above Mach 1.2, the handling characteristics might then change appreciably, particularly when carrying missiles. In this speed region, application of aileron might then induce a pronounced adverse yaw, causing reduced roll response and a feeling of control heaviness, and difficulty might be experienced in accurate lateral trimming. Therefore, throughout the acceleration up

to Mach 1.6, correct rudder trimming was important.

When Mach 1.6 was reached, the aircraft might be some considerable distance from base and a maximum rate turn using full re-heat could be commenced towards the dive circle once clearance to do so had been obtained. Bank would be applied and gradually increased while the turn was pulled tighter until 4½g was being pulled. Although the limitation was 5g, 4½ was normally used in training. This ensured that the fatigue meter did not record a 5g loading, and thus helped conserve the fatigue life of the aircraft.

An exercise was flown whereby the student would climb to service ceiling on cold power and re-heat to investigate the climb performance of the Lightning. (The

service ceiling was defined as that height above which the rate of climb became less than 1,000ft (300m)/min.) A normal cold power climb was carried out and continued at Mach 0.9 as far as possible on one heading, until the rate of climb on the RCDI fell to 1,000ft/min. Reheat was then selected and the climb continued until the RCDI again fell to 1,000ft/min rate of climb. It was pointed out to the student that when re-heat was applied, the aircraft would be very close to the boundaries of the Lightning's performance envelope. The approximate heights of cold-power and re-heat service ceilings were 42,000ft (12,700m) and 47,000ft (14,200m) (T.4).

The student had to be made aware that if the exercise was to be of any value, then accurate climbing speeds were essential and, if possible, no turns should be made until the ceiling was reached. This necessitated constant checks of fuel and position. Under certain conditions 50,000ft (15,000m), the limiting altitude of the aircraft with its current oxygen equipment without a Taylor high altitude helmet, could be reached before the re-heat service ceiling. In that event, the climb had to be discontinued and the aircraft levelled off.

When height was reached, a turn was made to show how little bank could be applied before speed reduced and the aircraft started to judder. The rate of turn was low and it would be noted that the IAS was below 250kt at Mach 0.9 and therefore the aircraft was on the wrong side of the drag curve. The operational implications were that in order to be manoeuvrable at height, the aircraft must be at a higher IAS in order to overcome the aerodynamics problem, and also provide better engine performance due to ram effect of air entering the intake. The acceleration to this higher speed was carried out at the tropopause, where the aircraft performed most efficiently. This then would lead into the energy climb (see below), which was performed during the same sortie.

The energy climb, or 'zoom climb', was the operational method of reaching the Lightning's maximum operational height (50,000ft, the maximum height with the Mk.20 oxygen regulator and P/2 type mask) and entailed an acceleration to Mach 1.5 at the tropopause, followed by a zoom at a fixed angle of climb until height was reached. Using an attitude of 15 degrees for the zoom, a speed of Mach 1.5 at the tropopause was sufficient to reach 50,000ft at Mach 1.3. To avoid exceeding 50,000ft, the level-out had to be commenced at 47,000ft. If the student commenced the level-out later than required, he had to avoid over-controlling on the pitch forward due to the possibility of illuminating the HYD (Hydraulic) alarm in the AWP (Auxiliary Warning Panel). Full re-heat had to be kept applied and the aircraft turned level at the maximum angle of bank to maintain speed. The rate of turn and the angle of bank would be compared with those which were attained when demonstrating the re-heat service ceiling, then the bank was increased to the judder to note how quickly the speed reduced to a figure too low to operate at.

The fast descent would be carried out at Mach 1.1 until 450 knots – airbrakes out and engines at idle/idle. Due to the high

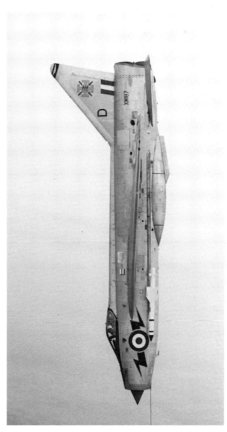

F.1A XM187 of 111 Squadron in a dive. Before carrying out aerobatics in the Lightning, the student had to be briefed on a few points. The Lightning was a heavy aircraft and it therefore had a large amount of inertia. If the nose was allowed to drop too much below the horizon during manoeuvres, a considerable height loss would result. Manoeuvres such as loops, barrel rolls and wing overs used up a large amount of sky. A very good lookout therefore had to be maintained during aerobatics. It is also very easy to overstress an aircraft unless a careful eye is kept on the airspeed and accelerometer. Without missiles it was difficult to hold the nose of the Lightning above the horizon when inverted. *Aeroplane*

rate of descent it was most important that full de-mist was set at the commencement of the descent and maintained until after the aircraft had been stabilized at low level. At 10,000ft (3,000m) the power would be set to idle/fast idle. Height was lost very quickly during this type of descent, the distance from 50,000ft (15,000m) to 2,000ft (600m) being approximately twenty-five miles (forty km) and the time taken, approximately three minutes. The fast descent therefore had to be commenced close to the dive circle and care had to be taken that the aircraft was initially heading away from land. The student had to allow approximately

5,000ft (1,500m) for the level-out. Within the context of the actual sortie, it was suggested that a descent to 20,000ft (6,000m) would be sufficient to demonstrate the most important points while still leaving the aircraft in a reasonable height/range position relative to base for the remainder of the recovery.

Advanced Training

During the conversion phase students would complete instrumentation flights using full instrumentation and the standby instruments. The Interim Integrated Flight Instrument System was fitted in the T.4 and F.1. It gave accurate indications of pitch and bank attitude on the attitude indicator. The G.5 compass virtually eliminated all turning errors and gave completely 'dead-beat' indications of heading. The Mk22C altimeter reduced considerably the lag experienced in older designs. In addition, the information provided by the attitude indicator, altimeter and, in the T.4, the compass was all duplicated for the second seat, giving the pilot full instrumentation as long as electrical power lasted. Nevertheless, the same principles applied for accurate instrument flying; a good instrument scan pattern, smooth control movements and accurate trimming.

Instrument flying would culminate in the instrument rating test which covered the climb, acceleration, supersonic precision turns (at Mach 1.2 at 60 degrees) and subsonic precision turns (at Mach 0.95 and 50 degrees), recovery on the standby instruments, and GCA and ILS approaches down to break-off height. The instrument flying sorties included certain parts of the recovery being conducted using the standby instruments, and though full instrumentation was available, difficulty would be experienced due to the different scan patterns required, particularly in the case of the Lightning T.4. The Mk.6H standby horizon presented no problems, but the altimeter had a presentation, particularly above 10,000ft (3,000m), that was difficult to read accurately and changes in height were difficult to notice. When using this instrument the student had to rely on the RCDI more than he had done previously. Unlike the Lightning T.4. the F.1 did not have a standby direction indicator system fitted. Consequently, timed turns, using the E2

All About Altitude

Altitude Feet	Pressure P.S.I.	Density lb/cu.ft.	Pressure Millibars	Temperature °F	Temperature °C	Speed of Sound M.P.H.	Speed of Sound ft/sec.	
80,000	0.36	0.002	25	-70	-56.5	660	971	Stratosphere
75,000	0.50	0.003	35	-70	-56.5	660	971	
70,000	0.66	0.004	46	-70	-56.5	660	971	
65,000	0.83	0.005	58	-70	-56.5	660	971	
60,000	1.04	0.007	72	-70	-56.5	660	971	
55,000	1.31	0.009	91	-70	-56.5	660	971	
50,000	1.68	0.011	116	-70	-56.5	660	971	
45,000	2.14	0.015	147	-70	-56.5	660	971	
40,000	2.72	0.019	188	-70	-56.5	660	971	
35,000	3.46	0.024	238	-67	-54.3	661	973	The Tropopause (approx.)
30,000	4.37	0.029	301	-49	-44.4	677	997	
25,000	5.46	0.034	376	-31	-34.5	693	1,013	Troposphere.
20,000	6.77	0.041	465	-13	-24.6	707	1,035	
15,000	8.31	0.048	572	5	-14.7	723	1,058	
10,000	10.08	0.056	697	23	-4.8	739	1,081	
5,000	12.23	0.066	843	41	5.1	755	1,105	
Sea Level.	14.69	0.077	1,013	59	15.0	771	1,128	

FROM THE GROUND UP: A table to show the effect of height on the various properties which influence the performance of an aircraft. The stratosphere is defined as the area above such currents of air as are influenced by the earth's surface. The height at which the stratosphere begins, i.e. the tropopause, varies with latitude and season but can be taken as approximately 36,000ft, above which the constant temperature drop with altitude gain no longer prevails, the temperture remaining constant.

compass only, were practised. For these turns to be accurate, E2 readings had to be taken only in steady flight with the wings level and a constant speed being held. Timing had to commence after the bank had been applied and had to stop only when the wings were level again. Throughout the turns the angle of bank had to be held constant.

GCA and ILS approaches presented no difficulty in the Lightning and were simple to fly accurately, providing that the corrections were made positively and promptly. At speeds below 200kt the aircraft had a large nose-up attitude in level flight and the RCDI played an important part in maintaining height. Extremely accurate speeds and rates of descent could be maintained providing that the aircraft was correctly trimmed and power corrections were not over-controlled. During dual instrument flying sorties, approaches could be flown to well below the recommended break-off heights.

Before carrying out aerobatics in the Lightning, the student had to be briefed on a few points. The Lightning was a heavy aircraft and it therefore had a large amount of inertia. If the nose were allowed to drop too much below the horizon during manoeuvres, a considerable height loss resulted. Manoeuvres such as loops, barrel rolls and wing-overs used up a large amount of sky. Therefore, a very good lookout had to be maintained during these aerobatics. It was also very easy to over-stress the aircraft unless a careful eye was kept on the airspeed and accelerometer. Without missiles it was difficult to hold the nose of the aircraft above the horizon when inverted. For this reason, slow rolls were best performed at 370kt until the pilot was reasonably experienced. Slow rolls were not to be performed at less than 350kt.

With the Autopilot Master Switch 'OFF', it was possible to lose one degree of tailplane movement. The AMS was therefore always 'ON' during aerobatics, but the

Pitch and Roll/Yaw switches were 'OFF'. Loops were started at a speed which required re-heat for completion of the manoeuvre. Speeds were therefore at least 450kt with or without re-heat until experience was gained. A minimum speed of 200kt was aimed for at the top of the loop, but if the speed was less the back pressure was relaxed and the aircraft allowed to fly round the manoeuvre until the speed had built up to at least 270kt on the descent. Loops were never started at less than 400kt. Hesitation rolls were forbidden.

Students were given the chance to gain experience in flying the Lightning at low level, a cross-country being included in the OCU syllabus to be flown at 500ft (150m) AGL. This was comparable to the lowest height at which operational flying would be carried out on a squadron. The legs of the cross-country were flown at different speeds, thus providing experience in operating the Lightning at both range (ie: most fuel-economical) speed and at the

After the pilot had learned to fly the Lightning well, basic and advanced radar courses, using Canberras as targets, would follow. Then and only then, the embryonic Lightning pilot was posted to a front-line fighter squadron, such as 11 Squadron, seen here at Luqa, Malta in 1970. F.6 'L' is XR723 which was built originally as an F.3. This aircraft later served with 5 Squadron and 23 Squadron before being struck off charge on 18 September 1979. via Peter Winning

maximum which would be used during PI. In the same way, turns would be flown at different angles of bank.

The AFCS (Automatic Flight Control System) had also to be mastered, and the student learned the differences between the T.5 and the T.4. They were basically similar, although once the engines were started the student would find that the JPTs at idling RPM would be higher on the T.5 than on earlier marks, and when taxying, the higher idling thrust would require more use of the brakes. The take-off would not normally present any difficulty, providing that the student had been briefed on the greater stick force required to raise the nose-wheel when missiles were being carried.

Flying the F.3 after, say, the T.5, carried some minor, but important differences that the student pilot had to familiarize himself with. On take-off the F.3 had a much lighter nose and much lighter controls all round. It also accelerated faster than the T.5, was much noisier, particularly when accelerating after take-off. The 'cobbles' would start with less warning and were more intense. The student would quickly note, too, the improved visibility from the cockpit, and the fact that the approach was easier to fly, but that the lighter tailplane might lead to a high round-out. Equally, the brake parachute would pull the nose-wheel off the runway if it was streamed with the stick not fully forward.

After learning to fly the Lightning well, basic and advanced radar courses, using Canberras as targets, would follow. The basic course (when night flying would be carried out as well, with two additional handling sorties [one dual, one solo] and at least one solo Rad-ex) involved a total of fourteen hours' dual and five and a quarter hours' solo. On the advanced radar phase, nine hours, forty minutes (consisting of eight hours' dual and one hour, forty minutes' solo time), would be spent learning to use Red Top and automated and pilot-interpreted AI (airborne intercept radar). Additional sorties, probably one dual and two solo, would be flown starting with an ORP scramble and using targets.

Then, and only then, the embryonic Lightning pilot was posted to a front-line fighter squadron or, as in some cases, it was off to MU as a test pilot, or to OCU as an instructor. Whatever his destination, he could be sure of a thrilling, sometimes dangerous, experience in the hot seat of the 'Frightening' Lightning!

T.5 XS423 landing at Coltishall, where it joined 226 OCU on 1 June 1965. Simon Parry

CHAPTER FIVE

Prods and Brackets

Fighter Command first introduced the inflight-refuelling technique in June 1960, when 23 and 64 Squadrons, operating the Javelin FAW.Mk.9, began receiver training. In August, a 23 Squadron Javelin was flown to Akrotiri non-stop, refuelled and escorted by Valiant BK.1 tankers. Beginning in December 1960, the Lightning F.1A, which was fitted with a port-mounted probe for inflight refuelling, was issued to 56 and 111 Squadrons at Wattisham. In 1961, a joint RAF/USAF exercise was held to demonstrate the compatibility of the Valiant tanker with American fighters and fighter-bombers, and of the American KB-50J tanker with Valiant, Vulcan, Victor and Javelin receivers. Although the Lightning F.1As did not participate, the valuable close co-operation between the two nations did have benefits for the Lightning force the following year, as Sqn Ldr Dave Seward, OC 56 Squadron, recalls.

Now when the F.1A first entered service, each squadron was given various development tasks to perform. On 56 Squadron we were ordered, in December 1961, to develop air-to-air refuelling techniques for the Lightning force, using Vickers Valiant tankers. The timetable directed that during January–July 1962 we would work up six pilots in the AAR role and in July, send two Lightnings to Cyprus with tanker support. Full squadron deployment to Cyprus was scheduled for October 1962.

This sounded OK, but over the period August–December 1961, we experienced odd, unpleasant happenings with the Lightning. You would be flying along in cruise power when the re-heat fire warning lights would illuminate without having reheat selected. As the only method of extinguishing re-heat fires was to de-select re-heat and shut down the engine, it was rather thought provoking if both re-heat lights were on without being in re-heat, and the only alternative seemed to be to become a glider! Some pilots shut an engine

down and in some cases, the fire indication went out. To their cost, others hoped it was a spurious warning. We lost one of the AFDS (Air Fighting Development Squadron) aircraft when the back end burned off, and in another incident, all was revealed when an aircraft landed with the re-heat area on fire. The cause was traced to hydraulic pipes (which were aluminium rather than high-tensile steel) chafing inside the fuselage, causing the hydraulic fluid to pour back along the inside of the rear fuselage and swirl around the back of the jet pipes where it caught fire in the re-heat area.

Thus, in January 1962, it was decided to replace and re-route the hydraulic system in all aircraft and at Wattisham, 56 Squadron and 111 Squadron [and 74 Squadron at Coltishall] were modified. It was going to be a four week job for the lot; six weeks at the outside, so plans were made to have the air-to-air refuelling ground school in January and start flying in February. Unfortunately, the hydraulic modification was not completed in four weeks, but dragged on for sixteen weeks. However,

Fighter Command were adamant that two Lightnings had to be at Akrotiri, Cyprus in July and that the squadron would be there by October!

It was purely fortuitous that at Wattisham we had a social relationship with the American 55th Tactical Fighter Squadron, 20th Tactical Fighter Wing, at RAF Wethersfield, and over drinks one Friday, I mentioned our problems to their commanding officer, remarking that the flight refuelling system on their F-100F Super Sabres, although being on the opposite side (starboard) to the Lightning (port), it was basically similar and what a good idea it would be if we learned our flight refuelling on the F-100? Things must have been desperate, because on the following Wednesday, we had permission from both Fighter Command, and HQ USAFE, for six pilots from 56 Squadron to fly flight refuelling sorties in the F-100, using the KB-50J Superfortress tankers [of the 420th Air Refuelling Squadron]! Although the KB-50 flew at 180–200kt indicated and probes on the Lightning were angled to squarely hit a Valiant basket, the refuelling went remarkably

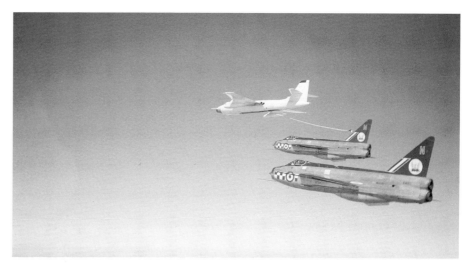

A pair of 56 Squadron's F.1As about to begin in-flight refuelling from a Vickers Valiant. When the F.1A first entered service 56 Squadron were ordered, in December 1961, to develop air-to-air refuelling techniques for the Lightning force, using Valiant tankers. Brian Allchin

well. From Aldburgh to the Humber we did dry, then 'wet' proddings. The USAF would have a KB-50 on station off Aldburgh flying a racetrack pattern and would listen out on a particular frequency. When a chap needed fuel he would call using his call sign and 'book in' and the fuel was then attributed to his squadron. In the half hour to go before the KB-50 had to dump excess fuel, refuelling during this time was free. They'd all come in then because the squadron would not get charged for the fuel.

Two of us were up one day on PIs and I heard this guy say he had half an hour to go and was throwing away the fuel. We gave the call sign for Wethersfield, which was 'Trout, Three-Five and Three-Six'; 'Roger, you're clear in astern,' he replied. He asked, 'What type of aircraft?' We said [untruthfully!], 'Foxtrot 100'! He said, 'Roger'. We flew in, lowered the flaps, and took on the fuel from the KB-50. Thinking about it afterwards, we knew we were taking on JP4 and our Avons were tuned for AVTUR, but we kept that to ourselves (our engineers were worried about the lubrication of the fuel pumps, but we had no problems). We each received six tanking sorties in the F-100 (needless to say, the Americans all had trips in the T.4 Lightning), before starting our own tanking with Valiants on 13 June.

The method we used, as recommended by both English Electric and the USAF, was to position the Lightning about 30yd behind the Valiant and synchronise speeds, with the Valiant at about 250kt indicated at 30,000 or 36,000ft. We then set the No.1 throttle at about 94 [per cent] and set up an overtake speed of about 5kt using the No.2 throttle to vary the speed. You lined up with the basket and edged forward, not looking at the basket, which is going up and down about 3ft but getting what is called a 'sight picture' of the Valiant and flying steadily in. As the basket passes the nose of the Lightning it is 'trapped' and if your line-up has been good, your probe goes into the centre of the basket and you make a good contact. You then move forward into a close formation line astern, keeping a slight bow in the hose and when contact and positioning is confirmed by the tanker, he passes the fuel to you. Fly too low and the hose becomes taut and the probe could break. (You could also break the probe by being too far left or right.) You could also break a probe by having too high an overtake speed and thus hit the basket too hard. On the other hand, if you are too cautious and hit the basket too slow with too low an overtake, you will get a soft contact, and end up being sprayed with fuel,

or, in extreme circumstances, have your engines flame out with fuel pouring into the intake.

A trick in getting at least the vertical position right was to fly in with the fin tip just 'burbling' along the bottom of the Valiant's jet efflux – a technique that we were to regret somewhat later. Still, all went well, and the schedule was met. We simulated the trip to Cyprus by going twice around the UK and got the first two aircraft (myself and John Mitchell, attached from AFDS) to Cyprus on time, flight refuelling to Akrotiri on 23 July (Exercise *Tambour*).

The second detachment, *Forthright One*, involving six other 56 Squadron pilots, went ahead on 6 October 1962, as Flt Lt Bob Offord recalls:

We went in pairs, three tankers per pair, and I flew XM183. Jerry Cohu and I flew at Mach 1.7 until Crete, where we carried out our seventh and last refuelling. In Cyprus the Turkish inhabitants took one look at our red aircraft and thought, 'Hooray, here comes the Turkish air force!'

We spent about eight weeks in Cyprus, carrying out low level PIs, one against one, and the odd Canberra at 60,000ft from Akrotiri's

four resident squadrons. We'd pull up to 36,000ft and zoom up to in excess of 50,000ft. We were also aided by the radar stations at Cape Gata and Mt. Olympus. We could not do low level work in the UK but the Mediterranean is much calmer than the North Sea and the radars could see better. The AI 23 was good for its day but at high level it was difficult to see the Lightning beyond twenty-five miles on radar, and even worse at low level, where it was down to just five–six miles because of the sea returns. Most days we worked in the mornings and swam in the afternoons. These were the best days of Lightning operations. We returned to the UK in April, and then spent the summer exercising and tanking, part of it at Coltishall for three–four weeks while Wattisham's runways were repaired.

When, in January 1965, 92 Squadron's turn to fly a detachment to Cyprus came, the requirement unfortunately coincided with the withdrawal from service of all Valiants, after dangerous metal fatigue had been discovered in their airframes in August the previous year. Flt Lt Alex Reed, one of the four pilots in 92 Squadron at Leconfield who would still fly the trip, explains how it was carried out now that the Valiants were unavailable:

The loss of the Valiant force in 1965 left the RAF with no tanking facilities so the USAF made available three KC-135s over a six- to nine-month period for much-needed in-flight refuelling practice. Operation *Billy Boy*, as it was called, began on 5 April 1965, with 1½ hour sorties with 23 and 74 Squadron's Lightnings, refuelling with 3,000lb (1,700kg) each sortie. The KC-135's rigid refuelling boom to which was attached a 7ft flexible hose-and-drogue called for a much different receiver technique to that used on the hose and reel-equipped Valiant Brian Allchin

We were going to 'puddle-jump' our way to Cyprus, four of us, in two pairs. We took off from Leconfield on 9 January (I flew XN792), made our first stopover at Geilenkirchen in West Germany before going on to Istres in southern France, then crossed the Mediterranean to land at Decimomannu, Sardinia, before stopping the night at Luqa on Malta. Next day we took off for El Adem in Libya, the last stop before Akrotiri. We thought before we went that this sounded a pretty good trip, and it was. We had a ball. At each stop we did a quick run in and break and we all received glowing tributes!

While on the detachment on Cyprus, we flew PIs, or 'Profit Sorties' against Canberras of 360 Squadron. Unlike in Britain we had the added benefit of the radar station on Mt. Olympus to help us. We would be scrambled off, go out and find the target, 'fire' two missiles and then, after the targets were 'splashed', we would break off and cream our way back to Akrotiri. Back on the airfield again we would go straight onto the ORP, ready to scramble again. This was the most exciting operational flying I did! I averaged twenty-three minutes per sortie (we did four sorties each). We were flying the Lightning to its maximum operational capability. Mind you, it was under optimum conditions, but tough work in the hot sun. Then Sqn Ldr Les Hargreaves, our CO, decided we would do low-level interceptions at night. Les said, 'I'll lead the first pair. We don't want to push it.' (Low-level PIs on a black night using AI 23 left a lot to be desired.) Les added that we would have the target at 1,000ft so we'd have plenty of room. It was pitch black. He came back, looked at us, and said, 'Right, we'll put the target at 1,500!' The rest of us heaved a big sigh of relief.

Tanking With *Billy-Boy*

Meanwhile, the conversion of Victor B.1 bombers to K.1A in-flight refuelling tankers was speeded up. The first to fly was XH620, on 28 April 1965. 55 Squadron, which had become non-operational as a Medium Bomber Force Squadron at Honington on 1 March, moved to Marham on 24 May 1965 to operate in the in-flight refuelling role. The Squadron's first two Victor K.1A two-point tankers, XH602 and XH648, arrived the following day, and two more, XH667 and XH620, arrived at the end of May. (These interim, two-point tankers severely limited long-range operations as they were unable to permit

On the end of the KC-135 boom was a basket which went into an Omega shape, and this put more stress on the Lightning's connection. The weak link safety device just behind the nozzle in the probe, which broke off in emergency, was too weak to mate with the KC-135. Dick Bell

Victor–Victor refuelling operations and would be withdrawn and be replaced with three-point tankers at a later date.) 55 Squadron's full complement of six Victors would not be reached until October but, like the 7th Cavalry, the Americans again came to the rescue. Arrangements had already been made with the USAF for the use of three KC-135s over a six to nine month period so that much-needed in-flight refuelling practice could commence immediately. Two KC-135s, from 919th Squadron, SAC, to be stationed at Upper Heyford, would begin in-flight refuelling with 23, 56, 74 and 111 Squadron's Lightnings in the UK, while another, from the 611th ARS, to be based at Adana, Turkey, would operate with 29 Squadron's javelin FAW.9s at Akrotiri.

Operation *Billy Boy*, as it was called, began on 5 April, with one-and-a-half hour sorties with 23 and 74 Squadrons' Lightnings, refuelling with 3,000lb (1,400kg) of fuel each sortie. Pilots discovered that the KC-135's rigid refuelling boom, to which was attached a seven-foot flexible hose and drogue, called for a much different receiver technique to that used on the hose and reel-equipped Valiant, as Flt Lt Bob Offord, now on 23 Squadron, who did his first 'bracket' with a KC-135 on 5 April, recalls:

This caused us no end of problems because we were not set up. On 7 April, I became the first pilot in the squadron to break a probe, which cost me a barrel of beer! However, my probe breaking was the first of many. [Of the twenty-two conversion and twenty-five continuation training sorties flown, the loss of probes on fifteen per cent of these sorties was 'unacceptably high'.] On the end of the KC-135 boom was a basket which went into an Omega shape, and this put more stress on the connection. Our weak link safety device just behind the nozzle in the probe (which broke off in emergency) was too weak to mate with the KC-135.

Initially, 23 Squadron's pilots, seventy-five per cent of whom had had previous experience of in-flight refuelling, had the lion's share of the KC-135s (by the end of April only nine pilots in 'Tiger' squadron had completed a minimum of three in-flight refuelling sorties). However, the CO, Sqn Ldr John Mcleod, admitted that it had also 'broken the largest number of probes – a weakness which would be largely eliminated by a current modification'. Bob Offord confirms, 'We had to have our probes 'beefed up' (the weak link was made stronger). From then on, the Americans would ask during tanking if we had a 'beefed up' probe.' Pilots in 111 Squadron at Wattisham, however, reported that,

A Tanker Training Flight was formed at Marham in July 1965 and 55 Squadron's Victor K.1As trained pilots in 74 Squadron prior to four pilots flying the receiver aircraft in *Forthright* 22/23 to Cyprus in August, the first occasion that the Victor tanker was used for an operational overseas deployment. RAF Marham

'initial contacts in the 'boomed' KC-135s proved relatively easy compared with the Valiant tanker'. However, the CO, Sqn Ldr George Black, wrote, 'the kinking and shortness of the KC-135's hose and drogue (seven feet) [had] proved more strenuous in probe rivets' and that remaining in contact for prolonged periods of up to five minutes had been 'more exacting and tiring than Valiant refuelling'.

Then, in May, several sorties were flown with the flight profile being one hour with the KC-135, followed by forty minutes on PIs. During 24–28 May, preparatory to their deployment to Cyprus, 56 Squadron at Wattisham, which had just converted from the F.1A to the F.3 in April, began their *Billy Boy* refuelling practice with five

F.2s XN730/B and XN784 of 19 Squadron refuelling from Victor K.1A XA918. In the summer of 1965 six pilots from 19 Squadron at Leconfield converted to high-level refuelling and then carried out low-level refuelling trials from five of the K.1A tankers. RAF Marham

The vortex coming off the Victor's wing always forced the Lightning's wing down, so when going in on the starboard side, a pilot had to feed in using left rudder and right aileron, while on the port side the problem was exacerbated because the probe's being on the left-hand side meant that the pilot had to be between the Victor's pod and his fuselage. via Gp Capt Ed Durham

The Victor's wing was prone to flexing in turbulence and the whip effect at the basket end of the drogue was quite frightening if a Lightning was not on the end to tone it down. Here, F.2 XN723 successfully engages the basket from a Victor tanker. While with Rolls-Royce XN723 crashed on 25 March 1964 at Keynham near Leicester after a fire in the No.2 engine bay. Mr D. Witham, the pilot, ejected safely. *Aeroplane*

Teaching 'probing and droguing' to a student using a T.5 (XS420 pictured) could cause a problem. Flying the T-bird from the right-hand seat when on the left wing of the Victor, trying to get between his pod and the fuselage, was difficult, especially since the pilot flew the T.5 with his left hand and he had to have his right hand on the throttle! Ronald Johnson

and the whip effect at the basket end of the drogue was 'quite frightening if a Lightning was not on the end to tone it down'.

Dave Seward agrees:

You had to refuel cross-controlled because the vortex coming off the Victor's wing always forced the Lightning's wing down (we always used the Victor's wing positions, the rear, central position only being used by the bigger aeroplanes), so, if you were going in on the starboard side, you had to feed in using left rudder and right aileron to keep your wings level and keep yourself from being thrown out of the wing vortex. If you went in on the port side you got the same sort of problem, but it was exacerbated in that your probe, being on the left hand side, meant that you had to be between the Victor's pod and his fuselage. You didn't have much room to play with if you started to buck up and down. People just got used to it. The problem came when we would demonstrate flight refuelling to a student using a T.5. Flying it from the right-hand seat when you were on the left wing of the Victor trying to get between his pod and the fuselage was difficult, especially since you flew the T.5 with your left hand and you had your right hand on the throttle! It worked, but you had to work hard at it.

You became more confident with practice but after becoming proficient at flight refuelling you got into a few bad habits. I, for instance, started off by religiously not looking

tanker missions involving three pairs of Lightnings being allocated to each tanker. However, one sortie was cancelled owing to Lightning unserviceability and two were lost when the KC-135 was forced to return to base with a probe end stuck in the drogue. Four probes in total were lost in the twenty-seven sorties achieved.

trials from five of the K.1A tankers in preparation for 74 Squadron's return to the UK in August. Low-level tanking was possible but extremely difficult, and was best carried out over the sea where conditions are relatively smooth. The Victor's wing was prone to flexing in turbulence

Enter the Victor

When a Tanker Training Flight was formed at Marham in July, 55 Squadron could get on with the task of training pilots in 74 Squadron. Nine successful sorties were carried out with nine pairs of F.3s. 74 Squadron's need was urgent as four pilots would fly the receiver aircraft in the forthcoming in-flight refuelling exercise *Forthright 22/23*), to Cyprus in August, the first occasion that the Victor tanker was used for an operational overseas deployment. The F.3s left Leuchars for Wattisham on 13 August, and took off from the Suffolk station the next day, in-flight refuelling to Akrotiri. All four Lightnings arrived on schedule after an average flight time of four hours ten minutes. In the meantime, six pilots from 19 Squadron at Leconfield converted to high-level in-flight refuelling and then carried out low-level in-flight refuelling

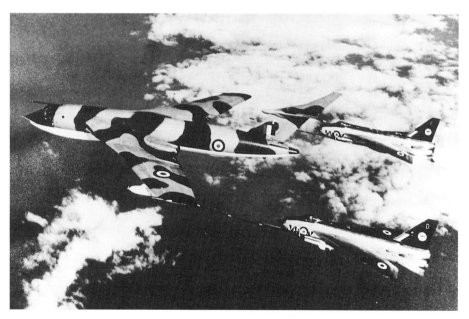

In October 1965, during Operation *Donovan*, four F.3s of 74 Squadron at Akrotiri, were refuelled all the way to Tehran and back, where, on 17 October, they took part in an IIAF (Imperial Iranian Air Force) Day. RAF Marham

Normally, Lightning pilots tanked from the Victor's wing positions, the rear, central position only being used by the bigger aircraft. In this photo F.3 XP747/S of 29 Squadron uses the central position on Victor K.1A XA932. XP747 had operated with 56 Squadron until it suffered Cat.4 damage on 11 May 1966 when the aircraft ran off the runway. After repair it was operated by 29 Squadron and was lost on 16 February 1972 following a collision over the North Sea with XP698. Flt Lt 'Chile' Cooper, the pilot of XP747, was killed. Dick Bell

By October 1965 the Lightnings were able to use all six Victor tankers. During the month four F.3s of 74 Squadron at Akrotiri, in Operation *Donovan*, were refuelled all the way to Tehran and back, where, on 17 October, they took part in an IIAF (Imperial Iranian Air Force) Day. That same month a 23 Squadron detachment was made to Cyprus to take the place of 29 Squadron's Javelins, which, when UDI was declared in Rhodesia, were sent to the troubled region. For Flt Lt Bob Offord, it meant a return to the island he had last visited with 56 Squadron:

This time we stayed three months, with crews rotating back and forth to the UK during this period. One of my interceptions, on 24 November, was against Turkish Air Force RF-84Fs, who as soon as they realized they had been intercepted, turned and headed for home. Little did they know it but my radar was u/s. The Turks were always friendly. In fact they would hold up a map and point to indicate that they were going home. [Bob Offord himself went home at the end of 1965 and in 1966 was posted to 226 OCU as an instructor.]

In June 1967, 74 Squadron and its thirteen Lightnings were posted to Tengah, Singapore, to replace the Javelins of 64 Squadron. Operation *Hydraulic*, as it was known, the longest and largest inflight refuelling operation hitherto flown, began on 4 June, staging through Akrotiri, Masirah and Gan, and using seventeen Victor tankers from Marham. Simon Parry

at the basket and kept a general sight picture but as you got more used to it once I had trapped the basket I would automatically have a quick look at the probe and nudge it in.

At OCU the instructors were all flight commander material but they did not practise flight refuelling at night so no-one was current. For this reason, 11 Group said that we couldn't be used operationally at night. However, we went up and did prods at night using a Victor until everyone was night qualified. When we told them, 11 Group demanded to know how we had become night qualified. I said we just went up and did it. How else did they think we had become proficient? It was rather like in the 1950s when you couldn't land at Gibraltar unless you had landed at Gibraltar before!

Just how difficult tanking could be was tragically brought home on 27 April 1964. Flt Lt George Davey had been the last of 92 Squadron's Lightnings to take his turn at air-to-air refuelling practice with Victors over the North Sea. Davey repeatedly failed to take on fuel and eventually had to abort. Unwisely as it turned out, he chose not to divert to nearby Coltishall, but decided to try instead to return to base with the rest of his squadron, which had now departed. He reached Binbrook, but

on finals his cockpit canopy failed to demist and he was prevented from making a visual approach. As Davey entered the circuit for a GCA approach, his Lightning crashed, out of fuel, at Beelsby, near Binbrook, too low for him to safely eject.

At the beginning of December 1965, 55 Squadron had been joined at Marham by 57 Squadron, minus their Victor K.1/1As. In fact the first of six, XA937, did not arrive until 14 February 1966. In 1966, 56 Squadron was tanked to Malta by 55 and 57 Squadron Victors to take part in the Malta air defence exercise, *Adex 66*. On 1 July 1966, the third and final Victor

At Farnborough in September 1968 two Lightning F.6s of 5 Squadron gave a fly-by demonstration paired with Victor K.1A XH614. A year later, XS926, the nearest F.6, crashed into the sea fifty-one miles off Flamborough Head. Major C. B. Neel USAF, ejected safely. Mike Flowerday

On 27 August 1968 the CO of 23 Squadron, Sqn Ldr Ed Durham, and Flt Lt Geoff Brindle, tanked from Leuchars to Goose Bay, Canada in seven hours twenty minutes for the first ever Lightning crossing of the Atlantic. Ed Durham is pictured taxying in XR725/A, and after arrival, right, with AVM Mike Le Bas, AOC 1 Group (the Detachment Commander), and Wg Cdr Liaison BDLS Ottawa. via Gp Capt Durham

1966 by the introduction of the F.6). Of course, intercepts were carried out at night and these posed some added considerations to take into account. Floodlights aboard the Victors lit up the under surface of the tankers' wings and could ruin a Lightning pilot's night vision. Normally therefore, receiver pilots asked for them to be turned off. All that were left were the tanker's navigation lights and a small triangle of blue lights on the receiver basket. Some found tanking in the dark that much easier because they could not see, and were therefore not distracted by, the refuelling probe whilst trying to engage the basket.

Long-Range Lightnings

In June 1967, 74 Squadron and its thirteen Lightnings were posted overseas, to Tengah, Singapore, to replace the Javelins of 64 Squadron. Operation *Hydraulic*, as it was known, the longest and largest inflight refuelling operation hitherto flown, began on 4 June when the CO, Wg Cdr Ken Goodwin, led six Lightnings off from Leuchars. Five more departed the next day and the last two flew out on the 6th. (XS416, the T.5 trainer which did not have overwing tanks, remained behind at Leuchars, while another, XV329, went by sea from Sydenham, Belfast. XV329 returned by sea to the UK in August 1971 and had to be written off in December when it was discovered that acid spillage from the batteries had corroded the airframe.) All thirteen Lightnings reached Tengah safely, staging through Akrotiri, Masirah, and Gan, and using seventeen Victor tankers from Marham, for what turned out to be a four-year tour of duty in the tropics. During this time, three 2,000-mile deployments were made to Australia non-stop using Victor tankers, the major one being Exercise *Town House*, 16–26 June 1969. The Lightnings also participated in *Bersatu Padu* ('Complete Unity'), a five-nation exercise held in Western Malaya and Singapore in July 1969. Regular exchanges were also flown with RAAF Mirages at Butterworth, Malaysia, and two Lightnings were flown to Thailand for a static display in Bangkok.

Meanwhile, 11 Squadron had practised in-flight refuelling (in 1967) and on 29 November, Flt Lt Eggleton had established a record, of eight and a half hours' flying, refuelling five times, flying 5,000 miles. By

Squadron, 214, formed at Marham, and by the end of the year was equipped with seven K.1/1A three-point tankers. In February 1967, Exercise *Forthright* 59/60 saw F.3s flying non-stop to Akrotiri and F.6s returning to the UK, refuelled throughout by Victor tankers from Marham. In April, 56 Squadron moved to Akrotiri to replace 29 Squadron's Javelins, a posting which would last seven years (May 1967–September 1974). The Lightnings' journey from the UK to Cyprus

involved six in-flight refuellings for the fighter versions, and ten for the T-birds, which were often taken on detachment to Cyprus to familiarize new pilots on target interception.

In-flight refuelling from Victors also became a feature used often on QRAs, 74 Squadron sharing the northern IAF (Interceptor Alert Force) defensive duties at Leuchars with 23 Squadron's F.3s (the Lightning's operational range and endurance being improved from August

Victor K.1A XH650 of 55 Squadron refuels F.3 XP700/K of 29 Squadron. XP700 crashed during take-off from RAF Wattisham on 7 August 1972 after the tail bumper and ventral tank made contact with the runway. Flt Lt E. Fenton ejected safely, the wreckage of the aircraft landing at Newton, near Sudbury. Richard Wilson

now a further twenty-four Victor K.I/1A three-point tanker conversions were in RAF service, and in 1968, twenty-seven B.2 and SR.2 versions were converted as K.2 tankers to replace the K.1 tankers at Marham. In May 1968, four F.6s of 5 Squadron from Leconfield flew non-stop from Binbrook to Bahrain, in eight hours, refuelled along the 4,000-mile route by Victor tankers from Marham.

In August 1968 two Lightnings from 23 Squadron, fitted with overwing tanks, were required to fly the Atlantic to Canada non-stop to enable RAF solo display pilot Tony Craig to take part in the International Exhibition at Toronto. He would use one of the Lightnings for his solo display – the other was a spare in case of problems with the first Lightning. On 26 August Sqn Ldr Ed Durham and Flt Lt Geoff Brindle of 23 Squadron took off in XR725/A and XS936/B respectively, and rendezvoused with their first tanker off Stornaway at

Lightnings of 29 Squadron, at the end of their training period at RAF Akrotiri in June 1974, prepare to return to RAF Wattisham by courtesy of the Victor tanker force. At the end of the year 29 Squadron began re-equipping on the Phantom. *Aeroplane*

XM171 is towed back to its hangar at RAF Wattisham on 6 June 1963 after Flt Lt Mo Moore managed to nurse the F.1A back with nothing more than a few dents in the fuselage and minus both Firestreaks, following a mid-air collision with Fg Off Mike Cooke in XM179 during a *Firebirds* practice bomb burst. Brian Allchin

F.1A XM173/C of 56 *Firebirds* Squadron, one of only twenty-four built, and the first Lightnings to be fitted with a production in-flight refuelling probe, closes in to refuel to tank from Vickers Valiant XD814, January 1964. In 1965 the Valiants were scrapped following metal fatigue problems. Brian Allchin

T.5 XS418, which was delivered to 226 OCU on 25 May 1965, at RAF Coltishall in September 1967. XS418 crashed at RAF Stradishall on 23 August 1968. Flt Lt Henry Ploszek and SAC Lewis were unhurt. The aircraft's last flight was in September 1974 and it served as a surface decoy until being scrapped in September 1987. Ron Clarke

Flt Lt Brian Mason of Treble One Squadron suffers a landing mishap in XM215 at RAF Wattisham in January 1964. The F.1A later served with OCU and the Binbrook TFF. Brian Allchin

XM147/J of 74 'Tiger' Squadron, one of the twenty-strong F.1 production batch, pictured at RAF Leuchars in July 1964. Gp Capt P.T.G. Webb

Flt Lt Brian Allchin of 56 Squadron poses by the side of his F.3 at Luqa in October 1965 during the Malta **ADEX**. Brian Allchin

A Lightning F.3 refuels from the centreline tank of a Handley Page Victor K.1A during a tanking exercise in the summer of 1972. Sqn Ldr Dick Bell

Over the Alps F.3 XP756/E of 29 Squadron moves in to refuel from Victor K.1A XH649 of 57 Squadron during an exchange exercise to Grosseto, Italy, in 1970. This Lightning crashed into the North Sea on 25 January 1971; Captain Bill Povilus, its American exchange pilot, was picked up safely. Sqn Ldr Dick Bell

F.6 XR725/A of 23 Squadron, which Sqn Ldr Ed Durham flew non-stop to Goose Bay, Canada, (with Flt Lt Geoff Brindle, in XS936/B), in seven hours twenty minutes, on 27 August 1968, using in-flight refuelling. When both Lightnings returned to Leuchars on 3 September 'A' had been 'zapped' by Air Canada and a maple leaf emblem added to the tail fin! Gp Capt Ed Durham

F.3 XP763/P which joined 29 Squadron at RAF Wattisham from 23 Squadron in 1972. Sqn Ldr Dick Bell

F.6 XP750/H of 111 Squadron crossing the coast of Suffolk inbound for Wattisham in the early 1970s. This aircraft, which was built originally as an F.3, joined Treble One in 1972 and finished its days as 'AQ' at RAF Binbrook from 1983. Sqn Ldr Dick Bell

F.1A XM214 of 226 OCU in flight from RAF Coltishall in July 1969. Sqn Ldr Dick Bell

F.3 XR718/P of 5 Squadron and F.6 XR752 of 11 Squadron (the first interim F.6 delivered to squadron service) from RAF Binbrook, in flight over the North Sea in August 1978. Gp Capt Ed Durham

92 Squadron line-up at Gütersloh in April 1977. The Lightnings spell out the words of the squadron Rugby team – 'The King Cobras XV'! Ed Durham

T.5 55-712/B of the Royal Saudi Air Force taxies in at RAF Coltishall in 1968. This aircraft arrived in Saudi Arabia in July 1969 and was lost on 21 May 1974 when it crashed into Half Moon Bay after an inverted low-level pass over some sand dunes. Colonel Ainousa and Lt Otaibi were killed. Adrian Savage

T.5 XS459 of 226 OCU taxis by the control tower at RAF Coltishall in July 1968. This Lightning went on to serve with 29 Squadron and the LTF as 'X' at RAF Binbrook. It crashed on approach to Binbrook on 21 March 1981. Repaired, it last flew on 15 March 1987 and is now on display at the Fenland and West Norfolk Aviation Museum at Wisbech, Cambridgeshire. Grp Capt Mike Hobson

T.5 XS451 of (2T Sqn) 226 OCU, airbrakes out, comes in to land at RAF Wattisham. Registered G-LTNG, this Lightning is owned by Barry Pover at Plymouth, Devon. Pete Nash

Flt Lt Roger Pope in F.6 XS897/K comes up close to Flt Lt Dave Roome in F.6 XR773/F during the flight from Tengah to Gan on 6 September 1971. Following the disbandment of 64 Squadron, all remaining Lightnings were flown on the 6,000m, thirteen-hour trip to Akrotiri, Cyprus, staging through Gan and Muharraq and completing seven air-to-air refuellings with Victor tankers, for transfer to 56 Squadron. XR773 flew for the first time on 23 December 1992. Registered G-OPIB, it is now owned by Barry Pover of the Lightning Flying Club at Exeter, Devon. XS897 is preserved at the South Yorks Aviation Museum at Firbeck. Gp Capt Dave Roome

F.2 and F.2As of 19 Squadron with a F-104G Starfighter of the Belgian Air Force during an air defence competition at RAF Gütersloh, Germany in the summer of 1968. Del Holyland

F.6 XR727/'BH' and XR725 off 11 Squadron from RAF Binbrook during a summer 1987 inflight refuelling exercise with F.3s and a VC-10 tanker of 101 Squadron on one of the 'tow lines' over the North Sea to Aberdeen. No.5 Squadron proved the longest operator of the Lightning, finally disbanding at Binbrook on 31 December 1987 and reforming as a Tornado F.3 unit at Coningsby in 1988. 11 Squadron finally disbanded on 30 April 1988 and reformed as a Tornado F.3 Squadron at Leeming in November 1988. Mick Jennings

0800. Geoff Brindle, however, could not take on fuel and his overwing tanks were venting. Both pilots aborted and it was decided to re-mount the operation the following day after repairs to Brindle's aircraft.

At 11.40 hours on 27 August, Sqn Ldr Durham and Flt Lt Brindle set out again with their supporting Victors. The first bracket went well, but at the second bracket, about 300 miles west of Stornaway, Brindle again could not take on fuel into his 'overburgers'. Ed Durham continues:

> We decided to carry on. Geoff would just have to refuel more often. I refuelled seven times across the Atlantic. Geoff Brindle did more like twelve or thirteen! The flight took seven hours twenty minutes. Apart from the refuellings, and bad weather at Goose Bay, it was otherwise bloody boring. Craig took XS936 back with me in XR725 on 3 September and he had trouble with the overwing tanks on the first refuelling bracket! I said, 'We force on'. If a tanker did not get airborne we could always divert to Goose Bay. The Victors did arrive every time and after several tankings we reached Scotland again safely.

On 6 January 1969 Exercise *Piscator*, the biggest in-flight refuelling exercise so far mounted by the RAF took place when ten Lightning F.6s of 11 Squadron, refuelled by Victor tankers of 55, 57 and 214 Squadrons from Marham, deployed to RAF Tengah, Singapore (staging through Muharraq and Gan) and back, a distance of 18,500 miles. During the two-way journey, 228 individual refuelling contacts were made during which 166,000 imperial gallons (754,630 litres) of fuel were transferred.

Twelve months later, Christmas 1969, Exercise *Ultimacy* was mounted when ten F.6s, of 5 Squadron this time, flew to Tengah for joint air-defence exercises with Lightnings of 74 Squadron and RAAF Mirages there. Only one stop, at Masirah, was made *en route*, the first Lightnings leaving Binbrook before dawn on a foggy 8 December morning. At 0345 hours they made their first rendezvous with their Victor tankers over East Anglia in the dark. Then it was on, across France and the Mediterranean and a rendezvous with more Victors from Cyprus. They continued eastwards, finally crossing Muscat and Oman and on to Masirah, the overnight stop. Next day a pre-dawn take off saw the

The Victor K.2 increased the fuel available to receiver aircraft. Here, a K.2 of 232 OCU at Marham refuels two F.6s of 11 Squadron, XR724/K and XR769/J, during an exercise in September 1974. MoD

Lightnings away on the last leg of their trip, across 4,000 miles of ocean, south-east to Gan (where Victors rendezvoused on schedule to refuel them), and then due east to Sumatra. 5 Squadron were escorted into Tengah by 74 Squadron. While in Singapore, 5 Squadron participated in local defence exercises, which began with Exercise *Antler* on 18 December, before

exchanging some of their Lightnings for those of 74 Squadron which were in need of major overhaul. Pairs of Lightnings began leaving Tengah daily from 8 January onwards, and by the 15th all were back safely at Binbrook after stop overs at Masirah and Akrotiri *en route*.

In February 1971, 23 Squadron tanked from Victors to Cyprus, to take part in

Victor K.1 XH621 prepares to receive a 19 Squadron F.2A from RAF Gütersloh in 1976. Richard Reeve

practice air defence of the island and ACM (air combat-manoeuvring exercises). On 25 August that year, 74 Squadron disbanded at Tengah, Singapore, and 56 Squadron acquired all of the 'Tiger's' remaining F.6s, which, starting on 2 September, were flown over the 6,000-mile (1,600km) route, a thirteen-hour trip, to Akrotiri, staging through Gan and Muharraq and completing seven air-to-air refuellings with Victor tankers. 56 Squadron was relieved in June the following year by 11 Squadron, which deployed to Akrotiri for a one-month detachment, enabling 56 squadron to fly to Britain to complete MPC (Missile Practice Camp) at Valley before returning to the island.

Cyprus featured high on the agenda again in 1974. In January six F.6s were sent to the island where, on 15 July, a Greek-led coup by the Cyprus National Guard overthrew President Makarios of Cyprus. Five days later, Turkey invaded the northern part of the island. After two days of fierce fighting, the United Nations arranged a ceasefire. The coup led to a dramatic increase in Turkish air activity around the island and Lightnings of 56 Squadron flew over 200 sorties, 20–27 July, 110 of them fully armed battle sorties, to protect the Sovereign Base Areas.

Following a subsequent Whitehall defence review, all 56 Squadron's Lightnings had gone by the end of January 1975 and only the SAR helicopters of 84 Squadron remained on the troubled island. However, Lightnings did return to Cyprus again, albeit on five-week detachments, when its importance as an Armament Practice Camp was fully realized. Each pilot would fly a series of cine camera work-up flights against a banner towed by a Canberra. When the pilot was considered safe, he would fly nine live gun firings on the banner. Scoring was completed by tipping the head of each 30mm round in a special semi-drying paint, which, when it hit the banner, left a stain around the hole that left no room for doubt. To avoid confusion on multiple sorties, each pilot's bullets would be tipped with a different colour paint.

The APCs continued right up until 1987, tanked there and back, as always by the ubiquitous Victors, who were always on time and on target!

A Victor tanker and Lightnings taking part in the 25th Anniversary celebrations at RAF Binbrook, September 1979. Flt Lt Tony Paxton

QRA: Keeping the Bears at Bay

The Lightning's most demanding role was to intercept, supersonically, enemy aircraft penetrating NATO airspace at altitude and, if called upon, shoot them down with air-to-air missiles and cannon. If the deterrent was to work effectively, RAF Fighter (later Strike) Command had to station Lightnings, and later Lightnings and Phantoms, on immediate readiness, twenty-four hours a day, 365 days a year. Quick Reaction Alert (QRA), as it was called, was just that, with intercepts possible at 40,000ft (12,000m)+ just minutes after a re-heat take-off. It was all very well having the world's most advanced supersonic interceptor with this capability, but if sorties were to be successful, then pilots needed to apply completely new techniques *vis-a-vis* radar and weaponry.

Initially, the missile and radar systems were beset with teething problems, and it fell to pilots like Bruce Hopkins at the AFDS at Coltishall to carry out trials work on the Lightning's radar and fire control systems. 'At the start, in 1960, we had problems with the fire control computer', he recalls,

Once the radar was locked on we had a very simple analogue computerized steering programme to do the intercept. The theory was that we tracked the 'dot' on the scope to obtain the optimum pursuit path for firing. The trouble was, it was bloody useless! You could do a manual intercept far better. So, we threw the steering programme away and developed a system of intercept using the basic B radar scope display. This became the basis of

Initially, the Lightning's missile and radar systems were beset with teething problems, and it fell to the pilots of the AFDS at Coltishall to carry out trials work on the radar and fire control systems. Posing for the camera in front of XM137/F on 26 April 1961 are: Flt Lts Jim Reynolds and Bruce Hopkins, Major Bill Cato USAF, Sqn Ldr E. Babst, Wg Cdr D.C.H. Simmons, Sqn Ldr D. Vasse, and Flt Lts Pete Collins, John Mitchell and Don Lamont RCAF. Bruce Hopkins

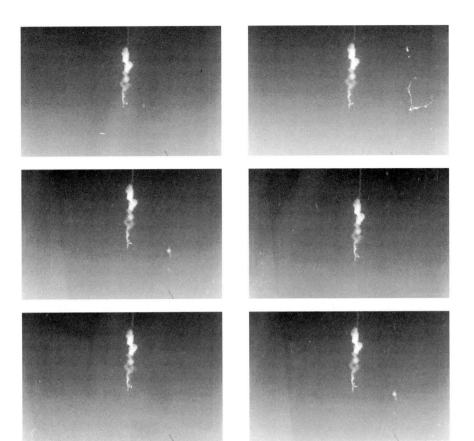

From February 1961 onwards work started on ILS and weapons' systems work at Boscombe Down as well as missile firings. At first, telemetry-fitted Firestreaks with the explosive removed were used against pilotless, remotely-controlled, Meteor targets, then, Jindiviks (pictured). Tony Aldridge via Pete Nash

A 23 Squadron Lightning shadows a Soviet 'Bear' over the North Sea during June 1968. via Ed Durham

all Lightning AI (Airborne Intercept) work. Unless you had a high closing speed, the intercept bracket was about two miles from the target. The skill came in making the intercept at subsonic speed. If you got it wrong, you had to go to re-heat to make up the distance.

We did a hell of a lot of work on intercepts, high-level then low-level, where the radar did not perform too well due to ground clutter. (Although the AI pulse radar at this time had a maximum range at height of twenty-five miles, at sea level it was less than five miles.) Once we had got what we thought were the basic techniques we started flying the super-sonic intercept mission. Now we really had fuel problems! It meant that there was far less time to get the radar intercept right. Our radar scanned horizontally at ± forty-five degrees with a beam width of two to three degrees, so we had to search vertically for the target by use of a scanner elevation control. As we moved the elevation lever the radar dish looked up and down. This is known as the 'elevation search'. Of course supersonically, we had less time to search for the 'blip'. Then we had to lock on to the target using the trigger switch and we went into the intercept with it locked on.

From February 1961 onwards we started

This operations room at an RAF 11 Group Master Radar Station in the 1960s with its plotting table and RAF clock reminiscent of World War Two was one of several radar stations in the UK responsible for early warning of aircraft and missile threats within the UK Air Defence Region. RAF Neatishead

de Havilland Firestreak

The first Firestreak missile was successfully flight tested at Larkhill on 17 January 1953 and the first air-launch of a fully guided and controlled round took place at Aberporth when a Firestreak fired from a Venom destroyed an unmanned radio controlled Firefly. First Mk.1 production versions entered service with FAA Sea Venom squadrons in 1958. The infra-red guidance system consisted of a cassegrain IR telescope with fifteen degree squint angle located behind an eight-faceted all glass nose-cone. Cooling of the seeker head and onboard electronics carried out by nitrogen in the launch aircraft. Target lock-on (rear only attack) was effected by two rings of sensors behind the main seeker head. The 50lb (23kg) warhead was wrapped around the motor tube just forward of the fins.

Dimensions:
Length: 10ft 5.5in (3.18m)
Diameter: 8.75in (0.22m)
Wingspan: 2ft 5.5in (0.76m)
Weight: 300lb (136kg)
Speed: Mach 3
Range: 0.75–5m (1.2–8km)

A Gütersloh based F.2A of 92 Squadron taking off in 1976. An awe-inspiring sight and sound never to be forgotten, the sheer power of the Avons, with their ear-splitting roar, would leave ears ringing for hours afterwards! Richard Reeve

Two F.6s, XR713/C and XR716/F, of 111 Squadron at operational readiness on a wet night ready for interceptor duty. These two aircraft joined Treble One Squadron early in 1965 and both later served with 5 Squadron. via Jean Stangroom

A 23 Squadron F.6 with overwing tanks pictured at Leuchars while on QRA duty. Dugald Cameron via Bruce Hopkins

For QRA duty four armed Lightnings (from September 1969, Lightnings and Phantoms) sat in a 'Q-shed' near the end of the runway, two fighters at Leuchars in the Northern QRA all year round, and the other two at alternately Wattisham and Binbrook (later, Coningsby's Phantoms were also used) in the Southern QRA. via Hugh Trevor

missile firing trials at Boscombe Down. At first, we used telemetry-fitted Firestreaks with the explosive removed, against pilotless, remotely-controlled, Meteor targets. Then, in March, on the Aberporth ranges in Wales, I fired at Australian-built 'Jindiviks'. Major Bill Cato, our American exchange pilot, Jim Reynolds and I carried out a whole series of Firestreak firings during 1961. Jim Reynolds and I would fly a Javelin FAW.8 to Boscombe Down on the Monday (which we also used to go back and forth to Coltishall for spares etc), and fly back to Coltishall on the Friday after a week of missile firing exercises. We must have been the most expensive 'commuters' in the world. We had competitions to see who could transit between Coltishall and Boscombe the fastest. The ground rules were, you were not allowed to break any airframe limits or air traffic rules. After take off from [runway] '22 SW', you would cruise in re-heat at about Mach 0.94, and make a straight-in approach at Boscombe. Jim Reynolds finally got the time down to eighteen minutes seven seconds!

We fired a total of five Firestreaks. This all proved very successful. Then we did quite a bit of gun firing, which wasn't so successful! All we proved was that the pilot attack gunsight was very basic. It was OK if we did approaches from behind, but it was not so good under g conditions using lots of angle. In fact, it was only any good from line astern. Still, guns were a very useful weapon to have, the basic philosophy being missiles for long range (one mile minimum), and guns for within a mile of a target. I was always a member of the 'let's keep the gun' lobby. The Lightning, though, was never a good aircraft for gun-fighting. All our air-to-air gunnery was done on the 'flag' ie. the quarter attack. With a couple of hundred rounds you were lucky to get twenty per cent of the rounds on target in a Lightning; this, compared with forty to fifty per cent on Hunters.

Bruce Hopkins left AFDS in September 1962, being posted as a Weapons Instructor on T.4s to the Lightning Conversion Squadron at Middleton St. George. Promoted squadron leader, he left 226 OCU (the LCU had expanded) at the end of January 1964 on a posting to the Air Ministry. A series of staff appointments, and a two-year exchange tour with the US Navy on the F-4J Phantom meant that he would not return to the Lightning force until 1972, when he was given command of 23 Squadron at Leuchars.

The System

23 Squadron was a key element in Britain's air defence. The front-line squadrons were backed up by a first-class ground controlled defence system. No.11 Group's Air

In Germany in September 1965, 19 Squadron's F.2s began performing a QRA role at Gütersloh and, in December that year, 92 Squadron's F.2s joined them in the role, at Geilenkirchen. This photo, taken on 24 March 1970, is of F.2A XN773 of 92 Squadron (which had moved to Gütersloh in January 1968) flown by Sqn Ldr John Bryant, passing the Möhne Dam in formation with a Hunter FR.10 of No 2 (AC) Squadron piloted by George Lee. Built as an F.2, XN77 was operated originally by Rolls-Royce at Hucknall and 60 MU, when, in July 1967, it was converted to F.2A standard at Warton. Wg Cdr John Bryant Collection

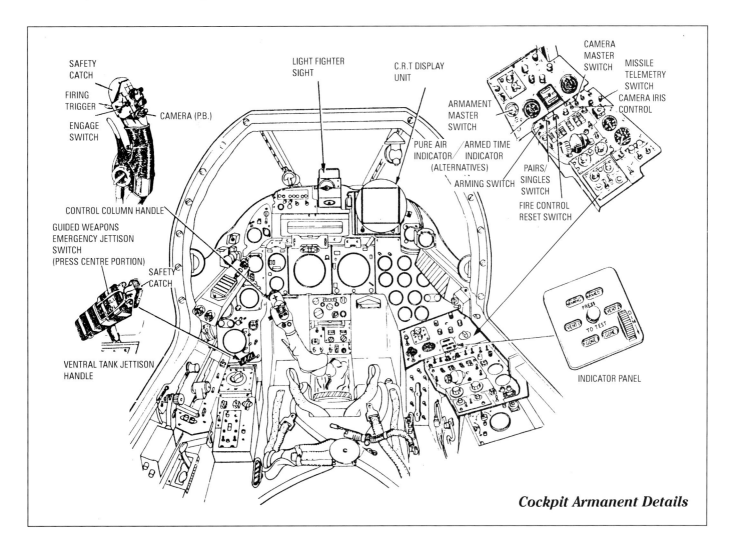

Cockpit Armanent Details

A Lightning of 5 Squadron at Binbrook taking off on 25 March 1971 in preparation for the squadron's defence of its unofficial title of 'Europe's Top' in the annual NATO Air Defence Competition. The usual starting level for PIs (Practice Intercepts) was 36,000ft or, more correctly, Flight Level 360. The tropopause was normally somewhere near there, and the Avon 200s liked that. The ventral tank would run dry about six minutes after levelling off, then the fuel in the flaps (yes, flaps!, about 250lb in each) would have their fuel consumed before the main wing tanks came on line. About four PIs could be carried out subsonically, with the 'fighter' at Mach 0.95 and the 'target' – usually another Lightning – at Mach 0.85. If a high-flyer (50,000ft and up) or supersonic target was on the menu, only one PI was likely, as the fighter would have to use re-heat. The fuel consumption was then increased six-fold, which was alarming in an aircraft that was at 'Mayday' levels even on taxying out. via EDP

Defence Ground Environment (ADGE), with its Headquarters and operations centre at Bentley Priory, near London, provided early warning of Soviet aircraft and missile threats. Aircraft such as Tu-95 'Bears', Tu-16 'Badgers' and, occasionally, M-4 'Bisons' and Il-18 'Coots', of the Soviet Long-Range Air Force and Naval Air Force, flying reconnaissance missions around the North Cape of Norway and on towards the central Atlantic and the British Isles, would be investigated in the UK Air Defence Region by 11 Group using QRA interceptors. Usually the Soviet aircraft practised their war roles of maritime surveillance, anti-shipping and anti-submarine warfare, and simulated strikes on mainland Britain.

The UK ADR, contained entirely within NATO Early Warning Area 12, forms part of a unified air defence system under SACEUR (Supreme Allied Commander Europe), which extends to cover three other NATO air defence regions. Three Master Radar Stations (from 1975, key sector operations centres [SOCs]), with control and reporting facilities were grouped around radar units at Boulmer, Buchan, Scotland, and Neatishead, Norfolk. These were fed with data from six NATO Air Defence Ground Environment (NADGE) stations via digital link with the Air Defence Data

de Havilland Red Top

Originally designated the Firestreak Mk.IV, this collision-course missile, fitted with a new, more rounded seeker head, could lock onto the heat generated by the target aircraft's engines, and also the friction hot spots created by its flight path. An improved rocket motor gave a top speed of Mach 3+ with an in-control range of 7m (4.4km). The warhead carried 68lb (31kg) of explosive. The first Red Top entered RAF service in 1964 with Lightning F.6s of 74 Squadron.

Dimensions:
Length: 11ft 5.5in (3.18m)
Body diameter: 8.75in (0.22m)
Wingspan: 2ft 11.375in (0.9m)
Weight: 330lb (150kg)
Speed: Mach 3
Range: 7m (4.4km)

Wg Cdr Bruce Hopkins, CO of 23 Squadron, after a sortie over the North Sea. Bruce Hopkins

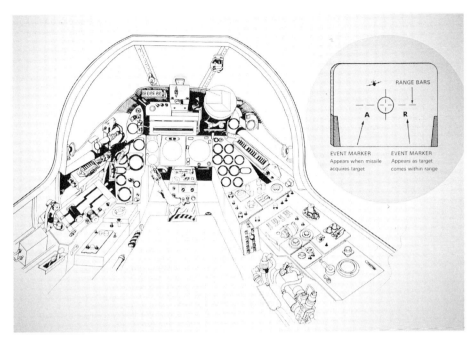

Centre at West Drayton and the Air Defence Operations Centre at Strike Command HQ, High Wycombe, forty miles west of London. Here sat the Air Officer C-in-C Strike Command, who also wore the NATO 'hat' of COMUKADR (Commander UKADR). Further long-range, low-level radar coverage was provided by twelve Shackleton AEW.2 AEW aircraft. From 1975 onwards, data was also fed into the system from the control and reporting post on Benbecula on North Uist, and from the reporting site at Saxa Vord. Additional links were provided by the Ballistic Missile Early Warning System (BMEWS) station at Fylingdales, Yorkshire.

At the 'sharp end' four armed Lightnings (from September 1969, Lightnings and Phantoms) sat in a 'Q-Shed' near the end of the runway, two fighters at Leuchars in the Northern QRA all year round, and the other two at alternately Wattisham and Binbrook (later, Coningsby's Phantoms were also used) in the Southern QRA. In Germany in September 1965, 19 Squadron's Lightning F.2s began performing a QRA role at Gütersloh, and in December that year 92 Squadron's F.2s joined them in the role, at Geilenkirchen. In January 1968 92 Squadron moved to Gütersloh and together with 19 Squadron carried out interceptor duties until replaced by Phantoms in December 1976 and March 1977, respectively.

On QRA, each pair of Lightning interceptors would be attended by seven groundcrew, one or two from each trade and a SNCO (Senior NCO) in charge. Two pilots dressed in full flying kit, minus their life preservers and helmets, but including their immersion suits during the winter, were at ten minutes' readiness.

This meant that an aircraft had to be airborne within ten minutes of the 'Scramble' order. (In keeping with the World War Two fighter spirit, 'scramble' signalled a take-off, while that other popular term, 'Buster', which originally meant 'through the gate', was used to describe re-heat. Targets were known as 'Trade', another throwback to the War.) At nights, it was relaxed to thirty minutes. Even then they had to don their flying kit.

At the Sharp End

Pete Nash, a ground crewman occasionally on QRA at Wattisham, recalls:

> Sometimes a klaxon, just like those World War Two submarine diving alarms, would rent the air, meaning that a scramble was imminent and cockpit readiness was required. The pilots would let us groundcrew rush out first, punching a button that opened the front and rear doors. First out would hit the button, even if his aircraft was the second and furthest away. Beforehand, all jobs were allocated so each knew what he had to do. One would start the Houchin (ground power set) and press the power buttons. The second would go round the other side and remove the Master Armament Safety Brake, then stand clear

Two of 92 Squadron's F.2As on QRA duty at Gütersloh with a pair of Firestreak missiles in the foreground.
via Gp Capt Ed Durham

F.3 XR751/Q of 29 Squadron pictured at the southern, Bildeston end ORP (Operational Readiness Pan) during an air defence exercise in the early 1970s at Wattisham. The long thin cable snaking out to the starboard wheel-well is the 'telebrief', a landline through which the pilot could talk to the Station Operations and to Sector Control and receive his initial interception instructions and the order to 'scramble'. With the cockpit vacant it would indicate a low level of alert with possibly another Lightning on the line at cockpit readiness. On these exercises 29 and 111 Squadrons would share the same ORP; at other times each would be at opposite ends of the runway. Pete Nash

High above the North Sea in 1974 a Soviet 'Bear' long range reconnaissance aircraft is intercepted by F.6 XR753 flown by Wg Cdr Bruce Hopkins, CO of 23 Squadron from RAF Leuchars. The photo was taken from a Phantom of 43 Squadron also based at Leuchars. MoD

while the third would help the pilot strap in. If a launch was ordered, then pilot only waited long enough for a thumbs up from the ground-crew to indicate that the 'fireman' had extinguished any flames from the starter exhausts before he released his brakes and taxied out. The power lines and telebrief [through which the pilot was given his orders] were anchored to the floor so as the aircraft moved forward, they were disconnected. As he left the 'Q-Shed', the pilot lowered his flaps and trusted air traffic to clear the runway for him because he didn't stop. Onto the runway he then engaged double re-heat, and away he went. A QRA scramble had priority over all other local traffic. Meantime, 'Q2' would sit at cockpit readiness until 'Q1' was well on his way and declared that his aircraft was service-able. Only then would he stand down to ten minutes.

For the groundcrews, QRA was a rest. We did a week continuous, sleeping in the accom-modation next to the aircraft shed, doing the flight servicings when required, an engine run every so often, and watching telly, playing board-games, or fixing our cars. It was the easiest job on the squadron! If an aircraft went unserviceable then it either had to be fixed or replaced; half an hour ago, if not now!

Before the flight servicings could start we had to contact the fighter controllers for permission to take the aircraft 'Off State', and then we were only allowed one hour to fix it otherwise we had to change aircraft. Another aircraft had to be armed and ready, usually on the flight line with a pilot close by, while the 'Q' aircraft was fixed. When it came to meal times we went to the head of the queue and our Land Rover was parked right outside the mess doors, ready for an instant call back for a scramble. Wattisham shared the Southern QRA with Binbrook. Leuchars was always on Northern QRA.

Flt Lt Bob Offord was posted from 56 Squadron to become the A Flight Commander on 23 Squadron at Leuchars in September 1964, a move that meant transition to the F.3:

The F.3 was a different aircraft in many ways. It had a totally different instrument layout, the engines were bigger, and it had a faster autopilot that worked. It had height and heading hold and could be used for turning. It also had a priority for automatic ILS, although it was set up for three degrees (the Lightning liked two and a half degrees), so it was very rarely used. Our preferred approach was GCA, which would be two and a half degrees, and in some cases, manual ILS. the autopilot was like having another pilot and it let the aircraft look after itself more while you looked after the radar. The AI 23B doubled the range and V-bombers now appeared on screen much sooner. I could also now carry Red Top.

At Leuchars 23 Squadron had sixteen pilots. Flt Lt Ian Thompson, the B Flight Commander, and myself did not operate as separate flights. We would chop and change and took it in turns to do the day and night shifts. We operated a pair of Lightnings on QRA, 8am to 8pm. It was intensive, especially

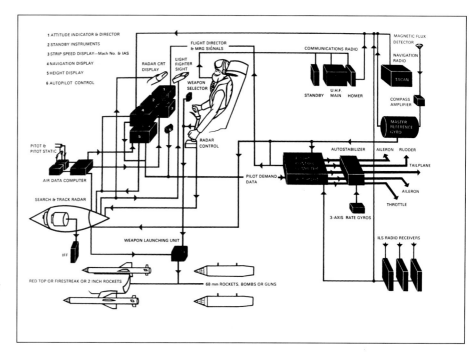

19 Squadron groundcrew in NBC (Nuclear, Biological and Chemical warfare) clothing, refuel and rearm a Lightning during an 'attack evaluation' exercise at Gütersloh in 1976. These were a regular feature of RAF life at the time when the base 'went to war' to test whether it was ready for any eventuality. The speed with which the groundcrew refuelled and rearmed an aircraft would put the average Grand Prix pit crew to shame! Richard Reeve

Scramble! Air and ground crew race to their waiting and fully armed F.2A at the start of another intercept sortie. On QRA, each pair of Lightning interceptors would be attended by seven groundcrew, one or two from each trade and a senior NCO in charge. Two pilots dressed in full flying kit, minus their life preservers and helmets but including their immersion suits during the winter, were always at ten minutes' readiness.
Richard Reeve

for the 'plumbers', though in the summer we gave up night flying, because flying at the heights we flew, it does not get dark enough. Normal take-offs were carried out on cold power, at 150kt IAS, and you became airborne at 165–170 IAS. (The front wheel would not retract above 165–170 IAS.) Then it would be a ten degrees climb out at 450kt, pitching up to twenty-two degrees on the Initial Altitude Indicator, invariably to 36,000ft (at the tropopause), where we did most of our work. QRAs used re-heat take-offs, so getting the gear up was more critical. So too was fuel, but from October 1965 onwards we used Victor tankers. (The Lightning was short of fuel the moment you started the engines!) Acceleration and the rate of climb was

phenomenal – from brake release to 36,000ft took just two and a half minutes. And you did it at a forty-seven degrees angle. Also, the seat was angled at twenty-three degrees, so the combination of the two made you feel that you were lying on your back!

On head-on supersonic interceptions (with another Lightning) we had a closing speed of Mach 3–4. Head-on attacks were very exciting and set-up had to be very good! For a successful 'shoot-down' to happen, three parameters were needed. First, the trigger had to to be pulled (first, because we had to do this up to fifteen miles range, then hold it until the interception), when the missile saw the target, in range, and 'fired'. There was no audible sound that the missile had 'locked-on' but a

circle in the sight, which collapsed once you were in range, indicated that you were in range (the Red Top would normally see the target before it was in range). I carried out head-on attacks in daylight, never seeing the target visually. After the attack we rolled down and went home. During my time on the squadron no Russian aircraft were intercepted, but from 1966 onwards they started in a big way, right around the clock.

With Firestreak the kill radius from the Lightning's base for a hostile aircraft flying at a speed of Mach 1.5 at an altitude of 45,000ft (13,720m) was 300nm (556km). With air-to-air rockets it was 390nm (722km). With rockets or Firestreak the

A 19 Squadron F.2A rolls out of the QRA hangar at the end of the Gütersloh runway. Crews spent twenty-four hours at a stretch on instant standby, living in accommodation just a few feet from their aircraft because aircraft had to be airborne within ten minutes of the 'scramble' order. Richard Reeve

kill radius against a hostile aircraft at Mach 0.9 at 36,000ft (11,000m) was 480nm (890km). Against a hostile at 350 knots (650kph) at 20,000ft (6,100m) the kill radius was 475nm (880km) with rockets or Firestreak. According to the sales brochure, from Lightning take-off a Mach 1.5 intruder at 45,000ft (13,720m) could be destroyed in 6.2 minutes with rockets, or in eight minutes using Firestreak. By the same token, an intruder at 36,000ft (11,000m) could be destroyed in 3.3 minutes, and a 350 knot (650kph) intruder at 20,000ft (6,100m) in 2.1 minutes.

Meeting the Oppostition

Sqn Ldr (later Gp Capt) Ed Durham flew several QRAs at Leuchars as a flight commander in 23 Squadron during 1968–70. 'It was one of the loneliest feelings there was,' he recalls, 'being 600 miles north of Lossiemouth and looking for a tanker to refuel from.' (As many as six inflight refuellings could be required on a long-range QRA sortie.) It could sometimes be quite hectic too, although in a given period, not all flights were QRA sorties. On 25 February 1970, Sqn Ldr Durham intercepted two 'Bear-Ds' on a night QRA. He had already flown four sorties the day before, and three more followed on the 26th, and the same

number two days after that.

Wg Cdr Bruce Hopkins, CO of 23 Squadron since May 1972, sometimes took part in his squadron's QRA commitment at Leuchars, as he recalls:

At one time all my pilots had done at least two

intercepts against Soviet aircraft. Eric Houston did twenty-four scrambles that resulted in intercepts, 1972–75. The QRA shed was at the end of the runway and we would go there for twenty-four hours at a time, and sit and wait. We'd sit in the crew room, kitted up, and sleep there in proper beds in our underclothes. Our immersion suit, g-suit and Mae Wests were laid out.

We would get a build-up – in other words, a recognized air picture. A typical scramble would begin with one of the Norwegian radars plotting a Soviet aircraft transiting the Northern Cape and on into the North Sea. It could be a training flight – Bears were always going to Cuba via the Faroes-Scotland-Iceland gap – or an intelligence gathering sortie. Every time we had a naval exercise in the area you could always guarantee Soviet aircraft would monitor it. Sometimes we would go weeks without any Soviet aircraft, then get a dozen in a four-day period. The plot would be picked up by Saxa Vord, who would 'tell in' to Strike Command at High Wycombe, who would organize resources. Tankers would usually be called in to support us. You therefore knew well in advance when you would be scrambled and if and when you would get a tanker. First we were brought up to cockpit readiness. All relevant information would be relayed by the ground controller, together with your call sign and that of the tanker. The type of call depended on the circumstances. The aircraft

F.2A XN731/Z of 19 Squadron in dark green low-visibility scheme is seen here in mid-flight over the northern plains of West Germany. Prior to 1973 XN731 had served with 92 Squadron. Richard Reeve

19 and 92 Squadrons carried out interceptor duties from Gütersloh until replaced by Phantoms in 1977. 19 Squadron disbanded on 31 December 1976 and reformed at Wildenrath on 1 January 1977 with the Phantom FGR.2. In this photo, taken in January 1977, an F.2A of 92 Squadron formates over Germany with a Harrier of 4 Squadron also from Gütersloh. Three months later, on 31 March 1977, 92 Squadron disbanded; its Lightnings were replaced by Phantom FGR.2s on 1 April when the squadron reformed at Wildenrath. MoD

was always fully armed. We would carry a hand-held camera in the cockpit.

Usually, one aircraft would be scrambled, but both pilots would be in their cockpits in case of a problem. Once airborne, we would first get to a tanker and then stay with him and refuel until the actual intercept. (A typical sortie would be five to six hours and involve several tankings, or 'brackets'.) Once the intercept was set up, we would cast off from the tanker and head for the target. We would intercept, investigate and shadow, take photos, and feed information on new aerials aboard an aircraft etc., back for intelligence gathering. Flying a Lightning and taking photos of a manoeuvering Bear was not the easiest job in the world but we developed a technique. First we would fly under the Bear, or the Badger, etc., and take photos from all angles. Sometimes, to make life even more difficult, they would turn in to you or away from you. Sometimes the guy at the back would wave. At night they shone lights at you to find out who you were. Although international airspace reached to within 12m of the coast of Britain, usually, the Soviet aircraft never came within 100m.

Squadron Leader Dave Seward was also asked to take photos of Soviet bombers from the cockpit while on QRA intercepts:

I think that the Lightning cockpit was built around Roley Beamont, a four-foot eight-inch 'monster' who had hands like meat plates, and not for six-foot tall chaps like me! Trying to turn around in the cockpit when your head is almost touching each side and wearing an

Wg Cdr Ed Durham, CO 92 Squadron, November 1975–31 March 1977. In April 1977 92 Squadron became a Phantom squadron and Wg Cdr Durham went to Brüggen to become a Bloodhound Missile Squadron commander where, to his misery, he saw the Lightning F.2A decoys on a daily basis. Gp Capt Ed Durham Collection

**F.2As of 92 Squadron, led by Gp Capt Ed Durham, pictured near Gütersloh in 1977 by the port-facing F95
nose recce camera of a 4 Squadron Harrier GR.3 flown by Flt Lt Bruce Monk.** Bruce Monk Collection

immersion suit and oxygen mask etc., to take a photo with your Vivitar was, shall we say, 'difficult'. Taking photos whilst flying the Lightning 1A, whose early autopilot was an AFCS giving just heading and attitude hold, was even worse. At that time QRA was a lot of sitting around on the ground. At Wattisham, whenever we were used 56 Squadron reinforced the Northern QRA. On Christmas Day 1962 the Russians put up a stream of Bears and the odd Bison round the North Cape and we were up and down and landed at Leuchars. The Russians could be sheer bloody minded. Commanding Officers did not do normal QRAs but generally speaking, we did Christmas Day and Boxing Day duty.

In December 1973, the 23 Squadron CO, Wg Cdr Bruce Hopkins, leading from the front and volunteering for it, did a Christmas and Boxing Day stint, from 9.00am on Christmas morning to 9.00am on Boxing Day. All was quiet until 4.00am on Boxing Day morning when he was scrambled to investigate a plot over the North Sea. As usual, he expected to first make a rendezvous with a tanker. (Tankers were usually available at a high readiness state, in order to keep the interceptors airborne for as long as required –

sometimes up to seven or eight hours.) 'However', he recalls,

There was no tanker available and so I did not have enough fuel to get to the intercept point. (It was a Bear making the Cuba run.) I flew out for forty minutes in the hope that I would get a look at it but the target profile probably turned away. A year later, on 17 September 1974, I intercepted two Badgers flying together, going north.

The training and probing flights continued and each time we would send Lightnings up to investigate. Sometimes they were one of 'ours'. Sometimes they weren't. It was hard work but I enjoyed it. Comparing the Lightning with the Phantom was like comparing a sports car with a ten-ton truck. The Lightning handled beautifully and had a responsive feel to it, whereas the Phantom did not have that precisesness of control.

Continental QRA

Bruce Hopkins left 23 Squadron in April 1975. Seven months later, in November 1975, Gp Capt Ed Durham arrived at Gütersloh having foresaken ('not reluctantly') a desk in MoD London earlier

that year, to take command of 92 Squadron at Gütersloh. Gp Capt Durham recalls:

I had spent some months refresher flying and was looking forward to taking my first command of a fighter squadron. All my time in the RAF had been spent in air defence in the United Kingdom and I had already flown three tours on the Lightning. To return to flying after an absence of some six years was a tremendous thrill in itself but to be given a famous fighter squadron to lead and at an overseas location was real icing on the cake.

In the UK the threat we faced was largely a long-range bomber one, at medium- to high-level and at some distance from the UK mainland. In Germany it was a totally different matter. The threat was at low altitude, had a substantial self-defence capability and could well be dedicated to defensive counter air – in other words we, the fighters, were their prime target. Generally speaking we were heavily outnumbered as well. Such considerations tended to concentrate the minds of 2 and 4 ATAF fighter crews and the impetus was skill though realistic training. Ground Control was a bonus and we spent much of our time in the low-level combat air patrol patterns although we talked to 'Backwash' and 'Crabtree' [GCI stations in Germany] occasionally.

'Lightning Alley' was some obstacle for the ATAF fighter bombers to penetrate and affiliation training was achieved regularly under the 'Dial a Lightning' concept. All we needed was a 'phone call from some base like Laarbruch or Brüggen to say that so many Jaguars would be south of Soest at 1200 and there would be at least two Lightnings on visual patrol ready to do battle.

There is no doubt in my mind that my flying at Gütersloh was some of the best I have done in my Air Force career. Low altitude operations are exciting and stimulating in themselves but to add to these the extra bonus of air combat not only increased the flow of adrenalin but also revealed the sense of responsibility innate in our young fighter pilots of the day. Mostly they were given free rein to do the job and with very few exceptions they responded in an effective and mature way. I was very proud of all my men on 92, aircrew and groundcrew alike and I felt very privileged to be their commanding officer. We met every challenge, such as tactical evaluation, which came our way. I would also pay tribute to the other squadrons on the base for their contribution to the outstanding combat capability of the base and also for the friendly rivalry that helped to make life as good as it was.

19 and 92 Squadrons carried out interceptor duties from Gütersloh until replacement in 1977 by McDonnell Douglas Phantoms FGR.2. 19 Squadron disbanded first, on 31 December 1976. To mark the retirement of their Lightnings (the squadron reformed at Wildenrath on 1 January 1977 with the Phantom), Grp Capt Ed Durham led a 92 Squadron twelve-ship formation over the snow covered fields of Gütersloh on 30 December. Then it was the turn of 92 Squadron to disband and to replace its Lightnings with the Phantoms. Grp Capt Ed Durham was determined to mark the passing of the Lightning in RAF Germany in a manner befitting the occasion but had to content himself with just two aircraft. Shortly before midnight on 31 March 1977, he and Simon Morris took off from Gütersloh on a 55-minute sortie, during which time the CO called up each GCI station, and one by one bid them farewell.

'We landed,' he says,

back at Gütersloh and were then asked by the tower to stop for five minutes. There were no lights on at all, not even on the ASP. Then we got the 'Clear to taxi in' call and suddenly, all the lights came on at once. The ASP [Aircraft Servicing Pan] was filled with people! We were carried shoulder high to the hangar and a big 'hoolie' followed. It really was a wonderful moment.

By the end of 1977 only 5 and 11 Squadrons remained equipped with the Lightning. The rest of No 11 Group's interceptor force had converted from the Lightning to the McDonnell Douglas F-4M Phantom FGR.2. 5 and 11 Squadrons at Binbrook remained equipped with the Lightning, serving until 31 October 1987 and 30 April 1988, respectively, when they were replaced with Tornado F.3 aircraft. Binbrook remained equipped with the Lightning, and these served until 31 October 1987 and 30 April 1988, respectively, when they were replaced with Tornado F.3 aircraft.

Two Lightnings of 11 Squadron at RAF Binbrook in April 1988, only a few weeks away from the type's retirement from front-line duties. *Aeroplane*

CHAPTER SEVEN

Tiger Tales

Flt Lt Mike J.F. Shaw joined 74 Squadron, the 'Tigers', in 1962:

The Lightning F.1 had replaced the squadron's Hunter F.4s in June 1960 and had rendered all other European fighters obsoles-

cent; it was twice as fast and had more than double the rate of climb of anything else in service. This was brought home to me when I first saw a stream 'rotation' take-off of five F.1s at three-second intervals. The technique was something that could not be applied safely

to any other aircraft, namely, to lift off at 175kt, retract the undercarriage, push forward firmly to prevent too rapid a gain in height, then, at 220kt IAS, to pull the stick right back until the attitude reached seventy degrees. Provided both burners were still going, this

Ground crew hoist a Firestreak missile into place on the side of a F.1 of 74 Squadron at RAF Coltishall in 1961. It usually took between seven and eight minutes to refuel and rearm, from wheel stop to engines start. The pylons on which the missiles were carried contained ejector chargers so that they could be jettisoned in an emergency. via EDP

F.1 XM144/J at Farnborough in September 1962. This aircraft went on to serve with the OCU, Leconfield, Wattisham and Leuchars TFFs, and 23 Squadron before becoming 8417M and, in 1981, ending its career as the gate guardian at RAF Leuchars. via Ron Clarke

gave a climbing speed of 190kt and a feeling to the pilot of ascending vertically, as the ejection seat rails were inclined at twenty-three degrees. At 3,000ft the Lightning could be rolled onto its back and the nose gently pulled to the horizon before rolling out erect and cancelling reheat at about 250kt. At that point, the nosewheel, which retracted forwards, would finally lock up! To be anywhere in such a stream take-off was an unforgettable experience.

At first, all the two-seat flying was done in two Hunter T.7s which were beautiful aircraft to handle but had no resemblance to the mighty Lightning. Pilots were trained for that in the F.1 simulator, which had no freedom of motion but was more than adequate for the job, including radar interception work. So good was it that, on one occasion, descending through 10,000ft, when I felt a twinge of toothache, I remember thinking, 'Oh, it'll feel better when I get down to a lower altitude.' Pretty convincing simulation, obviously!

There were some downsides to flying Lightnings. First, there was 'practice death': being thrown into the sea at RAF Mountbatten. Pilots were towed behind a pinnace and had to release their harnesses when a whistle was blown, to haul in their dinghy packs, to inflate and then board their dinghies. After about an hour, a Whirlwind would appear, pick up a few 'survivors', disappear again, then come back and eventually retrieve all the bobbling sea-sick aviators –

often closer to the rocks off Plymouth Hoe than they would have liked.

Next, there was decompression training at RAF Upwood. The chamber took us up to 56,000 equivalent pressure altitude, requiring us to 'pressure breathe'. Bulging necks and arms full of stagnant blood, a squeezing mask, pressure jerkin and g-suit. Awful. Worse with the Taylor helmet – up to 60,000ft.

Then there was the drag across the airfield at RAF North Luffenham behind a rig on a three-tonner. This was to simulate being dragged by a parachute. Great.

I was one of the first students to undergo a course on the Lightning Conversion Squadron (LCS) at RAF Middleton St. George, where new T4.s had just been delivered. (The OC was Wg Cdr K.J. 'Ken' Goodwin, with, inter alia, Flt Lts Pete Steggall, Roly Jackson, and a huge navigator, Donaldson-Davidson, on the staff.) As I was to be 74 Squadron's QFI, it was important that I had some feel for the T.4. a model (XM974) which provided two-seat Lightning training for the first time and not wholly welcomed by the largely self-taught squadron pilots. I found, however, that all the pilots flew Lightnings very much in the same way thanks, presumably, to the flight simulator and its staff.

The Lightning was incredible. It climbed, initially, in cold (i.e. non re-heat) power at twenty two degrees attitude at 450kt IAS and, if a positive retrimming was not done at about 20,000 ft, would slip through Mach 1 in the climb. It took quite a strong pull at that altitude to counter the nose-down effect of the

Flt Lt Mike J.F. Shaw (far right) at the LCS RAF Middleton St. George in July 1962 in front of Flg Off P.J. Ginger's 111 Squadron Lightning. From the left are Flt Lts 'Bodger' Edwards, Chris Bruce and Dennis Luke. On 5 June 1973 Wg Cdr Chris Bruce ejected safely from XM988 after entering an uncontrollable spin. M.J.F. Shaw

74 'Tiger' Squadron's F.1s and a single T.4 arriving at RAF Leuchars on 29 February 1964. M.J.F. Shaw

rearward shift of aerodynamic centre when 450kt became Mach 0.9. With its beautifully made airframe, ingenious mainwheel retraction geometry, first-class engines and superb handling, the Lightning was a truly remarkable aircraft. It may have had a thirst for tyres and had operating costs far higher than those of its predecessors, but, in the 1960s, it was the queen of the European skies and its pilots knew that nothing could match it. If they kept their eyes open – and watched the fuel gauges – nobody could ever get close to them. It's not surprising that Lightning pilots were the most confident (and nauseatingly cocky) that could be found anywhere – with good reason!

What the Lightning did lack was fuel. It carried only 7,400lb at start-up, including a 250-gallon (2,000lb) ventral tank. The contents of this tank usually exhausted a few minutes after levelling off at 36,000ft, where most of the standard Practice Intercepting (PIs) took place – near the normal tropopause.

Recovery was usually via a 'dive circle', a circle centered on a point eighteen nautical miles out on the duty runway, with a radius in nautical miles equal to the height of the

F.3 XP754 which joined 74 'Tiger' Squadron (note the black and yellow striped probe) on 31 July 1964 and later served with 111 Squadron, pictured at RAF Coltishall. via Mick Jennings

F.1 XM135/B taxies in after a sortie. After service with the 'Tigers' and 226 OCU, this aircraft was one of several at 33 MU at Lyneham in 1966 which was prepared as a supersonic target for Fighter Command. While carrying out taxi tests on 22 July, Wg Cdr Walter 'Taffy' Holden, a 40-year old engineering officer and the CO of 33 MU, went for an unscheduled trip in this aircraft when, on the fourth taxi run, re-heat was inadvertently selected and the F.1 took off! Holden, who had never flown a jet aircraft before, was not wearing a helmet and the canopy had been removed prior to the taxi tests. Despite his lack of experience, Holden remained airborne for twelve minutes and he managed to land safely at the second attempt. XM135 was repaired and used by the Leuchars TFF before being retired to the IWM Collection at Duxford on 20 November 1974. IWM

In June 1967, thirteen Lightnings flew from the UK to Tengah, Singapore, in Operation *Hydraulic* for what turned out to be a four-year tour of duty in the tropics. They were led by the CO, Wg Cdr Ken Goodwin, right, being greeted by Gp Capt Phil Lagesen on arrival. Air Cdre Goodwin Collection

Lightning in thousands of feet. This gave a comfortable descent at 350kt at idle/fast idle (the No 2 – top – engine was kept at a fast idle setting to provide sufficient bleed air to drive the alternator fast enough to keep the aircraft services on line) for a feed into ILS, GCA, or visual rejoin. Further, the fuel used was only about 400lb from each wing, allowing a dive circle descent with 1,200/1,200lb to be completed to landing with the laid down minimum of 800/800lb. That gave a reserve, to tanks-dry, of little more than ten minutes, enough to cause an airline captain to have a heart attack. Indeed, he would have collapsed before take-off!

In 1964, 74 Squadron was posted from Coltishall to Leuchars, to help 23 Squadron's Javelins to cover the northern part of the UK Air Defence Region, and shortly thereafter, re-equipped with the F.3. This had Avon 300s in place of the 200s, and an increase in the fin area. The radar was improved, provision was made for Red Top IRAAM and the guns were deleted. The aircraft was cleared to Mach 2 (the F.1 was limited to Mach 1.7 for reasons of stability, not thrust) and all the pilots did at least one run to that speed. The fuel content was not increased, however, and the bigger engines were even less economical, so the practical use of this top speed was doubtful. Provision was made for in-flight refuelling, and the flight instruments were to [RAF standard]

OR946, including a strip (harder-to-read) Airspeed Indicator cum Machmeter. Further, the air intake was not really large enough for the Avon 300s and cockpit floor would vibrate on take-off as they gasped for air. Overall, the F.3 was not the advance we had hoped for,

although it still flew nearly as well as the F.1 but with a CG (centre of gravity) which was noticeably further aft (heavier engines, no guns?).

My average length on a sortie on the Lightning F.1 was forty-two minutes. During

Parade held at Tengah on 22 March 1968 to mark the fiftieth anniversary of 74 Squadron. Six months after this photo was taken F.6 XS896, to the right of the parade, was lost when it crashed on approach to Tengah on 12 September. The pilot, Flg Off Thompson, was killed. Air Cdre Goodwin Collection

my tour with 74 Squadron I flew just over 350 sorties, about a quarter of them at night. We lost two aircraft during the period: one F.1 (XM142) on 26 April 1963 indicated a double power controls failure after an inverted check during an air test, and its pilot, Flt Lt 'Jim' Burns, ejected successfully, over the North Sea. The second loss was [on 28 August 1964 near Leuchars] an F.3 (XP704) which failed to complete a loop overhead the airfield at Leuchars, killing the pilot, Flt Lt G.M. 'Glyn' Owen.

I had two anxious sorties myself, both due to the fact that our T.4 was really an F.1A rather than an F.1 and was fitted with UHF radio, as opposed to VHF. The squadron had all twelve F.1s and its T.4 at Farnborough in 1962, and on its return it was decided to fly VFR at low-level to Coltishall. We settled at 2,000ft AGL initially, with four vics of three, plus me in the T.4 with Fg Off Peter Clinton, the Junior Engineering Officer, tagging along behind, unable to hear any of the VHF transmissions. We flew over a town (Northampton) under a lowering cloudbase, then over Lakenheath at a rather alarmingly low altitude, but it was a Sunday and nothing else was stirring. Then I saw the vic ahead of me begin to climb, so I joined in as a No.4. We reached 30,000ft before we broke cloud. Nobody was talking to me on UHF, and I held on tightly to

F.6 XR771/D landing at Tengah in 1969. 74 Squadron participated in *Bersatu Padu* ('Complete Unity'), a five-nation exercise in Western Malaya and Singapore in July 1969. Regular exchanges were also flown with RAAF Mirages at Butterworth, Malaysia. Gp Capt Dave Roome

the No.2. The airbrakes extended, so mine went out too, and we went downhill until we broke cloud at 800ft, Coltishall in sight. I landed behind the other three in the sub-formation, still without any R/T contact. The other nine were still airborne, but appeared very shortly afterwards. The mission had not gone according to plan, but we were all safely home!

My next UHF problem was at night, when

I was flying with a pilot who was not a Lightning man in the right-hand seat of the T.4. All went well until recovery, when Coltishall did not answer my call on UHF and the station's TACAN was off the air. An adjoining station's TACAN was working, so I positioned overhead Coltishall using that and began a tear-drop (out-and-back, turning homebound at half the initial altitude plus 40,000ft) let-down. When we broke cloud at about 3,000ft, we were over land. But the TACAN had broken a lock during the inbound turn (not surprisingly, as the beacon was twenty five nautical miles away) and I could not see Coltishall, who spoke to us for the first time when I requested clearance to land straight in. We touched down, vibrated badly and stopped in 700yd. The mainwheels had not rotated at all. It later was proved that the Bowden cable from the right-hand control column had not released when the pilot on that side had retracted the wheels after take-off, so the brakes were still firmly on. My fault, of course – I should not have let an unqualified (though very experienced) pilot do the take-off. But there was no clue in the cockpit that the brakes had not released. Sometimes, you can't win. . . .

My next contact with Lightnings, after a tour in exchange with the US Marine Corps, flying Phantom F-4Bs, was on RAF Handling squadron at A&AEE, Boscombe Down in 1966–68. As the pilot responsible for the writing and/or amendment of the Lightning Pilot's Notes and Flight Reference cards, I had the opportunity to add the T.5, F.6 and, lastly, the F.2A, to my tally. The T.5 was an odd aircraft, based on the F.3, but with throttles (unlike the T.4) on the right-hand cockpit

During 74 Squadron's posting to Singapore three 2,000m deployments were made to Australia non-stop using Victor tankers, the major one being Exercise *Town House* on 16–26 June 1969. Here, XR761/B takes on fuel from a 55 Squadron Victor tanker. This F.6 was abandoned over the North Sea by Flt Lt Mike D. Hale of 5 Squadron on 8 November 1984 after pitch trim failure was followed by a reheat fire. Hale ejected safely. Mike Rigg

74 Squadron line at Tengah at the start of Exercise *Bold Robin* on 23 June 1970. Gp Capt Dave Roome

console for the right-hand seat. This meant that the stick had to be controlled by the left hand, the only fighter where this had been the case. Odd.

The F.6 was a Mk.3 with a long belly tank, non-jettisonable. It had extended leading edges which increased the wing area, improved the camber and compensates for the extra weight. It could also carry overwing fuel tanks, which would catch your eye and, until their presence was accepted, prove rather distracting. For ferry purposes only, these tanks made a great difference to endurance.

The F.2A was, in my view, the best of the lot. It retained two guns in the nose (the F.6 could carry two in its ventral pack, with the loss of some fuel), had the old Avon 200s which were much smoother than the 300s, and had the F.6-type long ventral tank and extended leading edges. The long tank deadened some of the sound of the No.1 (forward, bottom) engine, and increased the start-up fuel to over 10,000 lbs. It still had the old AI 23 radar, but that was quite good enough for the job.

When the F.2A was released to the RAF, I collected the first one from the English Electric factory at Warton, flew it to Boscombe Down and then, as was my brief, took it to the edges of its cleared flight envelope. It was a beauty, handling exactly as expected. Then, in January, 1968, I had to take it to RAF Gütersloh, and hand it over to 19 Squadron. It was not fitted with TACAN or IFF; that was a task for Gütersloh. For the first twenty minutes I could see the ground, but the continent had solid cloud cover and, oh dear, Lippe radar didn't answer my calls. I knew that I had a 90kt tailwind and, anxious not to plunge into the Air Defence Identification Zone just to the east of Gütersloh, decided to forget Lippe and call Gütersloh direct. They identified me, to my relief, twelve miles to the south after I had set up a prudent triangle; the subsequent let-down and recovery was immaculate, and the Squadron CO, Sqn Ldr Laurie Jones, later Air Marshal, intercepted me on the final approach. And that was the last time, as I knew it would be, that I ever flew a Lightning.

Earlier, in June 1967, thirteen Lightnings of 74 Squadron, led by the CO, Wg Cdr Ken Goodwin, had transferred to Tengah, Singapore, for what turned out to be a four-year tour of duty in the tropics. Flt Lt Dave Roome was posted to the 'Tigers' that same year. He relates:

During the three and half years that I was at Tengah, many events, both happy and sad, took place. These were the days when pulse doppler radar, track-while-scan, JTIDS [Joint Tactical Intelligence Information Distribution

Flt Lt Dave Roome in F.6 XR773/F and Wg Cdr D.E. Caldwell in F.3 XR723/A taking off from Tengah in 1970. Gp Capt Dave Roome

118

F.6 XS895 'H' of 74 Squadron at Tengah in 1968. Sqn Ldr Jimmy Jewell

System] and the god's eye view etc. etc., were still all only in the minds of the mad scientists. We used to sweat buckets in front of our trusty pulse radar on the Lightning to achieve successful intercepts. (This story starts with a short lesson in radar techniques, so QWIs can skip the next paragraph, unless you are under forty, in which case it'll all be news to you anyway!)

The pulse radar is not very good when looking down and painting a target behind which is the surface so, when doing intercepts against a low-level target (below 3,000ft) our technique was to fly at 3,000ft and rely on the GCI controlling us in a ninety degree collision (figuratively speaking, of course). We would then extend for fifteen seconds beyond the collision point and turn in thorough 120 degrees to be behind the target, descending to paint him on our own radar and fire the missile when in parameters. So if the target was coming from our left, we would extend fifteen seconds and then turn right through 120 degrees. All got the picture?

On this particular night over the Malacca Strait in 1968 – and a very black one it was, too – the target, which always flew at 1,000ft over the sea (no radalts in those days), was set up by the GCI as a slack ninety. In other words, it would cross my nose ahead of the collision, in this case by some two to three miles. There was me, ackling away (secret Lightning speak) like crazy and Lo! There it was, coming in off the

edge of the scope at eight miles.

More theory. At medium level, an ideal ninety degree intercept crossed the nose at four miles, allowing the fighter to turn in behind the target and fire. What I now did was to treat the radar picture as I always did at medium-level. By turning hard left I brought

the target across to the nose and then turned back at it, keeping it in scan in search as I did so. What I also did was to allow the target to go from below my altitude, through my level, to slightly above. It made it easier to paint in the radar (further away from all those sea returns), but I never thought what my own aircraft was doing.

I have already mentioned that there was no radalt in the Lightning. In order to fly at an accurate 250ft above the sea we set the regional pressure and flew with the main altimeter showing zero feet. We knew that the pressure error was 250ft at this speed and had proved it many times visually by day. It still works the same at night, by the way.

There I was, in a forty-five degree banked turn to starboard, looking in my radar scope, which was on the right hand coaming in the cockpit, when something made me look in, straight to the altimeter. To this day, I don't know what it was that got my attention but, to my horror, the main altimeter was reading 99,700ft. I was a submarine by fifty feet. The throttles went through the gate to full burner and I rotated the aircraft into what the fish probably thought was a very impressive display climb. As I did so, the target pilot, who had been looking back for me, saw the burner plumes with a bend in the flames. Almost certainly they were coming off the surface of the sea, as I was certainly that close to it! A few second later, when I was level at about 15,000ft, I announced that I'd done enough

Flt Lt Dave Roome with Buddist monks at Don Mauang AFB, Bangkok on 24 October 1970. Two 74 Squadron Lightnings had been flown to Thailand for a static display in Bangkok. Gp Capt Dave Roome

low-levels for that night and please could I go home now?

What I'd done is patently obvious – and patently stupid too –-but I know it's been done by others, too. Don't allow yourself to forget that the surface has a Kill Probability of 1 and keep you and your aircraft away from it unless the gear is down and you're planning to hit it!

On 23 October 1968 I had the chance to intercept a USAF RB-57F, a highly modified version of the Canberra with a 122ft span and 42,000lbs of thrust. This was in Singapore carrying out high altitude meteorological trials on turbulence prior to Concorde starting commercial services to Singapore. The abilities of this aircraft in the upper atmosphere were demonstrated graphically when he climbed 15,000ft, from 65,000 to 80,000ft, whilst flying a 180 degrees turn! He was surprised that the Lightning, which carried out the next intercept, overtook him in a descent through his altitude and advised us that his last run would take some time to set up. This time his altitude was into six figures and he was safe, but it left me with the thought that out in the

T.5 XV329 was sent by sea to Singapore from Sydenham, Belfast, in June 1967, when 74 Squadron deployed to Tengah from Leuchars. It returned by sea to the United Kingdom in August 1971, and had to be written off in December when it was discovered that acid spillage from the batteries had corroded the airframe. Gp Capt Dave Roome

74 Squadron finally disbanded at Tengah on 25 August 1971 and all the remaining Lightnings were flown on the 6,000m, thirteen-hour trip, to Akrotiri, Cyprus, starting on 2 September 1971, for transfer to 56 Squadron. Here, F.6 XS895, which is fitted with 'overburgers', comes in to land at Akrotiri after the long flight from Tengah. This aircraft finished its career with 5 Squadron. *Aeroplane*

A pair of 74 Squadron Lightnings are refuelled on 4 September 1971 *en route* from Gan to Akrotiri. The flight from Tengah to Cyprus staged through Gan and Muharraq and involved seven inflight refuellings with Victor tankers. Gp Capt Dave Roome

tropics where the tropopause is in the order of 55,000ft the Lightning could probably achieve above 85,000ft. I was determined to try it when I got the chance and some months later, that chance arrived.

There was a Victor tanker returning from Hong Kong and offering about 17,000lb of fuel to us. I went up the east coast of Malaysia almost to the Thai border and filled to full. I was now left with a straight run home and the east coast was the area in which we could fly supersonic. Initially, I climbed to 50,000ft, which was the subsonic service ceiling of the aircraft, and there I accelerated to Mach 2 and started a zoom climb, selecting about sixteen degrees of pitch. I levelled off at 65,000ft and let the aircraft have its head, reached Mach 2.2 before once again flying the same zoom profile. This time I held the climb attitude, though to do so required an increasing amount of aft stick as the reduction of the downwash over the tail increased. Eventually the stick reached the back stops and I gently topped out, 200ft short of 88,000ft. From there, Singapore looked tiny and I convinced myself that I could see from the very southern tip of Vietnam over my left shoulder, past the Borneo coast in my eleven o'clock, to the western coast of Sumatra on my right hand side. The sky was pitch black above me and all of a sudden I realized that I did not belong here. With idle/idle, I started a glide back down which would have carried me over 150 miles. A marvellous example of the Lightning's sheer performance, though the pressure jerkin, g suit

and normal oxygen mask would not have been sufficient had the pressurization failed.

We also took the Lightning to Australia, the first time in June 1969 for an exercise called *Town House* which was mounted in the Northern Territory and we were based at Darwin. This provided some excellent flying as the rules were few – the Base Commander was quoted by the local press as saying that, if they were to practise the defence of the area realistically, then the aircrew needed freedom and the town should 'expect to get boomed'.

Darwin was still used by the major airlines as a staging base and one sight that sticks in my mind is of a 707 taking-off whilst being overtaken by an 'attacking' RNZAF Canberra. Giving chase were one RAAF Mirage and one Lightning, which went either side of the 707 as it pulled into its normal, steep, noise abatement climb. The complaint of the 707 captain was met by the RAAF air traffic controller's statement to the effect that didn't he know there was a war on?

Although there were many problems with the aircraft during my time on it, and by far the worst problem was that of fuel leakage into the fuselage where it had a rather tiresome habit of catching fire (during my time at Tengah I had four fire warnings in flight) there was much fun to be had, not least because there was no QRA, very few exercises, and several detachments to places such as Butterworth in Malaysia, to Bangkok and across Australia. We had our own tactical air force in the Far East Air Force: Tengah had 20 Squadron with Hunter FGA.9s and three single Pioneers for FAC work, 45 Squadron flew the Canberra B(I)5 and 81 Squadron operated in the recce role with the Canberra PR.7. Elsewhere on Singapore there were Hercules, Shackletons, Bristol Freighters, Andovers, Meteors, Belvederes and Whirlwinds. North in Malaysia by some 330nm was Butterworth, which operated two RAAF fighter squadrons, eventually both with the Mirage III, and we used to have a regular exchange, called 'Tiger Rag'.

There was a long-standing competition for the fastest time from passing the ATC tower at

Flt Lt Dave Roome piloting XR773/F on 6 September 1971 *en route* from Gan to Akrotiri. Gp Capt Dave Roome

Flt Lt Roger Pope piloting F.6 XS897/K on 6 September 1971 over Iran whilst *en route* from Gan to Akrotiri. This aircraft first flew on 10 May 1966 and its last flight was on 14 December 1987. It is now preserved at the South Yorkshire Aviation Museum at Firbeck. Gp Capt Dave Roome

one base to arriving at the other, which had started way back in the days of Sabres and Meteors. The Hunter had brought the record back to the RAF but the arrival of the Mirage allowed Butterworth to regain the title, Eventually 74 planned an all-out assault, using four Lightnings on their way to start a Tiger rag. Each took-off at five-minute intervals and had several check points on the route north. If the lead passed a check point with more than the planned minimum fuel those behind left full burner in and so, of course, the back man slowly caught up the lead! Eventually, all four passed the Tower at approaching Mach 0.999 and the base commander, a somewhat irascible man, took umbrage at this hooliganism and ordered all four aircraft to return to Tengah the next day! They brought back the record though, of twenty four-minutes for the 330nm and it was to stay with 74 for the remainder of our time there.

On 22 October 1970 I was lucky enough to fly one of the two aircraft (the other was flown by the Boss, Wg Cdr Dennis Caldwell) up to

Bangkok for a display there. However, it wasn't all fun, for there were tragedies too, and in one four-month period in 1970 the squadron lost three aircraft and two pilots, a large percentage of a twelve aircraft, sixteen pilot squadron. But we always bounced back, a sure sign of a good squadron. On 26 May Flg Off John Webster was killed flying XR767 doing low-level practice intercepts over the Malacca Straits. He was, in fact, my No.2 that night and was on my radar scope until probably only seconds before impact with the water, though I was not aware that he had crashed for some time, as it was not unusual to see and then lose a radar return. The weather was stormy and he had just flown through a fairly bad rain shower although, as he should have been at 1,000ft above the sea, he should have had no problem. Only a section of overwing tank was ever found from the aircraft.

On 27 July Flt Lt Frank Whitehouse crashed in XS930 attempting a 'rotation take-off' at Tengah. Following a fire on start to XS928 in April, caused by a sticky overwing

vent valve, we had adopted the policy – agreed by BAC Warton – of selecting the Flight Refuel switch to Flight Refuel until after take-off. This prevented the ventral tank fuel pump from starting up on the ground, which normally occurred after 120–160lb of fuel had been burnt after start, and which had pumped the fuel out through the vent valve. Unfortunately, no-one had realized that burning fuel from the wings and not from the ventral had the effect of moving the aircraft CG aft and Frank had had a long wait on the ground and a long taxi to the take-off point. By the time he got airborne his CG was outside the aft handling limits, which had the effect of reducing markedly the stick force per g on the control column. When he 'snatched' the stick, as we used to for a good 'rote', the aircraft over-rotated and stalled. He should have ejected immediately but, with the aircraft virtually at the vertical (I watched the whole incident) it staggered up to some 4–500ft purely under the influence of two RR Avons before auto-rotating and falling, out of control. Frank ejected too late and was killed on impact with the ground.

On 12 August Flg Off Mike Rigg ejected from XS893/G off Changi when he could not get his port undercarriage leg to lower. The leg did not even leave the bay, as could clearly seen by the taxi light illuminating the bay as Mike overflew Tengah several times (I was OC Night Flying that night). The area into which the aircraft fell, the designated ejection area, turned out to have been used as an ammunition dumping area by the RN and the Army for years and no amount of pleading could get any salvage divers to go down! The ejection area, though never used again, was then moved to be south-west of Tengah by fifteen nautical miles.

Finally, the time came to fold up RAF fighter operations in south-east Asia, and we disbanded 74 and left Singapore in early September 1971. Our departure was in dribs

and drabs, too, for we ferried the aircraft in pairs via Gan to Akrotiri and gave them to 56 Squadron who had been operating the F.3. I decided that I wanted to go out with a bang rather than a whimper and talked over an idea for a final flypast on our departure. The Victor tanker captain was quite content, for he had plenty of spare fuel, and both OC Flying and the Station Commander agreed in principal. They attended the brief, at which I mentioned that I would take a line which would put me 'between the Victor on the main pan and the ATC tower'.

That is exactly what I did, but the two senior officers were watching from the Local, which was some sixty feet above ground level and I was out of sight to them both as I passed! I flew down the pan as low as I dared at about 330kt, and then plugged in the burners over the squadron for the last time and left for Gan not realizing the apoplexy I had left behind!

Luckily, OC Flying talked the station commander out of his plan to fall in two senior flight lieutenants and recall me for a court martial; instead my punishment involved removing my authorizing status (just prior to my last ever Lightning sortie). I'm still very grateful to Erik Bennett for that generous action.

So my last single-seat Lightning F.6 sortie, in 'my' aircraft, XR773/F, was 8.05, Gan–Akrotiri, with seven 'prods' taking on 36,000lb from the Victors. At the end of it I sat for a moment in the cockpit and thought back over all the good times I had experienced in the Lightning, what a marvellous, beautiful, powerful fighter it was, and quietly thanked it for giving me such never-to-be-forgotten experiences – then it was over and I went off to the JP 3 to learn to be a QFI!

An F.6 taxis in at Tengah. Sqn Ldr Jimmy Jewell

CHAPTER EIGHT

Linies

Lingua Franca (the lore of the service) defines 'linies' as 'non-flying personnel', one who works on the flight line, preparing the aircraft for flight, and recovering them afterwards. Almost exclusively they were, and still are to a great extent, the lowest ranks in the RAF: the LACs and SACs (leading and senior aircraftsmen). As such, they are invariably looked upon as the lowest form of life in a squadron, but they are amongst the hardest working tradesmen on a station.

Peter Hayward asks:

How many technicians who worked on the flight line at a Lightning base will remember the acrid smell and eye-watering after-effects of burnt AVPIN (isopropylnitrate starter fuel) and the ear-shattering blast of the engine starters, will remember being almost deafened out of their ear defenders by one of those big

silver bullets coming out of nowhere with both re-heats at full chat? The trouble was, they crept up on you. They crept up so fast that you didn't hear them coming until they'd gone. Then you heard them alright, but that ear-shattering roar of two Avons with the re-heat nozzles fully open and enough fire coming from their rear ends to make you realize that Hell was closer to Earth than you thought. The steely-eyed jockeys who flew them took great pleasure in showing off the awesome power of the engines and incredible rate of climb of the aircraft. Especially the aerobatic displays. A take-off with full re-heat would be followed by a few seconds of level flight a few feet above the runway until the landing gear was tucked away and the aircraft was clean and moving fast, then up into a near vertical climb until – for the mere mortals on the ground anyway – the aircraft was a speck in the sky. All this was accompanied by an

Linies pose for the camera at RAF Coltishall in 1960. Mick Cartwright

unimaginable din; it was simply shattering.

For the technicians who serviced them it was a love-hate relationship. The noisy beast of prey was difficult, the systems complex and it seemed that the designers had packed equipment in with hardly a thought as to how to get it out again. Oh, there were plenty of access panels but it seemed that for even the simplest of jobs one of the engines had to be removed, or the ejection seat, or the radar bullet. Top hatch off, ventral tank off, bottom hatch off. Fuel leaks, hot air leaks. Then it all had to be put back together again, tested, engines probably run and if you were lucky, if you were really lucky, the aircraft was cleared and handed over to the flight line.

The really hectic times would come during exercises. Aircraft would be serviced for the next flight in record time and from taxiing out, a turnround inspection could be done in nine minutes. This included completely refuelling the aircraft and installing a new brake chute, and a change of crew. The hive of activity continued even when the weather was too bad for flying. 'Clampers' was the term used. It meant bad visibility. The activity, however, was confined to the flight line hut and consisted of endless games of bridge and other card games, darts, innumerable cups of tea and coffee, erotic books and magazines, sleeping

'Linies', 'non-flying personnel' who work on the flight line, preparing the aircraft for flight, and recovering them afterwards. The LACs and SACs are invariably looked upon as the lowest form of life on a squadron, but they are amongst the hardest working tradesmen on a station. Pete Nash

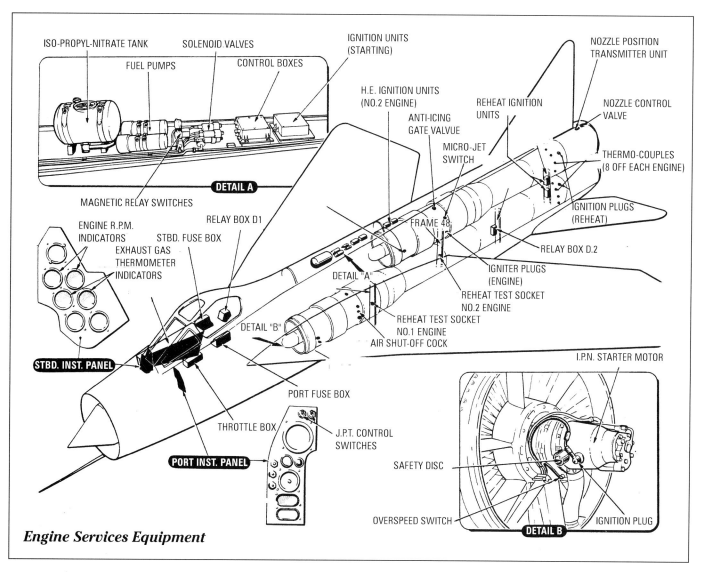

Engine Services Equipment

ISO-PROPYL-NITRATE TANK
FUEL PUMPS
SOLENOID VALVES
CONTROL BOXES
IGNITION UNITS (STARTING)
NOZZLE POSITION TRANSMITTER UNIT
H.E. IGNITION UNITS (NO.2 ENGINE)
ANTI-ICING GATE VALVUE
MICRO-JET SWITCH
REHEAT IGNITION UNITS
NOZZLE CONTROL VALVE
THERMO-COUPLES (8 OFF EACH ENGINE)
DETAIL A
MAGNETIC RELAY SWITCHES
ENGINE R.P.M. INDICATORS
EXHAUST GAS THERMOMETER INDICATORS
STBD. FUSE BOX
RELAY BOX D1
FRAME 48
IGNITION PLUGS (REHEAT)
RELAY BOX D.2
DETAIL "A"
IGNITER PLUGS (ENGINE)
REHEAT TEST SOCKET NO.2 ENGINE
STBD. INST. PANEL
DETAIL "B"
REHEAT TEST SOCKET NO.1 ENGINE
AIR SHUT-OFF COCK
PORT FUSE BOX
I.P.N. STARTER MOTOR
THROTTLE BOX
J.P.T. CONTROL SWITCHES
PORT INST. PANEL
SAFETY DISC
OVERSPEED SWITCH
IGNITION PLUG
DETAIL B

F.3 XP705/L of 29 Squadron being refuelled and rearmed at Wattisham on a practice operational turn-round in May 1968. Pete Nash works the winch while the other 'linies' go about their tasks. A hand brace was placed in the small hole just in front of the Ejector Release Unit (ERU) warning triangle, using the built-in winch to lower the missile pack. Whilst the ERUs were fitted, jettison cartridges were never fitted. If they were, the safety distances between aircraft would have meant that less than half of the slots on the pan could be used. Pete Nash

Corporal Winston 'Windy' Dekretser, who joined the RAF after emigrating to England from Ceylon, working on XM966 at RAF Coltishall in the early 1960s. XM966 was built as a T.4 and was converted to a T.5 at Filton. It crashed on a test flight over the Irish Sea on 23 July 1965 when Jimmy Dell and G. Elkington ejected safely. Jean Stangroom

Rocket Pack – Front Cross-Section

and asking if the squadron could stand down as the weather obviously wasn't going to improve was it?

Pete Nash joined the RAF in September 1967 and passed out as an LAC Aircraft Mechanic (Weapons) late in March 1968,

being posted to RAF Wattisham and then to 29 Squadron on 1 April. He well remembers his introduction to the squadron. As he was led up to the squadron armoury by a sergeant from the station armoury, he looked across the front of Hangar One (29 Squadron's Lightnings were in Hangar

Three), to see 29's T-Bird stuck in the grass alongside the runway after bursting a tyre on landing.

On a typical squadron the technical personnel would be split into two shifts: one on days, the other on nights. A typical working day for the 'linies' (about ten or twelve of us), Pete Nash recalls,

started at 0700, when we arrived at the hangar. The Line Chief, a Chief Technician of the Airframe ('riggers') or Engine ('sooties') trade would have drawn the keys from the guardroom and unlocked the centre fire doors. He would then go to Engineering Control, an office where all hangar servicing and rectification was controlled from, and where the Form 700s were kept, to find out which aircraft were available for that day's flying. Assisted by his two line corporals, usually from the rigger and sootie trades, he would detail off the towing teams and who was to take out all the ground equipment, etc. The hangar doors would be opened and the aircraft and ground power sets ('Houchins' – so called from the name of the makers in Ashford, Kent). The towing team would consist of three: a driver, brakeman, and chockman.

The tractor driver had an endorsement on his RAF driving licence stating that he had been examined and found sensible enough to tow aircraft, and that his colour perception was safe (CP1) ie. that he could tell red from

F.2A XN788/R of 92 Squadron on the line. This aircraft was built as an F.2 and was first assigned to the squadron as 'P' on 23 May 1963 and then loaned to 111 Squadron before returning to 'Ninety-Blue' late in 1964. After conversion to F.2A it was reassigned to 92 Squadron as 'P' and later 60 MU. The port main gear collapsed at Gütersloh on 29 May 1974 when the brake parachute failed. via Mick Jennings

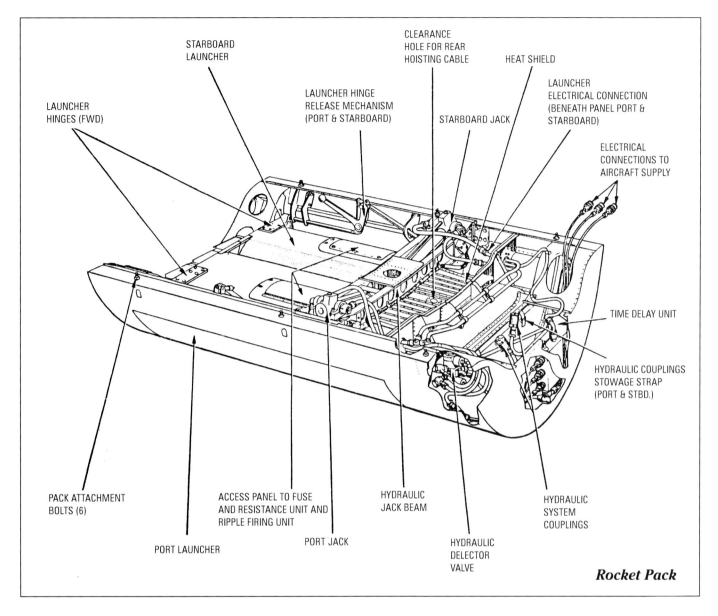

LAUNCHER
HINGES (FWD)

STARBOARD
LAUNCHER

LAUNCHER HINGE
RELEASE MECHANISM
(PORT & STARBOARD)

CLEARANCE
HOLE FOR REAR
HOISTING CABLE

HEAT SHIELD

STARBOARD JACK

LAUNCHER
ELECTRICAL CONNECTION
(BENEATH PANEL PORT &
STARBOARD)

ELECTRICAL
CONNECTIONS TO
AIRCRAFT SUPPLY

TIME DELAY UNIT

HYDRAULIC COUPLINGS
STOWAGE STRAP
(PORT & STBD.)

PACK ATTACHMENT
BOLTS (6)

ACCESS PANEL TO FUSE
AND RESISTANCE UNIT AND
RIPPLE FIRING UNIT

HYDRAULIC
JACK BEAM

HYDRAULIC
SYSTEM
COUPLINGS

PORT LAUNCHER

PORT JACK

HYDRAULIC
DELECTOR
VALVE

Rocket Pack

green as required by Air Traffic when they changed the traffic lights, or shone a red or green light at him, or, if he was in danger of annoying the Senior Air Traffic Controller (SATCO), a Very light across his bows. The brake man was certified as having been trained to sit in the cockpit and, if the aircraft broke free of the towing arm, to apply the aircraft brakes. On the Lightning this was a squeeze lever on the control column. Upon entering the cockpit he had to ensure that there was enough hydraulic pressure to operate the brakes. '1500 PSI' had to register on the gauge to operate the brakes at least once. If it was insufficient, then the manual pump handle was removed from the port wheel well and inserted in the pump just in front of and slightly below the port tail plane. Fortunately, it did not take long to pump the reservoir up

to the required amount. Sometimes, when a canopy lock had not been used, the canopy would droop down and prevent entrance to the cockpit. When this happened, a small triangular panel behind the cockpit on the port side was opened. Inside was a two-position rocker switch and handle. The switch was pushed away and the canopy was pumped up using the external hydraulic pump accompanied by an audible warning. If the canopy was to be closed, then the switch was toggled towards the operator and the canopy would drop under its own weight. The handle was to lock the canopy, by pushing it inboard, inflating the canopy seal at the same time if there was enough air in the system.

The chock man would connect the towing arm to the towing pintle of the tractor, pick up the wheel chocks, throw them onto the back

of the tractor, and walk at the wing tips until the Lightning was clear of the hanger, checking that the aircraft would not hit any obstruction on the way. Outside the hangar he would jump on the tractor and ride out to the line. With the nose wheel on the painted mark on the line the two chock men placed the chocks in front or behind the wheels, depending on the slope of the pan, disconnect the towing arm, lower the wheels, fit the earthing lead, jump back on the tractor with the brake-man and go back for the next aircraft.

Meanwhile, more 'linies' would be taking out the Houchins, and the brake chutes, and wheel trolleys, and collecting the LOX (Liquid Oxygen) trolley from the LOX bay. Others would be taking out the fire extinguishers and earthing leads stored in and around the 'line

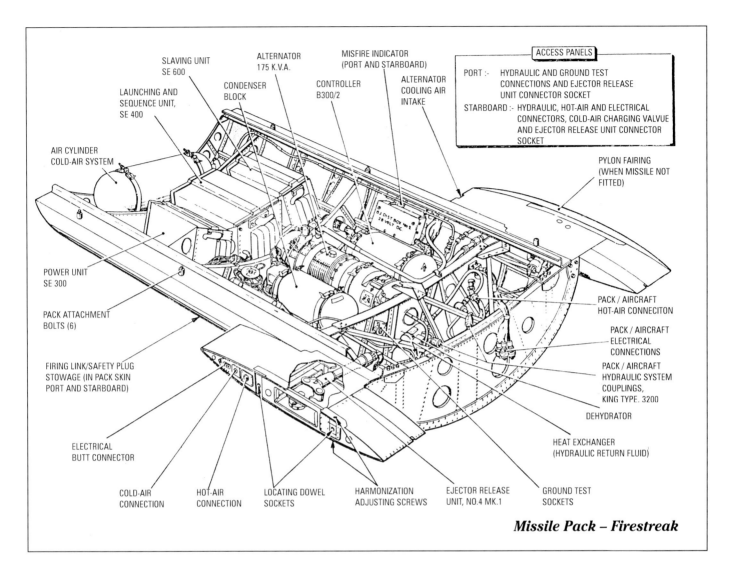

ACCESS PANELS

PORT :- HYDRAULIC AND GROUND TEST
CONNECTIONS AND EJECTOR RELEASE
UNIT CONNECTOR SOCKET

STARBOARD :- HYDRAULIC, HOT-AIR AND ELECTRICAL
CONNECTORS, COLD-AIR CHARGING VALVUE
AND EJECTOR RELEASE UNIT CONNECTOR
SOCKET

Missile Pack – Firestreak

hut'. Within half to three-quarters of an hour, the once empty line would get cluttered by all the paraphernalia needed to operate Lightnings.

The line is clearly marked out with lines and rectangles. The lines, in yellow, reach back to the taxiway, and indicate the ideal path an aircraft should take to arrive at a square where the nose-wheel should stop. At various places, red lines are painted, pointing at an angle to the yellow lines. These are for use when live missiles are fitted and indicate the 'safe heading', where a missile, if accidentally fired, can head off without damaging anything nearby. The rectangles delineated

Marie Fisher, Miss Battle of Britain 1968, brightens up the working day for two linies at RAF Coltishall on 14 September 1968. Gp Capt Mike Hobson Collection

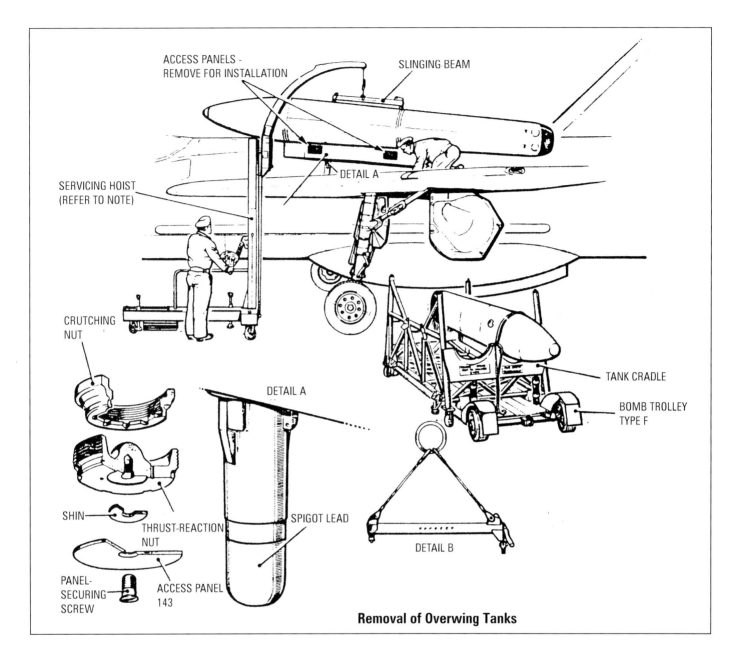

ACCESS PANELS -
REMOVE FOR INSTALLATION

SLINGING BEAM

DETAIL A

SERVICING HOIST
(REFER TO NOTE)

CRUTCHING
NUT

TANK CRADLE

BOMB TROLLEY
TYPE F

DETAIL A

SHIN

THRUST-REACTION
NUT

SPIGOT LEAD

DETAIL B

PANEL-
SECURING
SCREW

ACCESS PANEL
143

Removal of Overwing Tanks

the ground equipment areas, where the Houchin had to be, and where we could safely put LOX trollys and access ladders etc. With two Avon engines sucking through a narrow annular inlet, there was a very real danger of FOD (Foreign Object Debris) ingestion. Also, with the No.1 engine exhaust at about chest level, any loose, light articles were easily blown about.

While all this was going on, those not otherwise detailed to get the equipment out would start the 'B/F'. This was the 'Before Flight Inspection', where the Lightning was inspected and any replenishment done to prepare it for flight. The B/F lasted for eight hours and if no other inspection was done in

the meantime, another B/F was done. The riggers would check LOX levels, tyre pressures and the condition of the tyres, and check for hydraulic leaks and oil levels etc. The sooties checked fuel states, AVPIN starter fuel and engine oil levels etc. AVPIN (proper name, isopropylnitrate) was a mono fuel. It created its own oxygen as it burned, so it could be used in a totally enclosed ignition chamber. In its liquid state, it had a distinctive sweet smell. Burnt, it had a distinct, sharp odour, shared only with other select AVPIN-started aircraft. [The fuel is not shock sensitive and tests showed that armour piercing ammunition might be fired into tanks containing this fuel without any danger.]

As an Armament Mechanic, or 'plumber' as we were known, I ensured that the Master Armament Safety Break (MASB) in the starboard wheel well was fitted. Initially, this was a quick release electrical multi-pin plug, later modified to be a push in and turn key. It physically open circuited some of the armament firing circuits, preventing, along with the undercarriage microswitch, firing of guns or missiles when on the ground. During armament system tests the weight-on-wheels switch was operated by a special tool and the MASB fitted, or inserted, as required. Next, using a cocking indicator box, I made sure that the manual 4000lb bomb hook holding the belly tank on was correctly cocked. The missiles

F.3s of 29 Squadron line up. The nearest aircraft is XP695/L which also served 111 and 11 Squadrons. Air Cdre Ken Goodwin

were inspected for loose wings and fins. This became a problem with Red Tops later in their life. The wings often became loose on their mountings. This is why in some photos, especially late in the Lightning's career, the wings are missing.

The infra-red seeker head on the Firestreak was cooled using a combination of Stannag air and anhydrous ammonia. If the Lightning was fitted with Firestreak the missile pack air bottle pressure was checked and topped up if required and the ammonia bottle fitted. Air pressure was read off a small gauge just in front of the cooling intakes on the right-hand side of the missile pack. Upper and lower limits were 2,500 and 1,700psi respectively. The ammonia bottle formed the rear position of the launch shoe. It was screwed in via a worm drive engaging a thread on the bottle valve. Red Tops were cooled by a replaceable pure air bottle, fitted and removed using an inbuilt winch through a panel at the front of the pack. The pressure in the bottle was read off a cockpit gauge. Both Red Top and Firestreak missile packs had a misfire indicator viewed through a small round window below the stub pylon. It consisted of a solenoid and plunger that operated when the pilot squeezed the trigger, but the missile failed to launch. The

plunger was re-set by turning a cam. Checking it was required on the B/F because the hangar people would often forget to do it if they had been testing the pack. Also on the missiles, the shear bolts were checked for proper engagement.

The Lightning always flew with two missile 'bodies' fitted; a weighted drill round on the port side, and an acquisition on the starboard. It was always that way round to protect the glass seeker head from being damaged by the access ladder being fitted and removed. Sometimes, a metal cover was fitted over the glass to protect it when the aircraft was going to be used for in-flight refuelling. It was rather expensive to replace the seeker if it was smashed by a flailing refuelling hose if it got on the wrong side. The pilots also preferred to have the missiles fitted. The aircraft was better balanced.

Both the Red Top and Firestreak were launched forwards from launch shoes, the electrical services being provided by spring-loaded pins onto corresponding flush connectors. To stop the missiles sliding off they were held in position by a bolt between the missile body and the launch shoe. On rocker motor ignition, the bolt was sheared when enough thrust had built up and the

missile was launched. On one occasion a catalogue of errors and omissions occurred which allowed a shearbolt to be incorrectly fitted to a Firestreak drill missile fitted to XP755 'E' on 29 Squadron. A pilot reported feeling a jolt and a bang. He looked out of his cockpit and found the port missile missing. The inevitable board of enquiry was convened. It 'cogitated' and 'deliberated' and came out with its findings. One of its results was that torque wrenches in the RAF were inspected and calibrated on a more frequent basis. I didn't hear any more about the incident so I assumed that, as the last plumber to sign the flight certificate I 'escaped by the skin of my teeth'. The damage done to the aircraft was minor: a few cut wires in the external cable duct, and a few dents in the belly tank. The aircraft was soon repaired and back flying again.

After doing my external checks it was into the cockpit for the seat checks. Fitting the cockpit access ladder was not entirely without risk. On the F.3, 5 and 6, the cockpit access ladders were held in position by four balls on stalks engaging four elongated slots in the fuselage. Often, because of damage, the balls needed a little encouragement to engage the slots. In difficult cases it was accepted practice to jump up, grab the stalk or cross bar, and our

Good tyres were important; at fifteen tons the Lightning landed at about 140kt on tyres about six inches wide and inflated to 345 psi. They only lasted for seven landings, and many times less than that. For this reason, the Lightning never did a 'roller' touch and go landing. The ONLY time a Lightning took off again after touching down was on the rare occasions that the brake parachute 'candled'. Dick Bell

weight would pull the ladder into the slot. This had tragic consequences for one linie. We were all told of the dangers of wearing wedding rings. One linie had a rather ornate one with crinkled edges. He leapt up to grab the cross bar and his ring caught. He was left hanging, screaming in agony. We got him off and into a Land Rover to take him to sick quarters, where they had to cut the ring off before treating him. When we saw him a few days later he wasn't happy with his wife. She was more annoyed with the damage done to his wedding ring than the injury to his hand!

Once in the cockpit it was a quick look under the seat for loose articles (any found was by consensus claimed by the finder unless it had been reported beforehand). This is how I came to be the owner of an Aircrew Torch. It was left on top of the seat by Captain Ed Jordan, a USAF officer on an exchange tour. The seat inspection started with a look underneath to ensure that the leg restraint lines were anchored to the floor, followed by a look up the

One of the benefits of being in a front-line Lightning squadron in the 1960s was the overseas deployments and APCs (Armament Practice Camps) to exotic places like Cyprus. 29 Squadron look very pleased to be on detachment to the island in October 1968. Pete Nash

On 29 October 1971 F.3 XR711 of 111 Squadron, piloted by Flt Lt Eric Steenson, took off from Wattisham, retracted its undercarriage and then sank back down, dragging the tail along Runway 23. Tongues of flame and billowing smoke followed as the contents of his 360-gallon belly tank burned off. Dennis Brooks, directly behind Steenson (who was uninjured) for this nine-ship two-second stream departure, flew right through the fire and, undamaged, diverted to Coltishall. Peter Warren via Mike Cooke

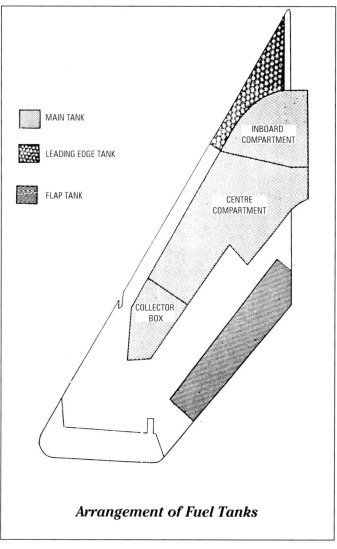

MAIN TANK

LEADING EDGE TANK

FLAP TANK

INBOARD COMPARTMENT

CENTRE COMPARTMENT

COLLECTOR BOX

Arrangement of Fuel Tanks

left side to make sure that all the pipes and connections were made, then across and down the right side before removing the seat safety pins from the guillotine, and the canopy jettison and seat firing sears. These were then placed in the stowage on the cockpit coaming port side.

Then it was turn around, sit down, and flick the battery 'on', if there was no external power running (third switch down on the outboard bank of switches by your right leg). Next, check the air pressure for the Red Top pure air bottle, and give a quick burst of up and down on the seat raises and lowering actuator. Pure air pressure was read off a gauge on the right console, by the knee. It had a red sector reading from 0–2500psi and green up to 3300psi. Below 2500psi the bottle was to be replaced. However, if the system was operating before it went into the red, it was sufficient for the air to liquefy and continue to keep the

head cooled. If the electrician wasn't about, or external power was on, I would take the seat pan down to its lowest limit and back up again to make sure that there were no obstructions. If a rigger was about, we'd call out the LOX contents. Below five-eighths would mean replenishment. Finally, I would stand up, turn around and re-tie the shoulder straps over the seat head box. Climbing out of the cockpit I would descend the ladder face first until I could grab hold of the refuelling probe and swing myself down to the ground, before going off to the line hut, sign up, and back out to do the next Lightning.

As the aircraft became available, flying started. A two-man starter crew comprising a marshaller and a fireman, both detailed by the line corporals, was required. While the marshaller followed the pilot on his walk round, stowing the MASB, the fireman removed the intake blank, started and ran up

the Houchin and fetched a CO_2 fire extinguisher and asbestos glove. Walk round completed, the marshaller would follow the pilot up the ladder and assist him strapping in, handing him his shoulder straps and pulling up the kidney pad to sit in his lumbar region. His final act before climbing down was to remove the face screen safety pin and pace it in its stowage. The ladder was removed and placed within the ground equipment area. Removing it entailed lifting it about half an inch and swinging it out and down clear of the refuelling probe. Being top heavy, it was hard to control, so it usually hit the concrete, bending the arms or the balls. All was then ready for engine start.

No.1 engine start was signalled by the pilot raising and waggling an index finger. The AVPIN pumps whined and a pitched scream assaulted the ear drums as the AVPIN ignited and spun the engine up to speed for ignition. After about five seconds the starter kicked out

Only mad dogs and Englishmen go out in the noon day sun. This photo, of 56 Squadron F.2s and crews on detachment, was taken at Akrotiri in 1969. Graham Vernon

and the engine ignited and became self-sustaining. The starter exhausted through the bottom hatch, any residual flames being extinguished by the fireman placing an asbestos glove over the exhaust port. The same procedure was followed for No.2 engine, its exhaust coming out just above the cable duct on the port side. The starter frequently failed to ignite. Three failed attempts and the mission was scrubbed as a half hour wait was required for the starter system to cool down. Sometimes it would start on the second try, and igniting any fuel from the previous attempt.

With both engines running, two hydraulic system checks were then carried out. Facing the aircraft the marshaller raised both hands, palms together, above his head, opening his arms as the airbrakes were opened and closed. Next, he turned sideways on with arms horizontal, one over the other, lowering his bottom arm to indicate that the flaps were operating. (Only once did I come across an occasion when the flaps operated differentially and the sortie was abandoned.) Checks over, there was a wave from the pilot, repeated by the marshaller, which indicated the time for the fireman to remove the power leads and chocks.

XP700/Z pictured at the Mildenhall Air Show in May 1967 in 111 Squadron colours. In July 1972 this aircraft joined 29 Squadron as 'K' and on 7 August 1972 was lost in a similar take-off accident to XR711 when Flt Lt George Fenton retracted his undercarriage and sank back down onto the runway, setting the ventral tank of fire. Unfortunately, the resulting fire destroyed all tailplane control and Fenton had to abandon the aircraft, which crashed at Great Waldingfield, Suffolk. Ron Clarke

T.5 XS422 which served on 226 OCU at Coltishall from June 1965, is pictured newly arrived on 29 Squadron in 1972. The small square panel open behind the cockpit gives access to the canopy raise/lower switch and external locking handle. In the foreground are two 45-gallon drums, the red and white striped one for FOD (foreign object debris) and the white one filled with water to be used for dunking anyone caught by the ammonia. In the centre are two old-style towing arms, heavy and awkward to use (later replaced by a NATO standard lightweight towing arm). The tilt on the Land Rover is painted yellow so that it can be seen by Air Traffic Control. The flat top trolley contains a main-wheel jacking adaptor, a bottle jack, two brake units, a nose-wheel and four main wheels. The small box contains a supply of split pins. Behind the wheel trolley is the canvas-sided brake 'chute trolley. The steps at the back of the aircraft are being used by a rigger to fit the cable for the brake 'chute in clips around the jet pipes. If he is following the normal practice he has climbed the steps until halfway and then stepped onto the starboard tailplane. XS422 was transferred to 56 Squadron in 1973 and later served with the ETPS at Boscombe Down. Pete Nash

Damage to XP755/E of 29 Squadron after the loss of its drill round missile in flight in June 1972. Note also the skin tear between the last two Xs on the Squadron insignia. The slightly misaligned rear part of the launch shoe is the ammonia bottle. At the front can be seen the flush contact pads supplying electrical current to the missile, while air and ammonia is supplied through the oval aperture. Just discernible on the pack below the electrical connectors is a vertically aligned safety panel with a quick release toggle. The missile safety breaks were placed here whenever the aircraft was carrying live missiles, so that if it landed at another airfield then the missiles could be made safe. The same idea was used on Red Tops, but using different plugs. Pete Nash

Most would then have a final check on the line of seat safety pins in the stowage, making sure that all five pins were in the stowage. The one usually missing was the seat pan pin. A reminder to the pilot was usually in order before allowing him to go any further. The marshaller then walked out to the other side of the pan centre line and would wait for a flash on the taxi lights to marshal the aircraft out.

On average, an F.3 sortie lasted forty-five minutes, unless air-to-air refuelling was involved, with a take-off about every fifteen minutes, so the line was a busy place. When an aircraft returned, it was subject to a turnround inspection (T/R). Like the B/F, it also lasted eight hours. If it didn't fly again, we had to do a B/F before it did. When it returned, the Lightning was taxied back onto the line, marshalled for the final turn and up to the nose-wheel mark. At first it was a frightening experience marshalling fifteen tons of metal travelling at about 20mph, especially if your only experience was a Chipmunk or Jet Provost at training school. About 18in from the final stop point the aircraft was stopped and the tread on the main wheels inspected for bald spots, cuts and depth. Once completed, the aircraft was marshalled forward for the final stop. Two stops were required because the part in contact with the concrete could not be checked.

Good tyres were important; at fifteen tons the Lightning landed at about 140kt on tyres about six inches wide, and inflated to 345psi. They only lasted for seven landings, on average many times less than that. For this reason, the Lightning never did a 'roller' touch and go landing. The ONLY time a Lightning took off again after touching down was on the rare occasions that the 'chute 'candled'. (The procedure for a 'chute that partially opened was to jettison it, take off again, wait for the 'chute recovery vehicle to retrieve it, then land again as close to the start of the runway and be followed by the fire section in case either the brakes caught fire or a barrier engagement was inevitable.) One day we were talking to one of the more experienced pilots about the way they slammed the aircraft onto the runway, so he taught us a lesson. On a later trip he eased it onto the runway. When he got to the end he called air traffic for a party to be sent out to inspect the wheels. The word came back to send the men and equipment to the end of the runway to do a double wheel change. When he took off the tyres were in good condition; they were bald when he stopped at the runway end. The lesson he taught us was that by slamming the aircraft onto the runway, the wheels got up to speed practically instantly. By

On its first flight at Wattisham after coming out of ASF, on 12 July 1972, F.3 XP694 of 29 Squadron suffered a double brake failure on landing and engaged the barrier. The top wire has taken off a small 'shark fin' aerial from the canopy and has ripped into the spine. Pete Nash

creasing it onto the runway, the wheels took longer to get up to speed and wore the tread off the tyres!

While the wheel checks were being done, the MASB was fitted, or removed if it was a pre-key MASB. Soon after engine shut down the bowser pulled up behind the aircraft.

These were mostly driven by civilian drivers and such was the relaxed, ready to help, atmosphere at the time, anyone would help the driver reel out and connect the hose to the refuelling point on the fuselage under the port wing. The sooty would replenish the AVPIN tank in the spine, and the brake 'chute under

Readiness on the ORP during exercises gave linies like these casually dressed – not wearing overalls – tradesmen reclining on the grass at the northern, Battisford end of the runway at Wattisham the chance to photograph aircraft like this F.3 of 56 Squadron, which had flown in from Cyprus and were at RAF Valley for Missile Practice Camp (MPC) to fire its missile allocation. ('P' was at Wattisham to have its radar bullet changed.) The white-painted spine was peculiar to 56 Squadron. It is the hinged section opened up to replenish the AVPIN tank and was no doubt to reflect the heat in the Mediterranean to prevent AVPIN from evaporating from the tank. On the left is the 75l Liquid Oxygen (LOX) replenishment trolley and the black objects 'growing' out of the ground are two telebrief terminals, the ends facing downwards to prevent water ingress. Pete Nash

the tail would be replaced. The plumber would straighten out the seat straps and carry out an inspection similar to the B/F. If it needed LOX-ing, the rigger donned a face mask and leather gloves and connected the LOX trolley to the charging point in the nose-wheel bay. Clouds of condensation would form on a warm day as the LOX in the aircraft tank was first vented out. The pipes and tanks were flushed and finally, when it was down to the proper temperature, liquid oxygen started to flow into the tank and it filled with LOX.

Sometimes we would get sprayed with fuel from the wing upper surface when the over-wing vents failed to shut off. A shout of 'Oi!' to the bowser driver would get the fuel shut off. Above the refuelling point was a rectangular panel with a perspex insert covering seven lamps. These lamps were the tank indicators; one for each main, flap and belly tank. When the tanks were full, the lamps extinguished. If the wing tanks vented and the light was out, then judicious and 'skilful' application with a General Service (GS) screwdriver handle to the vent shroud followed, to ensure that the valve would shut off. The belly tank shut-off valve also suffered from the same fault. Again, hitting or kicking it ensured that it operated properly. The remaining two lamps were the indicators for the overwing ferry tanks. These were rarely fitted to the F.6, and never on the F.3.

Another, potentially more serious, problem with a returning aircraft was a leaking ammonia bottle on Firestreak-equipped Lightnings. It wasn't hard to detect a leaking bottle. It stank, like 2,000 wet nappies put into a bin and opened two weeks later! The type used was anhydrous ammonia, a particularly nasty form, with a high affinity for water. It sucked up any moisture, including that of human flesh, if you stood near enough to it. To remove a leaking bottle we were provided with a fireman's breathing apparatus, complete with full face mask and cape over the head and shoulders, and a pair of full length rubber gloves. Another accoutrement of the armourers was a two-wheeled barrow to keep Red Top wing and fin covers. This came in handy for changing ammonia bottles. It was the right height for standing in. So, wearing breathing apparatus and gloves, pushing the trolley, I would approach the leaking bottle, remove it, and carry it, hissing and spluttering like an angry cobra, to the grass area behind the line. Along the back of the line and at each squadron line hut was a 45-gallon oil drum with the top cut off and filled with water. If anyone got a burst of ammonia in the face they were meant to be dunked head first into the

A Coles crane is used to move Lightnings at Binbrook with Phil Curtis (left) and a fellow linie holding the guide ropes. A. B. Curtis

barrel. Fortunately, in five and a half years, I never saw them having to be used.

Once all the consumables had been replenished and all trades signed their boxes on the flight servicing certificate, the Lightning was ready for another flight. However, if it was unserviceable and had to go into the hangar for rectification, then an After Flight (A/F) inspection was carried out. This inspection was valid for seventy-two hours, and once completed, required a B/F before it could fly. If it didn't, then another A/F had to be done. It wasn't unusual for an aircraft that had been in the hangar for a long time, say four days, to require an A/F and B/F before it could fly. This was because the last A/F was over seventy-two hours old and therefore invalid. It had to be done again.

In practice, the differences between the two servicings was small. For instance, on the A/F the armourers did not have to straighten the seat straps, or ensure that the missile was above limits. So what tended to happen was that one inspection was carried out by each tradesman covering both A/F and B/F inspections, after which he would sign the certificate and start on the next aircraft. Personally, I used the one inspection to cover all three servicings, except on an A/F the ejection seat safety pins were fitted to all five places required to make the seat 'safe for servicing' ie. seat pan and face blind firing handles, main gun, canopy jettison, and guillotine sears. For the other servicings on the face screen and seat pan safety pins were fitted. In the line hut were the servicing schedules. We were each meant to have a copy and follow them every time, but there were insufficient copies to go round, so each inspection was memorised.

One day [29 October 1971] I finished a turn round and standing at the top of the cockpit access ladder I watched a 'Tremblers'

Two linies at work on a Lightning. An acquisition round is fitted to the port side only, no doubt because, with the rundown of the Lightning fleet, there were not enough to have more than one per aircraft. In earlier years the 'acqui' was always fitted to the starboard side so that if the aircraft went inflight refuelling there was no danger of the basket hitting and breaking the glass nose. A white painted metal flyable 'cap' over the missile seeker head was used during long transit flights, or when inflight refuelling was planned. MoD

(111 Squadron) Lightning take off, retract his undercarriage, and sink back down, dragging his backside along Runway 23. Tongues of flame and billowing smoke followed as the contents of his 360-gallon belly tank burned off. I later learned that it was XR711 and the pilot was Flt Lt Eric Steenson [who later managed the Red Arrows]. [Dennis Brooks, directly behind Steenson for this nine ship, two-second stream departure, flew right through the fire and, undamaged, diverted to Coltishall.] On 7 August the following year, XP700 'K' of 29 Squadron did exactly the same thing, but this time the pilot successfully clawed his way into the air. Unfortunately, the resulting fire destroyed all tailplane control and the pilot abandoned the aircraft. I didn't witness this event; I was on leave.*

So flying continued throughout the day. Wheels were changed and brake 'chutes were replaced. On one particular day we were flying hard and by mid-afternoon, things were getting a bit frayed between the flight sergeant in Engineering Control and us on the flight line. D-Delta required a double wheel change and was delayed for its next sortie. The squawk

box buzzed. The flight sergeant, irrascible and irate, called, 'What's going on with Delta?' 'Wheels', came the cryptic reply from a harassed line corporal, before he switched the box off.

After the landing run, the 'chutes were jettisoned at the end of the runway, picked up and bundled into the back of a Land Rover operated by the brake 'chute section. They were taken back and hung for a period to straighten out and dry, then re-packed into their curved, metal-backed containers and re-issued. Sometimes, they would fail to release and be dragged back to the line by the

*Flt Lt George Fenton of 29 Squadron was taking part in a formation rotation take-off when he scraped the belly of XP700 on the runway and set the ventral tank on fire. He climbed to 3,000ft at 250kt when the controls began to stiffen, but which were still operative when he ejected using the SPH. There was some tearing of the pilot 'chute and main canopy and Fenton, who had done a parachuting course in 1967, landed heavily in a cornfield and suffered crush fractures. He had not tightened his harness straps as he felt they were already tight enough for take-off. The F.3 crashed at Great Waldingfield, Suffolk.

Lightning. The container was fitted under No.1 exhaust and two wires led, one either side of the jet nozzles, to a socket at the base of the rudder. Wattisham was meant to be the inspiration for one of the exercises held one time at the RAF School of Personnel Management at RAF Newton (called 'Little Snoring', after a World War Two airfield in North Norfolk). The exercise was about packing brake 'chutes with random chance selected by cards. Apparently, the Wattisham brake 'chute section was having a hard time meeting its commitment so a time and motion team was sent in. They arrived at about twelve o'clock as everybody was leaving. When asked where they were all going, they received the reply that it was lunch time! This did not please the time and motion team, who quickly came up with the answer that, 'if they had time to shut down for lunch, then there was no point in them being there to help them with their problem'. Whether this was true or not, I do not know, but it was a strong rumour from 'rumour control' when I did my management course.

On days our shift ended officially at 1700 hours (five o'clock), but the night shift started

F.6 XS897 of 11 Squadron on the line at Binbrook in 1981. Originally ground equipment was painted 'ground equipment blue', then, on introduction of the new model ground power unit, everything became yellow, which in turn was superceded by green on the tone down of airfields and equipment. Ron Clarke

at 1630 hours, so we were away soon after they arrived. Night shift was just a continuation of days with one exception – *Magic Roundabout*! Somehow, it became a tradition that all line work, including see-offs and seeing aircraft in, ceased, so that we could see the *Magic Roundabout*. Eventually, even the pilots joined in and watched with us. On the few occasions they got their timings wrong, they would wait for us, engines running round the back of the line hut for it to end before we would go out and marshal them in. Oh! haylcon days of ground crew power!

Finally, flying for the day ended. Noise restrictions meant that flying finished at about 2330 hours (or 1130pm for those non-24 hour clock readers). One night [10 December 1972] we on 29 squadron had finished flying. The last A/Fs were being done and some of us were sitting in the line hut waiting to tow the aircraft into the hangar when we saw a blue flash light up the north sky, rapidly followed by the crash alarm sounding over the tannoy system. We rushed to the windows and saw a Lightning [XP738, of 111 Squadron] sliding on its belly along the runway amid a shower of yellow sparks. Some of us on 29 shared a block with people from Air Traffic and 'rumour junction' was soon alive with the 'gen'. Apparently, the pilot had done one practice approach, overshot, retracted his undercarriage, gone around again and on his final approach, had called 'Finals, three greens', and plonked his belly on the runway.

Normally, at night, the pilots would switch on their taxi lights, which were on the main undercarriage legs, but not all did this, so when the pilot called 'three greens', telling everybody that all three undercarriage legs were extended and locked, the runway controller in his caravan thought that the pilot had left his taxi lights off, so did nothing. After every incident there is, usually, a procedure change, and so it was in this case. Pilots were now to switch their taxi lights on when landing and the runway controller was instructed to fire off a red Very light if he didn't see them. At least this is what 'rumour control' said was what was to happen.

As the aircraft landed from their last sorties they were given the final flight servicing. Any landing sooner and turned round were also A/F'd. Unserviceable aircraft were put into the hangar as soon as possible while the serviceable ones were left for last so that they were down the centre of the hangar and were first to be pulled out in the morning. At about 0100 or 0130 hours, with all the aircraft put away for the night, we linies would go home, leaving the hangar night shift to work on for another couple of hours before they too packed up, locked up and went home also.

Towards the mid-seventies NATO started to increase its alert and exercise status, calling no-notice exercises. I remember that on one of the first we were involved in, the 'Directing Staff' (Di-staff) put a cardboard sign on a Houchin that was being used in the hangar to supply power to an aircraft. It read; 'Fire!' The Di-staff approached a tired, harrassed, tradesman with the query, 'What are you going to do about that?' The tradesman took one look at the sign, picked up a piece of paper, and wrote 'Foam', placing it over the 'Fire' sign, and walked away!

In March 1974 I left the Lightnings to go on Jaguars with 54 Squadron to form at Lossiemouth and come south to Coltishall, just as 226 OCU was winding up in July/August of '74. By this time, practically all of the Lightnings had gone, the few that were left going to fire dumps. Years later, when on 56 Squadron, we were detached from Wattisham to RAF Leuchars for Red Flag build up. I drove a Sherpa north. One of my refuelling stops was at RAF Boulmer, near Alnwick, in Northumberland. Arriving at the main gate I was surprised, and delighted, to see XP745 still in 29 Squadron markings; an 'H' standing guard over one of the fighter control stations that had, no doubt, controlled it in earlier years. I remarked to my passenger that I wished I'd had a pound for every time I'd serviced it. He brought me back down to earth by sarcastically remarking that I must be old if I'd worked on a gate guard!

CHAPTER NINE

Lightning Strikes

One of the very best kept secrets during the Lightning's service career was the very high loss rate, which some place on a par with that of the notorious Lockheed F-104 Starfighter. (The Belgian Air Force lost thirty-nine Starfighters, the Dutch Air Force forty-four, and by late 1982 the Luftwaffe had lost 252.) Dave Seward comments, 'If you look at the numbers we lost, the numbers were not great, but you have to look at the total we had and the total number was not great.'

Of the 339 Lightnings built, 109 were lost or written off by a combination of many things, including pilot error, under-carriage failure, and fuel or hydraulic leak-related fires. In the late sixties and very early seventies, this became a 'disease' known as 'LFS' ('Lightning Fire Syndrome'), which in 1972 reached epidemic proportions. One of the first instances of LFS occurred on 16 December 1960, when Flt Lt Bruce Hopkins of the AFDS had a lucky escape in F.1 XM138:

I was on a trial sortie from Coltishall with a Javelin as my target when, suddenly, there was a big thump. I felt it on the rudder bars. Then, nothing. I called the Javelin pilot to check me over. He looked and said he could see nothing wrong. I decided to abandon the sortie and recover to Coltishall. During the approach I had restricted elevator control so I knew some-thing was wrong. I did a straight-in approach using elevator trim. The landing was normal. I was rolling out with the brake 'chute deployed when the 'Attention Getters' started clanging. One of the fire warning lights was on. At the same time ATC told me I was on fire! I completed the landing run – what else could you do? I stopped, switched off everything, unstrapped, stood up in the cockpit, looked back, and saw a conflagration; a great twenty-foot sheet of flame was spewing out! I hurriedly exited. Usually, you needed a ladder to climb down. I just leapt out onto the dummy Firestreak and onto the ground in one bound.

I ran! By which time, the fire engines had arrived.

What had happened was that there had been a hot gas leak from the No.1 engine near the jet pipe and it had impinged on the fire extinguisher bottle. Of course the inevitable happened. It cooked it and exploded it. The blast had bent the elevator control rods and fractured a fuel pipe. The fuel had spilled all down the underside of the fuselage but the air flow had kept it from igniting, until that is, I landed and slowed. This incident was very unusual and as a result, fire extinguishers were modified to include a pressure valve.

On 28 June 1961 F.1A XM185 of 56 Squadron was safely abandoned by Flg Off Pete Ginger, near Wattisham, after the undercarriage failed to lower. It was the only Lightning casualty that year. In 1962 six Lightnings were lost, and in 1963 four more were written-off. In 1964, another six Lightnings were lost after in-flight fires, undercarriage failures and pilot- or fuel-related problems.

In 1965 another four Lightnings were lost. On 11 January XG335 was abandoned by Sqn Ldr J. Whittaker, an A&AEE test pilot, over the Larkhill Ranges in Wiltshire, after the undercarriage had failed to lower. Whittaker ejected safely and the F.1 crashed at Woodborough. On 26 June Flt Lt Tony Doyle of 111 Squadron ejected safely after XR712 shed pieces of

F.2 XN723 was abandoned on 25 March 1964 near Hucknall after an in-flight fire and crashed at Keynham near Leicester. Mr D. Witham, the Rolls-Royce test pilot, ejected safely. BAe

1

2

3

4

5

6

This series of photos show the unfortunate path of devastation to F.3 XR721 which crashed on 5 January 1966 in the garden of Elm Tree Farm Cottages on the B1079 Otley to Helmingham road, near Woodbridge, Suffolk, after Flg Off Derek Law of 56 Squadron had suffered an engine flame-out. He had tried to eject but the canopy jammed, and despite a successful belly landing he was killed when his ejection seat fired him through the branches of a tree.

F.3 Lightnings of 23 Squadron in formation. XP760 was abandoned on 24 August 1966 after an ECU failure and crashed in the North Sea 35nm off Seahouses, Fife. Flt Lt Al Turley ejected safely. XP761 and XP758 went on to serve with 111 Squadron. via Tony Aldridge

tailpipe during the Exeter Air Show. The F.6 crashed near Padstow, Cornwall. On 29 September another 111 Squadron pilot, Flt Lt Hedley Molland, safely abandoned F.3 XP739 on approach to Wattisham after a double engine flame-out.

Earlier, on 22 July, XM966, a T.4 used to test the Microtell SNEB air-to-air rocket pack and crewed by English Electric test pilot Jimmy Dell and Graham Elkington, a Flight Test Observer (FTO), was lost over the Irish Sea when its fin disintegrated during rolling manoeuvres at Mach 1.8 at 35,000ft (11,000m) with the rocket pack extended. Dell was able to slow the T.4, hoping to recover it to Warton. Elkington ejected without any order to do so from Dell, who had his seat adjusted to the highest position and was thus exposed to high air blast as his head was above the top of the windscreen frame. His eyes were severely air blasted but his subsequent ejection was normal.

1966 was another bad year, with seven Lightning losses. The one on 5 January was fatal. Flying Officer Derek Law of 56 Squadron was piloting XR721 when it suffered an engine flame-out. Law, a Rhodesian pilot whose tour in the UK was almost up, tried to eject, but the system malfunctioned and his canopy would not separate after he pulled the ejection seat

pan handle. With no option but to try to belly land, a procedure which was normally out of the question in a Lightning, he skilfully put his crippled F.6 down in a ploughed field at Helmingham, near RAF Bentwaters in Suffolk, after avoiding high tension cables. XR721 shed its tail and careered out of control across the fields before clipping a tree on the B1079

Helmingham–Otley road. However, the young pilot was then ejected through the branches of the tree and was killed, his Lightning coming to a halt barely a yard from the front door of Elm Tree Farm Cottages on the other side of the road.

Gp Capt Antony J. Barwood of the Institute of Aviation Medicine at Farnborough explains what probably happened:

The cockpit canopy jettison system had fired when Law initiated ejection but one lock or shoot bolt had failed so that the cockpit canopy could not lift from the front and it had remained held by that shoot bolt. Law would then have had no option but to attempt a crash landing. The ground impact was sufficient to shake the cockpit canopy off and thus to remove the interdictor. It would have required a further seat pan or face blind pull to extract the ejection gun sear after the interdictor had been removed by the separating cockpit canopy. Law may have realised that the canopy had separated and that he could now eject or he might have retained a pull on a handle throughout the incident but this is unlikely as he was flying the aircraft so successfully to effect his crash landing. An unlikely alternative was that it was an impact ejection – the seat being forced up at ground impact, breaking the top lock to allow the sear to move up, displacing the sear to fire the gun, but we had no reported evidence of this.

Dave Seward, Law's commanding officer, recalls his loss:

F.1A XM184, seen here in 111 Squadron livery, suffered a fire on landing at RAF Coltishall on 17 April 1967 when it was operated by 226 OCU. Flt Lt Gerry Crumbie escaped unharmed. via Mick Jennings

Martin-Baker Series 4 Ejection Seats

The Mk.4 ejection seat was a lightweight seat specially designed for the light fighters in service with air forces throughout the world. The first emergency ejection using a Mk. 4 was from a Fiat G.91 in March 1957. Its construction was considerably modified from previous seats, but it retained the 80ft/s (24m/s) ejection gun and guide rail assembly, and the Duplex Drogue system which was deployed by the half-second time delay drogue gun, together with a re-designed barostatic 1½ second time-release unit. A guillotine system of disconnecting the parachute withdrawal line from the drogue rendered unnecessary the need for and operation of two D-rings on the parachute harness.

The conventional type of guide rail was eliminated and superseded by channel members mounted on the sides of the ejection gun. Steel slipper pads mounted on the seat booms located the seat in position in the channels and guided it out of the aircraft on ejection. Although fitted primarily with the face screen firing control, an alternative firing handle was fitted to the leading face of the seat pan. This enabled the occupant to eject when g forces made the use of the face screen control impossible.

The parachute and dinghy pack were located alongside the seat. The parachute pack was a back-type, horseshoe in shape and mounted high up on the back of the seat in the best position for automatic deployment together with a high degree of comfort. The parachute harness was redesigned to combine with it the safety harness all in one, with only one quick-release fitting which was fastened by the occupant when strapping in the seat, and remained fastened throughout any subsequent ejection until released by the occupant at the conclusion of the parachute descent. This combined harness was attached to the seat by two locks in the rear of the seat pan and another lock in the back of the seat at shoulder height, the locks being released by a redesigned time-release unit at the correct instant after ejection, through a linkage system installed in the seat. The locks could also be operated manually in the event of failure of the time-release unit by a manual separation lever on the seat. Late Mk.4 seats were fitted with a snubbing unit in the top lock and a release lever which permitted the occupant to lean forward in the seat but ensured that he was firmly held in the event of an ejection or crash landing.

An explosive canopy jettison system, powerful enough to force the canopy clear under all conditions, was linked to the ejection seat handle. The canopy jettison equipment consisted of a unit bolted to the rear of the ejection seat guide rail and containing a canopy jettison breech, together with a one-second delay mechanism. On pulling the ejection seat firing handle the sear of the canopy jettison gun was withdrawn, the cartridge detonated and the gases passed through piping to the two canopy jettison jacks. The expanding gases forced the pistons of the jacks upward, first operating the canopy locks and then raising the canopy for the airstream to carry it clear of the aircraft. (A later modification was the installation of a by-pass valve which could operate the canopy locks instead of the initial movement of the jacks.) At the same time as the firing of the canopy jettison cartridge the time-delay mechanism was tripped. This ran for one second, at the end of which the main ejection gun was fired, thus allowing the canopy to be well clear of the aircraft structure before the seat and occupant were ejected.

The time delay required for safe ejection at ground level had been found to be 1½ seconds, but this was only the case if ejection took place at low speeds. At high speeds this period of delay was insufficient to permit the seat to decelerate to a speed at which it was safe to deploy the main parachute. A unit called the g switch, which incorporated a delay varying in accordance with the speed at the time of the ejection, was therefore introduced. This made it possible to provide safe ejections at all speeds likely to be encountered by modern aircraft.

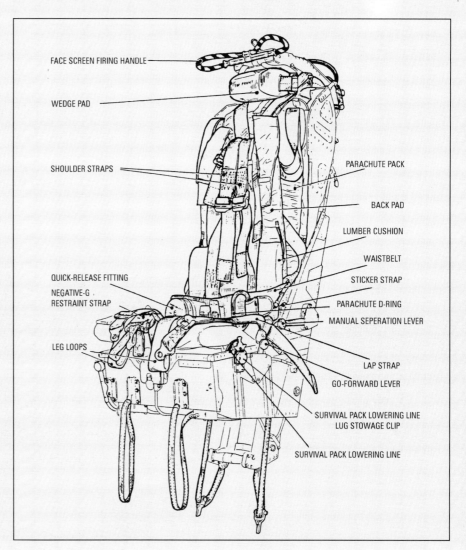

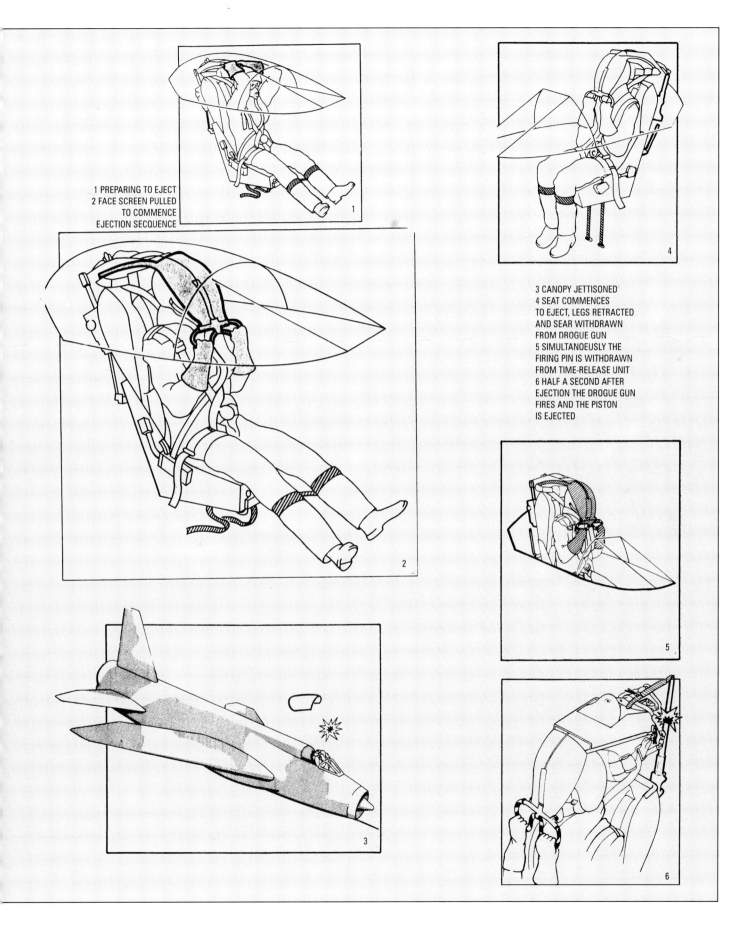

1 PREPARING TO EJECT
2 FACE SCREEN PULLED
TO COMMENCE
EJECTION SECQUENCE

3 CANOPY JETTISONED
4 SEAT COMMENCES
TO EJECT, LEGS RETRACTED
AND SEAR WITHDRAWN
FROM DROGUE GUN
5 SIMULTANOEUSLY THE
FIRING PIN IS WITHDRAWN
FROM TIME-RELEASE UNIT
6 HALF A SECOND AFTER
EJECTION THE DROGUE GUN
FIRES AND THE PISTON
IS EJECTED

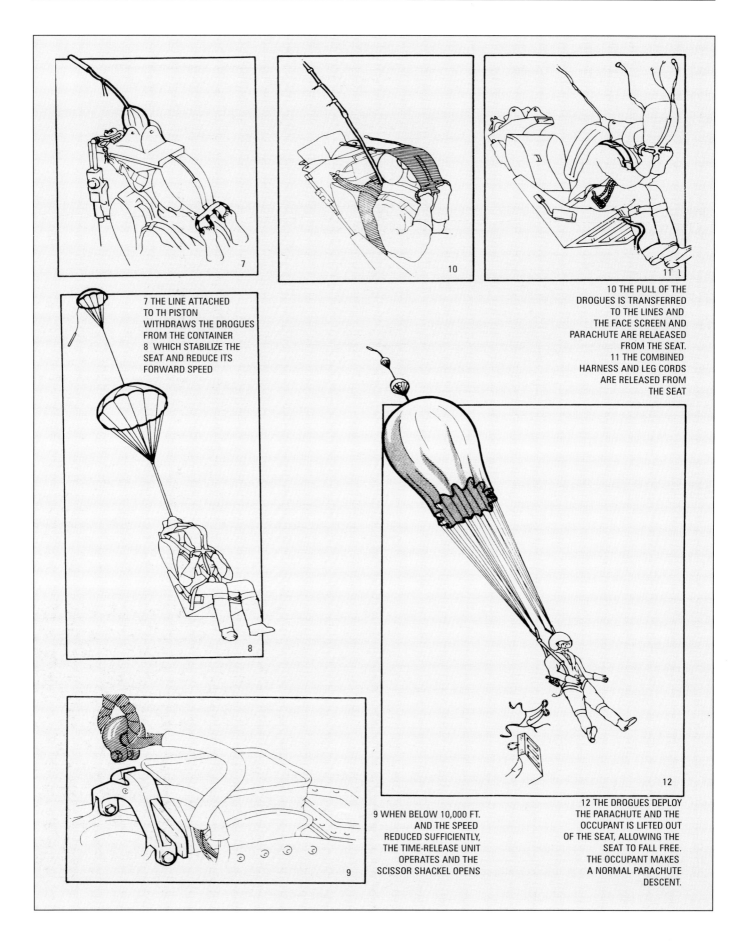

7 THE LINE ATTACHED
TO TH PISTON
WITHDRAWS THE DROGUES
FROM THE CONTAINER
8 WHICH STABILIZE THE
SEAT AND REDUCE ITS
FORWARD SPEED

10 THE PULL OF THE
DROGUES IS TRANSFERRED
TO THE LINES AND
THE FACE SCREEN AND
PARACHUTE ARE RELAEASED
FROM THE SEAT.
11 THE COMBINED
HARNESS AND LEG CORDS
ARE RELEASED FROM
THE SEAT

9 WHEN BELOW 10,000 FT.
AND THE SPEED
REDUCED SUFFICIENTLY,
THE TIME-RELEASE UNIT
OPERATES AND THE
SCISSOR SHACKEL OPENS

12 THE DROGUES DEPLOY
THE PARACHUTE AND THE
OCCUPANT IS LIFTED OUT
OF THE SEAT, ALLOWING THE
SEAT TO FALL FREE.
THE OCCUPANT MAKES
A NORMAL PARACHUTE
DESCENT.

T.5 XS418 of 226 OCU at RAF Coltishall crashed on 23 August 1968 while landing at Stradishall after the undercarriage was retracted on landing. Flt Lt Henry Ploszek and SAC Lewis were uninjured. In its final years XS418 was used as surface decoy before being scrapped in September 1987.

It was part of the bloody game I'm afraid. He did everything right. Somehow, against all the things in the book, he made a copybook wheels-up landing despite having two dead engines and seized up controls. It was a great shame. He was a great pilot and a lovely lad who had great potential.

During March–June, three Lightnings belonging to 226 OCU at Coltishall were lost, but all three pilots were uninjured. Then, on 27 July F.6 XR714 of 111 Squadron crashed on the runway at RAF Akrotiri, after being caught in jet blast during formation take-off. On 24 August Flt Lt Al Turley of 23 Squadron was forced to eject after F.3 XP760 developed ECU failure, to crash into the North Sea thirty-five nautical miles off Seahouses in Northumberland.

In 1967 another six Lightnings were abandoned including, on 3 March, XP699. Flt Lt Ian Fenton of 56 Squadron ejected from the F.3 near Wethersfield, Suffolk, after a fuel line failure had started a fire. The aircraft crashed at Finchingfield in Essex. Four days later, on 7 March, T.55 55-710 of BAC crashed on landing at Warton in a strong crosswind. On 7

September XR766 was abandoned near Leuchars by Sqn Ldr Ron Blackburn of 23 Squadron, after an uncontrollable spin. Blackburn ejected safely, the F.6 crashing in the North Sea, twenty miles east of Montrose.

F.6 XS900, which was abandoned on 24 January, was the first of five Lightning

losses in 1968. The pilot, Flt Lt Miller of 5 Squadron experienced trouble after take-off from Lossiemouth when his controls were jammed by FOD which caused a total loss of power. He ejected safely. F.53 53-690, which was destined for the RSAF, caught fire at 400ft on its first test flight on 4 September. The BAC test pilot, John Cockburn, climbed to 4,000ft, intending to ditch the aircraft in Morecambe Bay, when he lost elevator control and had to eject. Cockburn was uninjured but Bill Lawrenson of Stakepool, Pilling, twelve miles north of Warton, who was inspecting the newly laid concrete drive to his cottage, had a lucky escape when 53-690 plunged vertically through his nearby greenhouse! The explosion created a crater thirty-five feet deep and hurled Mr Lawrenson into the air. His wife, who had been working in the kitchen, was thrown into a corner when the wall blew in. The Lawrensons were taken to hospital and treated for shock and lacerations. Obviously believing that lightning does not strike twice in the same place, the Lawrensons still reside in the same cottage thirty years later!

A Lightning fatality occurred on 12 September in Singapore. 24-year old Flg Off Pete Thompson, of 74 Squadron, was approaching Tengah in XS896 on the downwind leg and was heard to call, 'Three greens', then, 're-heat light on – shutting down No.1'. The F.6 was seen to pitch up, then roll twice and enter a spin. The No.1 in the formation told Thompson to eject. The aircraft was now at low level, and in

F.1A XM174 which was abandoned on 29 November 1968 after Flt Lt Edward Rawcliffe of the Leuchars TFF suffered a fire in the air. He ejected safely and the aircraft crashed into a quarry at Bulmullo, near the airfield. via Mick Jennings

F.6 XS930, pictured here at Coltishall in September 1969, flew with 11 Squadron before being assigned to 74 Squadron. It crashed near Tengah, Singapore, on 27 July 1970 after Flt Lt Frank Whitehouse, who was killed, climbed too steeply after take-off. Ron Clarke

the airfield circuit. Thompson's canopy was seen to leave the doomed aircraft but the unfortunate pilot was later found dead twenty feet from the seat, which landed in a mangrove swamp north of Tengah.

To discover the cause of the crash, Gp Capt Antony Barwood of the Institute of Aviation Medicine at Farnborough and Brian Limbrey of Martin-Baker Ltd were despatched by RAF VC10 to Singapore. Barwood, who joined the RAF in 1941, had seen his first crash, a Vickers Vimy which fell near his prep school at Aldburgh in 1926. He recalls:

There were several witnesses to the Lightning accident, some of them aircrew on the ground and in the air, but the key witness was a corporal's wife, who was hanging out her washing. She told us *what she saw, not what she thought we wanted her to tell us*. (The best witnesses to aircraft accidents are schoolboys!) She saw the aircraft invert and the pilot eject downwards. All the seat systems had functioned correctly until the seat hit a mangrove tree and slithered to the ground with the pilot just detaching from it. He had a technical problem and presumably hoped to land the aircraft, but had left it too late.

Two months later, on 29 November, F.1A XM174, flown by 43-year old Flt Lt Edward Rawcliffe of the Leuchars TFF, and a simulator instructor, was abandoned after the pilot received a series of fire warnings. These were as a result of a hydraulic

fire caused by leaking fluid, which then burned through the controls. As the Lightning pitched downwards Rawcliffe, who had ejected from a Javelin FAW.4 two years earlier, tried, but failed, to pull the face blind. However, he managed to use his seat pan handle, which he activated at 1,000ft while the F.1A was doing 190kt in a 40–60 degree nose-down attitude and in a 30 degree bank to port. Both wheels and the flaps were down, and the dive brakes out. The ejection seat rotated once, then separated and the 'chute deployed. Rawcliffe landed in a hilly scrub 50yds from the Lightning, which crashed into a quarry at Bulmullo, near Leuchars. A rescue helicopter arrived within five minutes and airlifted the downed pilot to Leuchars, where his only injury was a bitten tongue.

The fire integrity programme begun in 1968, to fit 'Fire Integrity Package' modifications to Lightnings, and which went hand in glove with improvements in servicing procedures and engineer and groundcrew training, seemed to have an immediate effect, for in 1969 only one Lightning was lost. XS926 was abandoned 51m east of Flamborough Head on 22 September by Major Charles B. Neel USAF, an exchange pilot attached to 5 Squadron, after he failed to recover from spinning during ACT. Neel, who had previously ejected into the sea in a F-100 in November 1967, ejected from the F.6 safely and clambered into his dinghy after just four seconds in the water! He was

picked up and whisked back to base in a helicopter with nothing worse than two grazed fingers.

In the next twelve months eight Lightnings were lost. XS918 was abandoned over the North sea on 4 March 1970, by 31-year old Flg Off Tony Doidge of 11 Squadron, after a jet pipe fire overhead Leuchars. Doidge climbed the F.6 to 12,000ft and an aircraft fire was confirmed by his No.2. Doidge called, 'Ejecting'. His No.2 saw the canopy go and pilot and seat leave the aircraft, which crashed in the Firth of Forth. The pilot's PSP (Personal Survival Pack) was recovered five hours later floating in the sea, but the lanyard had not extended and Doidge's body was recovered soon after. The weather at this time was very cold indeed and Doidge was wearing no underclothing or other insulation beneath his Mk.10 immersion suit.

Two months later, on 2 May, a RSAF Lightning piloted by 'Slim' Wightman, who was uninjured, was lost. Five days later, on 7 May, F.3 XP742 was abandoned over the North Sea off Great Yarmouth, Norfolk, after an uncontrolled ECU fire during a pairs supersonic attack at 28,000ft. Flg Off Stu Tulloch of 111 Squadron had just made a climbing turn to starboard at Mach 1.3 in full re-heat when both re-heat fire warnings illuminated. Tulloch pulled back the throttles, called, 'Mayday! Mayday! Mayday! Double re-heat fire – ejecting!' and pulled the seat pan handle. The oxygen hose to his mask was broken and his helmet blew away in the ejection but Tulloch, who next remembered being in his dinghy, had nothing worse than a bruised forehead and bruising on the back of his shins and right ankle.

In a four-month period, May–August 1970, 74 Squadron, based at Tengah, lost three Lightnings, two of the crashes proving fatal.* On the night of 26 May Flg Off John C. Webster, flying XR767, was killed when he crashed into the sea after becoming disorientated during low-level practice intercepts over the Malacca Straits. On 27 July, two 74 Squadron pilots, Flg Off Roger Pope, and 25-year-old Flt Lt Frank Whitehouse, were briefed for a sortie. Pope had not done a rotation take-off for about a year, so the brief for this seemingly almost vertical climb to height was left to Whitehouse. The minimum

---

*In 'Tiger Tales' Gp Cpt Dave Roome details all three crashes.

Lightning Write-Offs by User/Type

Type	RAF	Contractors/Test Aircraft	KAF	RSAF	Total
P.1B/F.1	1	3			4
F.1	5				5
F.1A	9	1			10
F.2		1			1
F.2A	4				4
F.3	19				19
F.6	31			1	32
T.4	7	2			9
T.5	4				4
T.55		1		1	2
F.52				3	3
F.53		1	2	13	16
Totals	80	9	2	18	109

Loss Record (Write-Offs) by Year (All Users)

1959	1	1969	1	1979	5
1960	3	1970	9	1980	3
1961	3	1971	13	1981	2
1962	2	1972	8	1982	0
1963	4	1973	3	1983	3
1964	5	1974	4	1984	3
1965	4	1975	3	1985	3
1966	7	1976	3	1986	1
1967	6	1977	1	1987	2
1968	6	1978	0	1988	1

N.B. Write-off figures include crashes, abandoned aircraft, collision, enemy action and Cat.5 (written off after severe damage caused by any of the above, or corrosion, etc.).

speed for rotation was 260kt with a maximum pull of 3g. However, both pilots agreed that the more normal speed of 290kt was preferable, although they would observe the 3g limitation. Having entered a climb of around 60 degrees the recovery would be effected by a wing-over to port. As they walked to their aircraft Whitehouse jokingly said to Pope, 'Don't overstress it.'

Whitehouse wanted to make his rotation take-off as spectacular as possible because he had arranged for a photographer to be stationed at the end of the runway to capture his rapid climb to 20,000ft on film. The two Lightnings lined up in echelon port and Pope released his brakes and accelerated down the runway. At 290kt IAS, he rotated as briefed. Unfortunately, perhaps because he was rusty, he overdid it a little and registered 4g. However, he was safely airborne and as he gained height he waited for a call from Whitehouse in XS930, which took off just

five seconds behind. Unfortunately, the call never came. Whitehouse rotated while still some 300ft short of the runway barrier and snapped into an almost vertical climb before starting to roll left. In doing so he probably pulled 5g or more. (Onlookers reported that it was the fastest rotation they had ever seen.) Having reached a height of about 600ft, the F.6 started down again and after what looked like an attempt at recovery, disappeared behind some trees, where it crashed into a Malay village and exploded. Whitehouse and a Chinese farmer, Cheong Say Wai, were killed, 100 buildings were destroyed and two villagers were injured.

On 12 August Flg Off Mike Rigg of 74 Squadron was returning from a low-level pairs night interception sortie when the port undercarriage of F.6 XS893 failed to lower. Happily, Rigg ejected safely off Changi and suffered only bruising in the process. Even so, lessons were learned, as Gp Capt Barwood explains:

With plenty of time, the pilot tried everything; high g, 'bunting' and so on, to no effect. He was then vectored out to the ejection area off Changi and ordered to eject. This he did at 12,000ft and at 300kt. He was surprised to find himself hanging in his parachute harness, his life preserver hard up under his armpits, and nothing, apparently, between his legs. It was dark and he was aware of 'something' flapping around in front of him. He could see the lights of Singapore and of fishing boats and he could feel the quick release box of his harness high up on his chest compressing his life preserver onto his face. He inflated his life preserver before entering the water and then undid his QRB to get rid of his harness. He inflated his dinghy and got into it and was quite quickly recovered to Changi, as all the rescue services had been alerted. He was uninjured, apart from scuffing on the side of his body where the straps appeared to have pulled up and across his skin. His harness was not recovered.

I spent about three hours with this pilot, getting a detailed narrative which he gave very

F.6 XS894, which crashed into the sea off Flamborough Head on 8 September 1970, is lifted ashore at Grimsby (for movement to RAF Binbrook) from the bows of the recovery vessel *Kinless* after recovery from the sea bed. The air brakes are extended, indicating that the pilot, Major Bill Schaffner, was flying very slowly when he hit the sea. Jonathan Falconer

Capt Bill Povilus USAF, an American exchange officer who was attached to 29 Squadron, was forced to eject from a Lightning on the night of 25 January 1971. Col Bill Povilus Collection

well. Then I questioned him and we had a discussion. He wanted to know what went wrong as much as I did. Next morning I visited the Safety Equipment Section and had a look at an identical harness. From the design of that harness and the way in which the back riser webbing was sewn to the seat loop, it seemed obvious that a load applied at anything but a right angle could overload the corners of the sewn webbing and that it could then peel off. We had no sophisticated method of measuring the load to peel a strap like that. We suspended the pilot with the crutch loops torn and this was exactly the situation he had during his parachute descent. I sent signals to the UK, which were copied to Martin Baker's factory at Denham, where I went as soon as I got back. A large gathering of all those concerned were waiting. Sir James Martin was livid that I had

dared to suggest that one of HIS harnesses had failed, as he said that it had never happened before, in use or on test. I reminded him that two naval Scimitar pilots had ejected over the sea and were never recovered. 'This could be the same thing', I said. Steam was coming out of his ears. 'Anyway, we have got a dummy fixed up to drop and to simulate the seam parachute opening load.'

I had a look at the harness where I thought that it had failed. It was just as I thought. It was not at right angles. The dummy was dropped and fell straight through the harness into exactly the position described to me by the Lightning pilot. It was like an H.M. Bateman cartoon – so many mouths dropping open! Sir James had gone back to his office and did not witness the drop. I persuaded them to take photographs of the dummy in the failed

harness and of the load areas of webbing stitching failure so that I could send these back to the Board of Inquiry in Singapore.

The modification to prevent this recurring was extremely simple, well within the capability of every unit with a fabric workshop sewing machine. I sent copies of the photographs to Tengah, together with some of the drop tests we did at Farnborough. The pilot's mistake was that he opted to eject too high – 12,000ft – and too fast – 300kt. The suggested speeds for a controlled ejection at this time were 9,000ft and 250kt. The higher altitude and speed produced a MUCH higher parachute opening load, resulting in the damage to his harness. This may have occurred before, but had never been seen, as the Navy pilots were not recovered, and possibly they fell through their harnesses.

F.3 XP756/C of 23 Squadron in close formation with Javelin FAW.8 XH886 near the Forth Bridge on a murky day during a sortie from Leuchars (where the local 'haar' can often prove troublesome to aircraft operations). 23 Squadron began replacing its Javelins with Lightning F.3s from August 1964. In May 1967, when 23 Squadron began conversion to the F.6, 29 Squadron at Wattisham received F.3s like XP756 from Leuchars to replace its Javelins. On 25 January 1971 XP756, now coded 'P', was abandoned by Capt Bill Povilus, a USAF officer on exchange, after a re-heat fire. He ejected safely and was eventually rescued from the sea by a USAF Jolly Green Giant helicopter. *via Tony Aldridge*

Another Lightning fatality occurred on 8 September with the loss of XS894. Major Bill Schaffner USAF had completed two tours on the F-102, and as an exchange pilot attached to 5 Squadron at RAF Binbrook had accumulated 121 hours on the Lightning, of which eighteen were at night. He had been declared limited Combat Ready after only eight weeks on the squadron, this unusually short period of time being based on his previous operational status as well as his performance thus far on the Lightning. Schaffner was qualified in two of the three phases of 'visident', which meant that he would be capable of carrying out shadowing and shepherding tasks only if he was in visual contact with the target. 5 Squadron was participating in a TACEVAL at Binbrook and Major Schaffner was one of the pilots who took part. The evaluation involved 5 Squadron's pilots identifying and shadowing a simulated 'intelligence gatherer' (in this case an Avro Shackleton flying at

160kt at the minimum authorized height of 1,500ft) during a period of rising tension. The 'intruder' entered the UK airspace during daylight and remained on station through dusk and into darkness. One by one, the 5 Squadron pilots were scrambled to identify the 'intruder'. Each subsequently completed the task before returning to Binbrook. The TACEVAL continued as darkness fell, by which time it became the turn of Major Schaffner. Schaffner had had to endure one hour at cockpit readiness before being scrambled but this was cancelled before take-off could commence. Later, he was scrambled again and got airborne at 2030. The American climbed to 10,000ft and was handed over to GCI. He was then given a shadowing task against a Shackleton at 1,500ft. At a range of 28nm he was told to accelerate to Mach 0.95 in order to expedite the takeover from another Lightning. Schaffner called that he was in contact with the lights, but would have to

manoeuvre to slow down. His voice sounded strained, as though he was being affected by 'g'. XS894 was seen by the other Lightning pilot and appeared to be about 2,000yd astern and 500–1000ft above the Shackleton, in a port turn. The Shackleton crew then saw Schaffner's Lightning, apparently very low. Shortly afterwards, Schaffner failed to acknowledge instructions and emergency procedures were initiated. He crashed into the sea 5m off Flamborough Head. A search by the Shackleton, and a further ASR search the following day, failed to find any trace of the F.6 or its pilot.

The Lightning was located within a few days, and was recovered on the seabed at a depth of 190ft, almost completely intact with the canopy closed. The cockpit though, was empty, but the seat was still in the aircraft, the harness release box undone and the harness still in position. The ASI read 176kt. Gp Capt Barwood, who was involved in the investigation into the accident, tells what happened next:

When the aircraft was raised, it was established that the seat firing mechanism had been initiated, but that the cockpit canopy jettison mechanism had failed to fire. The cockpit area was completely undamaged, but the visor attachment track on the pilot's flying helmet had contacted the instrument panel. This probably had no effect on the pilot. He had accidentally flown into, or onto, the sea, and the very large belly fuel tank with which the aircraft was fitted acted as a boat hull to take most of the impact load. [During salvage the ventral tank and the belly of the aircraft were found to be ripped open and there was under-tail damage.]

The pilot had attempted to eject, but the canopy mechanism would not fire as the firing mechanism had been incorrectly assembled. (The breech firing mechanism of the cockpit canopy jettison system had been clamped in a vice, partially flattening the threads, so that when assembled, it was not screwed completely home, so that the firing plunger did not contact the percussion cap with sufficient energy to fire it.) He then opened his cockpit canopy manually using the ordinary post-flight opening mechanism, which is hydraulically operated. He still could not eject as the interdictor wire had not armed his seat firing mechanism. He undid his combined harness quick release box and climbed out of the cockpit. His dinghy lanyard was still connected and as he separated from the cockpit this extended – fully. At full extension it would check his upward movement, so he released it.

The pilot's body was never recovered. The cockpit canopy hydraulic pressure system slowly decayed so that the canopy closed, trapping the extended dinghy lanyard line. We did find some broken visor transparency on the cockpit floor. This would have broken when the pilot's Mk.3 helmet had hit the coaming beneath the in-flight refuelling panel and it is possible that a sharp edge cut his life preserver. We shall never know.*

---

*Altogether, night visidents were responsible for the loss of three Lightnings, and Keith Murty had a narrow escape when he hit a twin-engined Cessna which had entered UK airspace and was unknown to the air defence network. Neither pilot realized that there had been a collision until the Cessna pilot saw the damage to his wing on landing and associated this with the bump he had felt in flight.

F.3 XP705, which began its front-line career with 74 Squadron, seen here whilst serving with 23 Squadron, went on to serve in 29 Squadron as 'L', and was abandoned near Akrotiri, Cyprus on 8 July 1971 after a jet pipe fire. Flt Lt Graham H. Clarke ejected safely. via Mick Jennings

The Worst Year

The year 1971 proved the worst on record, with no fewer than ten Lightnings lost. The first, involving Captain William 'Bill' R. Povilus, a USAF exchange officer, occurred on 25 January during a head-on night intercept in XP756. Povilus, who had flown 373 combat missions as a forward air controller in Vietnam, had been attached to 29 Squadron at Wattisham since 1969. He recalls:

It was a normal pairs take-off, climb-out and positioning, about 60m off the coast of East Anglia. Bawdsey GCI control was the radar agency overseeing the mission. (As an interesting note, another American exchange officer, Major Bud Manazir USMC, was on duty with Bawdsey that evening.)

After a 30m split to obtain separation, Bawdsey turned both aircraft toward each other and ordered acceleration. I pushed both engines into re-heat and accelerated through the Mach. After what was probably only a minute or two, a No.1 engine fire warning illuminated and I instantly pulled both engines out of re-heat (I had been checked out as a test pilot in the Lightning and had two previous instances of fire warnings – both had been false), In any event, all other indications appeared normal, but the fire light stayed on and I proceeded through the appropriate drills, shutting down No.1 engine, then jettisoning

the belly tank. The light stayed on, so in short order I informed Bawdsey of the problem, turned westerly and asked my wingman to try and catch up. The first indication that I might have real problems was an erratic hydraulic gauge that finally went to zero. Then the machometer motored ever so slowly also to zero – I had no airspeed!

I kept a hot microphone open to Bawdsey and kept them informed about what was happening. My wingman finally called to say he saw flames at the rear of my craft and recommended ejection. I guess the water temperature that January night motivated me to stay with XP756 as long as possible. As other gauges and indicators also began to fail I knew ejection was inevitable; then I became aware that the rudder pedals had gone totally slack, as if disconnected! Shortly thereafter the aircraft nosed over slowly and I was unable to change its course. A British exchange officer in the States had once told me that, 'Fail all else, you can always place your faith in God, Mother and Martin-Baker.' I left XP756 to determine its own fate.[The F.3 crashed off Great Yarmouth.]

I found that my preparations came automatically and without hesitation. I called 'Bailing out', locked my knees as I forced against the rudder pedals, and pulled the seat pan firing handle with both hands as I stiffened to receive the howitzer shell that was about to fire into my butt. The decisions I had made long before that night surely helped save my

F.3 XP736/F of 23 Squadron joined 29 Squadron in May 1967 when 23 Squadron began conversion to the F.6. On 22 September 1971 XP736, now coded 'G', crashed into the sea 30m off Lowestoft. Flg Off Phil Mottershead was killed. via Tony Aldridge

control of the situation – losing consciousness – and I made a last ditch effort to stop the spinning and tumbling by forcing my arms straight out. The motion slowed and then suddenly lurched the other way. A bang occurred behind me and then the opening shock of the parachute suddenly brought me into a completely different environment.

I was stable and could clearly see the village lights on the coast and the greyish cloud below. In contrast to the trauma of only seconds ago I was quite comfortable now, mentally and physically. The opening shock of the 'chute had pulled my feet out of the boots and up to the leg restrainers in the immersion suit. I corrected this and proceeded with pre-landing drills. The mask disconnected quite easily and I threw it away. I then checked the PSP connection (several times) and tried to locate the release connections. I had waterproof gloves on and just couldn't get hold of those releases. After trying many times I almost got panicky for fear of going into the water with the pack still strapped to my butt. I decided to take off each glove in turn and find the release mechanism. I had no trouble at all with my bare hands, but was very careful not to drop my gloves, and quickly the PSP was deployed.

Next was the Mae West inflation and then followed what seemed to me the next logical step. I pulled up the life raft lanyard, found the T handle, and inflated the dinghy. Again a

life. I have long legs and knew I must press as hard as possible against the seat in order to escape with my knee caps still attached – hence the locked knees. I had also long ago decided that the bottom handle was the only one for me regardless of situation – I always used it in simulator practices and virtually forgot that the top handle even existed.

As I pulled the seat pan handle I heard a swoosh of air as the canopy left the aircraft. [The American ejected at 28,000ft at 300kt.] Everything from then on appeared to happen in slow motion. I felt my hands able to pull just a bit more on the handle (double pull seat) and then I started rising slowly amidst a shower of sparks that were coming from alongside and below me. I can remember glancing at various instruments as I started up and the last I saw of my ship was the windscreen brace as it passed in front of my face. There was no sensation of windblast as I left, only a feeling of flipping over backwards. then everything happened in 'real time' again and I found myself spinning violently in a very unstable fashion. I tried desperately to focus my eyes on the lights that I knew to be the East Anglian coast but was unable to do so due to the spinning and tumbling. It is hard to describe the experience – it was almost intolerably unpleasant, my whole existence consisting of blackness interrupted by brief flashes of light that continually changed position as they streaked by. A dull greyness I interpreted as

being a cloud layer. I knew such cloud existed at about 5,000ft and I decided that as I approached it I would pull the manual separation lever; I even felt for the lever to make sure it was still there. Then I felt myself losing

A continuing problem with the Lightning was fuel and hydraulic fires. The two engines mounted above each other, No 2 above and No 1 behind, both had long jet pipes close to the external skin. In an attempt to solve some of the in-flight fire problems 29 Squadron's XS459/T was loaned to BAC in the spring of 1972 for trials, though it remained on the squadron. The safety equipment was removed from the right-hand seat and small reservoirs of blue dye were placed in strategic places around the airframe. A control box operated by the BAC test pilot took the place of the safety equipment and the fuselage was painted with white distemper so that the dye trails could clearly be seen. XS459 is now on display at Wellesley Aviation at Narborough, Norfolk. Pete Nash

decision I had made a long time ago; a decision that was reinforced by troubles other chaps had had with the dinghy T handle once in the water. (American exchange officers flying the Lightning had speculated about inflating the life raft in the air 'on the way down' and having it ready for use once splashdown occurred. I followed this alternate procedure and it was a likely factor in my survival. Interestingly about a year after my incident, the RAF adopted automatically inflating life rafts.)

I tucked that dinghy under my left arm with the large end facing rearward. I entered cloud, rotated the quick release box, grabbed it with my right hand and prepared to enter water. I remember coming out of the warm moistness of the cloud but could see nothing – total darkness all around. Hitting the water was a complete surprise and certainly the worst shock of the evening. My left arm rested over the side of the dinghy so I merely swung around and pulled myself inside. Total time in the water couldn't have been more than thirty seconds.

After about fifteen minutes a red flashing light appeared on the horizon and progressed toward me. I became somewhat elated and knew I must fire some flares for him [an RAF Whirlwind from Coltishall] to find me. That was when I started having trouble getting the pen gun to engage the flares in the kit. I just couldn't seem to screw the gun into the flares. A certain sense of urgency developed as the chopper came closer and closer. I managed to fire off about four flares as the chopper swung around within about a half mile of me and then headed toward the horizon again. As he left he fired a green flare, but by now he had caused me to foolishly waste half my mini-flares and I was mad at him. As I tried to screw another flare into the gun (just to have one ready) the pen gun came apart in my hand and the parts fell. I 'battened down the hatches' for a long night, pulling my head down into the dinghy and doing up the Velcro all the way to the top.

I spent a good hour inside my little self-created womb and did little things like try and arrange items in the raft – by feel of course. I knew it fatal to start thinking about my predicament so I kept busy by doing little mundane tasks over and over again. The SARBE antenna was blowing over in the strong wind. I could hear it whipping against the dinghy canopy. I detached the beacon from my Mae West, listened to the reassuring beep-beep and then fixed it down between my legs. I ran the antenna up through a small hole in the Velcro and thus had about 2ft of straight vertical length for transmitting. A squall came up and the rain pelted my back and the waves broke over me more often. Suddenly I found

F.6 XR724 of 11 Squadron was being flown for the first time following a major servicing by Sqn Ldr Dick Bell, a Leconfield test pilot, on 28 July 1972, when it suffered a fire in the No.1 engine which was caused by a hydraulic coupling not being tightened up sufficiently. The fire went out but the F.6 was heavy and the pilot had a 185kt threshold speed. There was no wind and no parachute. Dick Bell rejected the early hookwire so that the aircraft would not be stretched and was aiming for the far hookwire relying on brakes when the port tyre burst. Despite full maxarat on full right rudder he could not control it and he had to heave the aircraft onto the grass where it stopped. Dick Bell

myself going over into the water. I lunged in the opposite direction and managed to right the dinghy again. I became very afraid of tipping over and crouched down in my dinghy even more.

I first heard a noise that wasn't the wind and stuck out my head for a look around. Immediately I saw a great number of red flashing lights far off and then saw a large aircraft through breaks in the cloud. Several white flares were dropped about 5m away and my sense of elation was almost overwhelming. I knew it had to be the rescue chaps from RAF Woodbridge with the Hercules and Jolly Green Giants. One flare fired by me quickly brought the search pattern closer. Another flare and another until one chopper headed right at me. I fired off my day/night flare but the helicopter drifted away again. Finally the Hercules dropped a batch of white illumination flares right overhead and a Jolly Green Giant came right alongside. I fired my next to last mini-flare vowing to shoot the last one right into his cockpit if he moved away. A basket was lowered and the chopper pilot kept trying to get it near me. For the first time I realised how rough the seas were – 10–12ft waves and a whole lot of spray and white water.

I thought about getting out of my raft (stan-

dard USAF procedure) but was so entangled in the cords and lanyards that I couldn't get free. When the basket came within about 3ft I lunged for it, literally falling inside with the life raft still strapped to my back. Talk about happy – you have no idea. Up I went and let them pull me inside just like the book says. An NCO took out his knife and cut me free from the dinghy and I was able to stand up though on somewhat wobbly legs. I almost kissed the NCO. We got my immersion suit off (there was about ½in of water in the boots and my seat was damp) and I wrapped up in a batch of blankets. While laying there for the half-hour trip home I got the shakes – partly from the transition of warming up – but mostly I think from the fears that were finally catching up with me. As I lay there I kept on thanking God and Martin-Baker over and over and over.

What caused the fire? From the sequencing and timing of events as recorded by Bawdsey that night, the engineering staffs were able to locate quite precisely the source of the fire and the resultant loss of control. The fire originated in the proximity of an elbow in the main fuel line in the firewall between Nos. 1 and 2 engines. All F.3s were x-rayed for cracks in the fuel line elbow and I was told several were found to be close to imminent failure.

T.4 XM974, seen here at RAF Coltishall on Battle of Britain Day, 15 September 1962, was abandoned on 14 December 1972 near Happsiburgh after a ECU/re-heat fire. Sqn Ldr John Spencer, 226 OCU, and Flg Off Geoffrey Philip Evans, ejected safely before the aircraft crashed in the North Sea. Ron Clarke

Hydraulic, pitot, static and control cables also ran through the same firewalled area and as they melted or were burned, the respective instrument or control surface failed. I was told that ultimately the tail section probably burned off.

In Germany three days later, on 28 January, Fg Off Pete Hitchcock, of 92 Squadron at Gütersloh, entered a spin in XN772 at 32,000ft during combat training. The F.2A had still not recovered by 14,500ft and he decided to eject using the face blind ejection initiation. Hitchcock had some difficulty as his head was high in the canopy, but eventually he got his right hand to the blind handle and then his left. He descended normally with automatic separation and landed in scrub, suffering a crush fracture. The aircraft crashed near Diepholz.

On 28 April, Flg Off Alastair Cameron 'Harry' MacLean of 23 Squadron, in XS938, suffered a re-heat fire in the No.1 engine shortly after take-off from Leuchars. He turned back and then received a second fire warning. MacLean put out a 'Mayday' and said he was ejecting, making a face blind initiation at 4,000ft and 250kt, slightly nose-up. There were no problems but after separation from his seat one side of the PSP support was undone. He lowered it gently but it increased in oscilation, so he pulled it up again and inflated his life preserver. Then

he lowered the PSP again; this time there was no oscilation and he was able to clamber into the dinghy. He was picked up shortly afterwards, twenty-eight minutes after his Mayday signal. The F.6, meanwhile, had crashed into the River Tay.

In Cyprus on 10 May, F.3 XP744 was abandoned shortly after take-off by Flt Lt Robert D.Cole of 56 Squadron, near Akrotiri, after he received a zonal fire warning. Cole ejected safely and was picked up, uninjured, by a helicopter after thirty minutes. His aircraft had crashed 8m south-east of Akrotiri.

Flt Lt Tony Alcock had a narrow escape on 20 May, during a 111 Squadron detachment to Colmar in France, when XP752 was involved in a collision near the base with a French Air Force Mirage IIIE. The French jet hit the starboard side of the cockpit canopy and nose of the F.3 as they broke formation in cloud. The Lightning's pitot head was bent in the collision, which also jettisoned the canopy. Alcock, who received a blow on the right side of his helmet, decided it was time to eject, but he did not pull his seat pan handle hard enough, and the seat refused to budge. Obligingly, the Mirage pilot formated on Alcock's damaged Lightning and led him in to land without further incident. XP752 was later written off.

On 26 May, Flt Lt Alastair J. MacKay RCAF, attached to 5 Squadron at Binbrook, ejected safely from XS902 near Grimsby following Fire Warning 1 after take-off followed by Re-heat Warnings 1 and 2. The F.6 crashed 9m east of Spurn Head. MacKay's was a routine ejection and the Canadian was recovered by helicopter within the hour and treated for neck abrasions and bruising of the shoulder and crutch. Then, during a 29 Squadron detachment to Cyprus on 8 July, Flt Lt Graham Clarke safely abandoned XP705

F.3 XR715 first entered service with 111 Squadron on 8 January 1965 and transferred to 29 Squadron at RAF Wattisham in 1972. The aircraft was abandoned on 13 February 1974 after an ECU fire forced Flt Lt Terence 'Taff' A. Butcher to eject. He suffered no ill-effects and was flying the next day. Pete Nash

XR715 crashed at Watermill Farm, Mells, near Halesworth, Suffolk where the local fire brigade were quick to arrive on the scene and extinguish the fire. Richie Pymer

near Akrotiri after a Re-heat Fire Warning 1 followed by Re-heat Fire Warning 2. His ejection was copybook – straight and level at 230kt at 13,000ft – and Clarke was picked up with only a bruised front shoulder. He was flying again ten days later. The F.3 crashed in the Mediterranean.

On 22 September Flg Off Phil Mottershead, a 29 Squadron pilot, crashed into the sea 30m off Lowestoft. During a climb at Mach 1.3 to 35,000ft to intercept 'playmate' at 3m Mottershead's 'Mayday! Mayday! Mayday!' had been rapid and panicky before his F.3, XP736, fell away to port and spiralled into the sea. Gp Capt Antony Barwood recalls:

Nothing more was heard. About half an hour later a searching Phantom crew saw an empty, deflated dinghy floating on the sea. This was recovered by the ASR launch, and sent to the IAM [Institute of Aviation Medicine] Accident Laboratory at Farnborough. The dinghy pack had obviously been hit very hard with displacement of the CO_2 cylinder and obvious scuffing and some paint transfers and it looked as though it might have hit the outside of the aircraft.

The Radar Unit at Watton reported that they had a plot of the aircraft and that one item only left the aircraft when the pilot ejected. They had a plot from an earlier ejection in almost the same spot and that, normal ejec-

tion, showed quite clearly two items leaving the aircraft; the cockpit canopy first, followed briefly by the seat. It seemed likely that this young pilot's ejection seat had failed to fire. The Lightning cockpit canopy was a partly metallic structure which must be jettisoned before ejection can proceed. The jettison

system is operated by ejection initiation which unlocks the canopy locking mechanism by withdrawing two lock or shoot bolts, operated by explosive cartridges. Explosively operated jacks then lift the canopy from the fuselage sill and the aerodynamic load takes it well clear of the aircraft. As the cockpit canopy separates, it removes the interdictor, which prevents the ejection seat from firing into the partly solid canopy. We had to assume that the interdictor had failed to operate, so that the ejection seat could not fire.

The pilot may have attempted manual abandonment. To do this he would operate his manual over-ride handle, unlocking his seat restraint harness from the seat structure. His dinghy pack would remain attached to him. This would considerably hamper his efforts to get clear of the cockpit in a high air blast situation. We assumed that he had disconnected it from both sides and from the dropping lanyard and that he pushed it out of the cockpit and that it picked up its paint markings as it contacted with the outside of the fuselage.

I went to Watton with the Board of Inquiry to see the plots for myself and then went on to Coltishall with the pilot's damaged dinghy and with an identical dinghy. They found me an identical aircraft with exactly the same paint finishes as the lost aircraft and by bashing the dinghy with a wooden mallet onto various parts of the side of the aircraft rear side of the

F.6 XR768 was the first full F.6 to be delivered, when it was assigned to 74 Squadron on 1 August 1966. In 1973 it was assigned to 5 Squadron but was lost a year later, on 29 October 1974, when Flt Lt T.W. Jones was forced to abandon the aircraft near Saltfleet, Lincs, after what was thought to be a double re-heat fire. The pilot was unhurt and the aircraft crashed into the North Sea, off Mablethorpe. Ron Clarke

XR765 was built as an F.3A and was assigned to 5 Squadron as 'M' (pictured) on 8 March 1966. It was brought up to full F.6 standard in February 1967 and reassigned to 23 Squadron on 25 March 1968 before joining 11 Squadron in December 1973 and finally 5 Squadron again, in 1981. On 23 July 1981 Flt Lt J.G. Wild was forced to abandon the aircraft over the North Sea after a double re-heat fire and the aircraft crashed 50m north-east of Binbrook. Ron Clarke

cockpit and on the inner edge of the wing leading edge, I was able to show that the paint transfers were identical.

About a month later, the pilot's bonedome was recovered by a Danish fishing vessel and returned to Farnborough. The break rivet on the chin strap had broken, so we assumed that it had been torn off by exposure to air blast. The remains of the aircraft were located on the sea bed and showed that the ejection seat was still in the aircraft at impact, but the seat systems had totally disintegrated and no evidence of a mis-fire or other malfunction could be found. Six months later, his cockpit canopy was dredged up. It was sent straight to the lab at Farnborough.

It was immediately obvious that the interdictor cable had broken. This cable is made of twenty-eight strands of stainless steel wire twisted into four smaller cables which are twisted together to form the interdictor wire. The ends of the cable are 'swaged' onto a steel sleeve (the wire being inserted into a sleeve and then subjected to high, all round pressure, a well established method of securing a steel cable into a connector). The broken end of each individual outer cable, six forming the

outside with one in the middle, had cracked, producing a six-sided facet. This cracking had occurred at the cable end of a swage and as this end was covered with a rubber sleeve, it was therefore not visible for routine inspection. Every time the cockpit canopy is opened, this cable is flexed slightly. Many repetitive flexings had produced the cracking of the outer six wires forming the strand, leaving one intact central wire in one of the four sub-cables – only one intact wire out of twenty-eight. This single strand of wire failed in extension when the interdictor wire tried to pull the interdictor catch off the seat firing mechanism.

We were able to reproduce this wire failure by clamping the swaged end so that it was firmly fixed and flexing the cable through 30 degrees, each side. It only required thirty-five flexions to reproduce the identical failure. This was one of the occasions when I went straight to the Director of Flight Safety to get him to ground all Lightnings until their interdictor wires had been tested under load. The interdictor wires were replaced and subsequently redesigned.

In Cyprus on 30 September, Flt Lt Richard

Bealer of 56 Squadron was forced to abandon XR764 near Akrotiri after take-off on full re-heat. At 22,000ft Bealer received a Re-heat Fire 1 Warning and he throttled back and turned toward base. His controls stiffened and the Re-heat 2 Warning Light illuminated. Bealer called 'Mayday! Mayday! Mayday!' as the warning lights refused to go out despite his completing the fire drills. He ejected at 22,000ft and 220kt and tumbled in his seat to such an extent that he believed his drogues had failed. Thankfully, however, the seat separated perfectly normally at 10,000ft and he entered the water with his PSP under his arm. A helicopter picked him up from a choppy, but warm (65–70°F) sea twenty minutes later. The F.6, meanwhile, had crashed into Limassol Bay, south-east of Akrotiri.

Improvements

Despite the Fire Integrity Programme, most of the losses in 1971 had been due to fuel leak-related fires and so the RAF

Flt Lt Mike Thompson, the pilot of XP753, who was killed on 26 August 1983 when the F.3 crashed into the sea off Scarborough during unauthorized aerobatics. Ken Johnson

redoubled its efforts to stamp out the problem. None of the Lightnings lost during 1972 were due to fuel-related fires, and the first casualty, on 16 February, was the result of a collision during a 29 Squadron night supersonic interception exercise from Wattisham. XP747, flown by Flt Lt Paul Reynolds, had slowed to Mach 0.9 at 35,000ft, turning onto 350 homing to Wattisham. As he descended, and 40m south-east of Harwich, Reynolds experienced a bump and pitched nose down but felt that he was being pushed upwards (XP747 and XP 698, flown by Flt Lt Patrick 'Chile' Cooper, who was killed, had collided). Reynolds' tail controls were lost and he was diving at 45 degrees so he put out a Mayday signal. At 31,000ft he put one hand to his face blind and pulled. Just fifteen seconds later, XP747 crashed. Dry and warm in his immersion suit, Reynolds was picked up by a fishing boat and a USAF Jolly Green Giant helicopter arrived to hoist him aboard, but the RAF pilot declined as he was sick and did not know how to use the Kaman winch used by the USAF. Two T.5s belonging to 226 OCU were lost, on 6 September and 14 December, and brought the year's Lightning losses to five.

The first Lightning loss in 1973 occurred on 3 April when XS934 was abandoned near Akrotiri, Cyprus, after an ECU fire during a general handling sortie. Flt Lt Fred Greer of 56 Squadron throttled back at 11,000ft and increased power on one engine. The fire went out but then recurred again and Greer experienced some stiffening of the controls. After pointing the F.6 towards the sea, he called 'ejecting' and left the aircraft safely. Another Lightning was abandoned before the year was out and two more, F.6 XR719, and F.3 XP738 of 111 Squadron, were declared 'Cat.5' after heavy landings on 5 June at Coltishall and 10 December at Wattisham respectively.

The fire prevention measures taken in the early seventies now began to pay dividends, for after 1973 fire-related accidents were halved, although XR715, the first of three Lightnings which crashed in 1974, on 13 February, was lost to 'Lightning Fire Syndrome'. Flt Lt Terence 'Taff' A. Butcher, one of a pair from 29 Squadron at Wattisham exercising at 7,000ft, experienced some difficulty in locating his face blind with his left hand. Butcher finally ejected at 8,000ft and 270kt. The Southwold lifeboat was alerted in case the Lightning came down in the sea, but it clipped two willow trees in a paddock at Mells, near Halesworth in Suffolk, and ploughed a 200yd furrow before ending up in three main sections across a barbed wire fence, just 100yds from Watermill Farm. Butcher, who landed in a field near the Norwich road, was flown to the RAF

Hospital, Ely, where x-rays revealed that there were effectively no injuries, and he was flying again the next day.

On 24 June Flg Off Kevin Mason of 111 Squadron took off from Wattisham in XR748 and did a slow roll over the station at 8,000ft when both hydraulic warning lights illuminated and remained on. Mason commenced a slow climb towards the coast, tightening his lap, shoulder outer and negative g straps, but after twelve minutes control was lost and Mason ejected near Coltishall at 18,000ft and 380kt. The F.3 crashed in the North Sea off Great Yarmouth and Mason also dropped into the sea, having separated from his ejection seat automatically at 10,000ft. Mason could not release his QRB, or inflate his life preserver, and he was dragged along for about fifteen seconds. He finally clambered into his dinghy but his harness pulled him out again. A Whirlwind arrived and the winchman managed to release Mason from his harness and pull him aboard the helicopter.

On 29 October, XR768 had to be abandoned by Flt Lt T.W. Jones of 5 Squadron, near Saltfleet, Lincolnshire, after his top engine flamed out off the Lincolnshire coast during banner firing. It refused to relight, but after a fire warning on No.2 was followed by a fire warning on No.1, it relit spontaneously. Jones, who had previously ejected from a Gnat on 23 May 1966 after flying into high tension cables, ejected at 3,500ft and 260kt. During his descent he dropped his PSP, and he was a non-swimmer. Once in the sea, Jones was in his dinghy in ten seconds flat! The F.6 crashed three miles off Mablethorpe.

Lightning losses, thankfully, now began to tail off. In 1975, two were lost, and in 1976 and 1977, only one a year was lost, although the first of these, in Cyprus on 7 April 1975, proved fatal. Sqn Ldr Dave Hampton, a very experienced pilot in 11 Squadron, took off from Akrotiri in XR762 on an AI exercise with another Lightning. Hampton climbed up to 40,000ft and carried out a tail chase down but then lost contact in a barrel roll. Hampton recovered but later lost it again. His No.1 saw him spinning through 12–10,000ft and called, 'Eject, eject, you are below 12!' No.1 thought he saw Hampton recover and pull out but the F.6 hit the sea with one large and two smaller splashes. It hit at a shallow angle and the seawater rushed up through the air intake and burst through the cockpit floor, forcing the seat upwards and firing the canopy jettison system. No.1 called 'Mayday' and alerted the Akrotiri helicopter, which arrived at the scene in fifteen minutes. There was no sign of the aircraft but Hampton's body was seen floating face down, his PSP up but without any sign of a parachute canopy. The crewman turned the body over, inflated his life preserver and undid the QRB and tried to resusitate the unfortunate squadron leader but to no avail.

In June 1975 T.4 XM991 was written-off after a ground fire at Gütersloh. In 1976, on 29 July, F.6 XS937, piloted by Flg Off Simon Manning of 11 Squadron at Binbrook, suffered an undercarriage failure overhead Leconfield. Eighteen minutes later, off Flamborough Head, he ejected at 7,000ft and 300kt. A SAR helicopter in the descent area picked up Manning ten minutes after he entered the sea. Manning got his feet tangled in his rigging lines and took a minute to free himself. Apart from some low lumbar pain, Manning suffered no lasting injuries.

In 1977, on 24 February, Sqn Ldr Michael Lawrance of 92 Squadron at Gütersloh was giving Lightning experience to Sqn Ldr Christopher 'Hoppy' Glanville-White, the 4 Squadron Harrier operations officer, in T.4 XM968 when, on the descent to circuit altitude, the undercarriage would not lock down. Lawrance closed down No.2 engine to conserve fuel and applied positive g to try to shake the wheels down, but to no avail. Glanville-White and then Lawrance ejected after the canopy jettisoned, the Harrier pilot sustaining crush fractures and Lawrance spinal injuries.

No Lightnings were lost in 1978, the first clean sheet since 1958. In 1979 though, three were lost. The first occurred on 25 May, when XS931 of 5 Squadron was abandoned by Flt Lt Pete Coker near Flamborough Head after a control restriction caused by FOD and the F.6 crashed off Hornsea. On 17 August Fg Off Raymond Knowles, a 5 Squadron pilot, was on a normal transit flight in XP737 from Binbrook to Valley where the F.3 was to be part of a ground display for an open day. In the circuit west of the airfield the port undercarriage warning light came on when the gear was operated and the tower confirmed that the port undercarriage was only 20 degrees down. Knowles completed all his emergency drills and attempted to fling the gear down with g, to no avail. Positioned four miles off Anglesey with a 22 Squadron Wessex alerted, Knowles, who had made four previous parachute drops, pulled the SPH and ejected at 9,000ft and 250kt over the Irish Sea. His PSP finally dropped at 500ft and the life preserver inflated at 300ft. The winchman aboard the Wessex saw Knowles dragged along for fifteen seconds before safely picking him up. Knowles suffered a very minor neck injury and was in a collar for seven days.

On 18 September XR723, a 5 Squadron F.6 which was on detachment to Akrotiri and was piloted by the Station Commander, Gp Capt Pete Carter, received fire warnings on both engines followed by aircraft failure. Carter, who had made a previous parachute drop, corrected his posture, tightened his straps, adjusted the seat height and checked arm and leg clearance as he climbed from 4,000ft to 7,500ft before pulling the SPH and ejecting at 250kt over the sea. He

F.3 XP753 first flew on 8 May 1964 and was assigned to 74 Squadron at RAF Coltishall on 23 June 1964 before being transferred to 29 Squadron in 1972. It went from 60 MU to 11 Squadron in 1973 and ten years later was serving with the LTF at Binbrook. It was lost off Scarborough on 26 August 1983. via Peter Winning

suffered back pain as the seat fired but managed to scramble into his dinghy after just twenty seconds and was helicoptered to land in minutes. XR723 crashed 15m south of Akrotiri.

The Last Few Years

There were no Lightning crashes in 1980, and just one in 1981. On 23 July, XR765 was lost when Flt Lt Jim Wild of 5 Squadron abandoned it over the North Sea after a double re-heat fire. The F.6 crashed 50m north-east of Binbrook. Wild ejected safely. The next Lightning crash occurred on 26 August 1983, when XP753 plunged into the sea off Scarborough during unauthorized aerobatics. Flt Lt Mike Thompson of the LTF was killed.

In 1984 two more Lightnings crashed. A 5 Squadron pilot was killed on 13 July when XS920 was lost near Heuslingen, West Germany, after the F.6 hit power cables during air combat manoeuvres. On 8 November, XR761 of 5 Squadron was abandoned by Flt Lt Mike Hale over the North Sea after pitch trim failure followed by re-heat fire. The aircraft crashed 8m north of Spurn Head.

These losses were followed by two more in 1985. On 6 March XR772 of 5 Squadron was abandoned off Spurn Head after a possible structural failure, and crashed into the sea, 20m north-east of Skegness. On 19 September, XS921 of 11 Squadron crashed 30m off Flamborough Head after an uncontrolled spin. Almost exactly a year later, on 15 September 1985, XR760 of 11 Squadron was safely abandoned by Flt Lt Bob Bees after a rear fuselage fire. The F.6 crashed into the North Sea 7m north of Whitby.

On 1 July 1987, during the last Lightning APC, XR763 of 5 Squadron was abandoned by Flt Lt D.K.M. 'Charlie' Chan near Akrotiri. He was flying an air firing sortie on a target banner towed by a Canberra when the upper wheel from the banner spreader bar came off and was ingested by the Lightning's No.1 engine, which promptly seized. Chan shut it down

and headed back to Akrotiri with the No.2 engine now running at abnormally high temperature due to debris damage. At about 2½m from the airfield the engine began to lose thrust. When Chan applied full power, the JPT rose to 900°C (the normal maximum allowable JPT being 795°C). XR763 continued to lose speed and at about 250ft and 150kt, Chan ejected safely. The F.6 crashed in a vineyard close to some houses and exploded in a fireball. (The fin, later recovered almost intact from the wreckage, was erected in the grounds of a bar used by service personnel.)

It was an ignominious end for XR763, which had first flown over twenty-two years earlier. So too had XR769, which was safely abandoned over the North Sea by Flt Lt Dick Coleman RAAF of 11 Squadron on 11 April 1988, after an engine fire during practice air combat with a 74 Squadron Phantom. (The Phantom crew landed and marked up their aircraft with one 'kill'!) XR769 was the eightieth and last RAF Lightning lost to all causes.

LTF Lightning on its belly, covered in foam. Martin Chorlton

CHAPTER TEN

The Yellow Gate

B.J. Madden

Ironically it is mostly very quiet and peaceful at this place. At the moment there is little sound apart from the seemingly ever-present but unobtrusive song of a skylark in the wide blue heaven above us. It is pleasing background noise, a perfect companion to the dozy warmth of a summer's day upon which my son has accompanied me to a small, unfrequented country lane. Progress is terminated abruptly after a few hundred yards by a bright yellow gate beyond which is the vast expanse of the airbase. There is little sign of life but through the shimmering heat haze, on the far side of the expanse, we can discern the distorted and disembodied image of the brisk, relentless swirling radar; the planes are flying.

The planes are why we are here, me with my arms resting on top of the gate, my young son clambering up so he can sit beside me astride the top bar, legs swinging idly. We are here to see the jets, to witness the experience and the thrill of several tons of high-tech avionics hurtle through the air not 50yd from where we stand and somehow make contact with the tarmac runway and remain in one piece! It is a thrill we share now and again when the mood takes us and we can spare the time.

A few minutes later as I scan the distant horizon for the umpteenth time I see a small speck which can only be our quarry. I trace with my practised eye the line of its approach from the edge of the runway through the tall sentinel landing lights, across the flat open country and eventually to its slowly enlarging image. 'Hey, James! Here comes another one!'

'Where, dad?'

'Over there, look, you can see its light.' What began as an infinitesimal speck in the far distance is now appreciably larger and a faint smoke trail can be seen in its wake. The bright lights shining powerfully from its nose wheel flaps provide a disproportionally large reference point to track its progress. There is no noise as yet but as the seconds pass the image becomes larger and it is possible to discern the distinct shape of a modern jet aircraft. Perhaps thirty seconds pass, a passage of time that seems far, far longer as the anticipation mounts.

'What is it dad?'

'A Jag, I think.' Its approach seems much quicker now but it is still strangely silent until it almost pounces upon us and zooms past with a tremendous cacophony of sound. Within moments it hits the runway at over 100mph, smoke flying from its tyres on impact. My lad has his hands over his ears but I can see he enjoys the moment. The Jaguar recedes into the distance and is soon lost to view. Silence reimposes itself over the scene. Loud sounds are the things I suppose that really impress, and the evocative smell of spent aviation fuel. I love it and I doubt that the excitement will ever pale.

There is now a lull in the action and I begin to think back to when I first discovered this place in the late summer of 1968. I can still remember the day vividly, the day when we first encountered a *real* jet; the magnificent, magical and majestic Lightning.

My friend and I, my very best friend, the inseparable and unquestioning kind you can only really make as children, had gone fruit picking with my parents. We were unimpressed with this obviously overrated pastime and decided to seek our fortune elsewhere. We chose Coltishall as the honoured destination of the day for no other reason than we had never been there before and were curious as to what it was like. At the local village shop we pooled our meagre resources to purchase a drink and some choc bars and then we first heard the thunderous roar of a Lightning. We realized that we were close to the famous RAF base where the wartime hero Douglas Bader had flown Spitfires and it at once became an irresistible lure. We walked further along the then almost deserted country lanes to get a closer view, if we could, of the powerful monsters that now inhabited the station. All the time the sound of jets got louder and louder and our expectations mounted. We arrived at the western end of the runway where the landing lights straddle the road, stopped and watched for the first time one of these magnificent silver machines come in to land. So loud, so fast, and so exciting. This was real fun! We just had to get a closer look.

It was high summer and even now I can capture the sights and sounds that assaulted us as we swam through a sea of corn. It was a real adventure, complete abandon; we did not have a care in the world.

We climbed an oak nearby and for the next thirty minutes or so we had a great time wedged side by side, safe and secure, in the boughs of the sturdy tree waving to the pilots as they taxied by. One or two waved back, which gave us great encouragement and which, I suppose, hastened our inevitable downfall.

There comes a point in every adventure where your luck runs out but on this particularly occasion ours didn't just run out – we gave it a pretty hefty kick out the door! But we were young and exhuberant and because of this determined that we would get closer still to these wonderful aircraft. We set out on a stroll across the airfield! Needless to say, we didn't get far and looking back we were extremely fortunate only to find ourselves explaining our presence to a somewhat bemused RAF sergeant whose powerful shouts had brought us shamefaced into his realm. It could have been much, much worse. Anyway, having decided the likelihood of us being communist spies was small the sergeant took pity on us, dumped us in the back of his truck and deposited us at the main entrance (exit in our case) of the station. This was a mixed blessing. On the one hand we had escaped the firing squad but on the other hand we had an extra couple of miles to walk home. On balance we decided that we had probably gotten off lightly and, resigned to our fate, tramped home.

Far from deterring us, this episode only served to spur us on: from that moment we were firmly hooked. Over the next couple of years we made regular excursions to the station discovering various vantage points from which to watch the Lightnings. Most of these spots ended in a yellow crashgate.

Although our excursions were restricted to school holidays, small things like the seasons bothered us not in the least. We visited the airfield come rain or shine and I particularly remember one freezing cold crisp midwinter day when every time a Lightning passed low overhead and plummeted onto the runway we held out our numb hands to gratefully receive a blast of warm air. To think that we were so close that the hot air could temporarily alleviate the numbness brought on by the cold.

For a time we lived Lightnings. We watched them, made models of them – whole squadrons adorned our bedroom ceilings – drew pictures of them, took photographs of them, and probably bored our friends stupid with our talk of them. But it was good, it was harmless and it gave us a focal point upon which to channel our ever increasing need for mental stimulation and practise our creative talents.

But then it all changed. We 'grew up'. Suddenly, there was a very urgent need to disassociate ourselves with any pastime that could be linked with childhood. More serious obligations began to impose themselves upon us and at sixteen we left school and largely went our separate ways. The cycle rides to RAF Coltishall, like so many other simple fun-filled things, ceased and were never resumed.

Looking back it seems almost terrifying to think of the way in which one takes things for granted. I didn't realize at the time that this was the last I would ever see of the old war-horse which had given me so much pleasure and had been such a feature of my life all those years ago. Its subsequent fate – I've seen the photos of rusting,

'We arrived at the western end of the runway where the landing lights straddle the road, stopped, and watched for the first time one of these magnificent silver machines come in to land. So loud, so fast, and so exciting. This was real fun! We just had to get a closer look.' Simon Parry

'I didn't realise at the time that this was the last I would ever see of the old war-horse which had given me so much pleasure and had been such a feature of my life all those years ago. Its subsequent fate – I've seen the photos of rusting, vandalized, dismembered hulks – almost makes me sick.' XS933 looks forlorn as the Farewell to the Lightning Flypast roars overhead at Binbrook on 13 April 1988. The Lightning did have weaknesses, and most stemmed from its origin as a pre-research aircraft: lack of fuel, limited accommodation for radar and a small weapon load clearly feature, together with the difficulty of engineering further development. But it was still a terrific machine to fly and with which to dominate the local skies! *Aeroplane*

vandalized, dismembered hulks – almost makes me sick.

My son was born in 1988. He is unlikely ever to see a Lightning fly. He will never witness its ability to ascend straight from take-off vertically towards the heavens until it is lost from view. A red hot silver bullet fired from a Cold War gun. For me, one era ended that year and another began.

I am brought out of my trance by the approach of another Jaguar. Although it is a worthy aircraft I can't help thinking that it is a poor replacement for the silver beast. As frightening as it is unexpected, an unwelcome longing has bubbled slowly to the surface. I feel as though the breath has been knocked out of me. The memories of those now extinct halcyon days of the 1960s are at this point so vivid I could almost touch them. I can recall wild laughter as we cycled along, the wind streaming through my hair, fever pitch excitement as we got closer to the yellow gate, legs pounding the pedals in a desperate attempt to be the first to reach the goal; always a race to see who could reach it first.

My son, catching something of my sombre mood, says, 'Come on dad, let's go home.' I help him down from the gate and take his hand in mine. As we walk away I take a look back over my shoulder at the yellow gate, and there for a brief moment I see the image of three young lads sitting astride their bikes propped against the gate laughing and joking together. They turn to look at me and they smile and raise their hands in greeting. I almost raise my hand in response but then see only the yellow gate. It is still there, unchanged in thirty years, smiling at me in the sunshine.

The yellow gate. Author

Lightning Units

5 Squadron

Motto: *Franges non flectas* (Thou mayest bend but shall not break)
Command Assignments: Fighter Command Interceptor Alert Force; UK Air Defence Region (Southern)
Aircraft: F.6 (12.65–12.87); F.1A (6.70–9.72); (10.72–9.87)
Station: Binbrook, 12.65–1.5.88

History

Disbanded, Geilenkirchen, RAF Germany (Javelin FAW9), 7.10.65, reforming the next day at RAF Binbrook to begin re-equipment with the Lightning.

T.5 XS451/T arrived first, on 19.11.65, followed on 10.12.65 by XR755/A and XR756/B, the first (interim) F.6s, so becoming the first RAF squadron to operate the type. Last of twelve interim F.6s arrived 8.3.66, the squadron becoming fully operational late that year. XS894/F, first full F.6 standard aircraft arrived 3.1.67; full complement being completed by spring 1967.

Took part in ADEX 67, being based at Luqa; Malta, 6–26 October. Four F.6s flew non-stop from Binbrook–Bahrain, May 1968, in eight hours, refuelled along the 4,000m route by Victor tankers from RAF Marham. Won the Dacre Trophy (awarded to the top UK fighter squadron in weapons proficiency) in 1968 and 1969. Ten F.6s flew to RAF Tengah, Singapore, 12.69, for joint air-defence exercises with other Lightnings and RAAF Mirages there. Participated in local defence exercises in Singapore, 1970, exchanging and returning with some Lightnings from 74 Squadron, which were in need of major overhaul. Won the Huddleston Trophy (best interceptor squadron in NATO) in the AFCENT Air Defence Competition, 1970 and 1971.

No.5 Squadron proved the longest operator of the Lightning, finally disbanding at Binbrook, 31.12.87, reforming as a Tornado F.3 unit at Coningsby, 1.5.88.

11 Squadron

Motto: *Ociores acrioresque aquilis* (Swifter and keener than eagles)
Command Assignments: Fighter Command Interceptor Alert Force; UK Air Defence Region (Northern)
Aircraft: F.6 (4.67–5.88); F.3 (10.72–5.86)
Stations: Leuchars, 4.67–1972. Binbrook, 1972–5.88

History

Disbanded, Geilenkirchen, end of 1965, reforming at Leuchars, 1.4.67, when it re-equipped with the Lightning F.6, the third RAF squadron to operate the type.

With the move by 74 Squadron to Singapore, became the main air defence squadron at Leuchars, 15.5.67. With 23 Squadron, formed the Leuchars Lightning Wing, part of the Interceptor Alert Force (IAF) or QRA (Quick Reaction Alert); the long-range interception of Soviet aircraft in the Northern UK Air Defence Region. One day, April 1970, no less than 40 interceptions were carried out on *Badgers* and *Bears*. Meanwhile, in-flight refuelling was practised. Flt Lt Eggleton established a record, 29.11.67, of eight hours' flying, refuelling five times, flying 5,000m. Took part in the biggest air refuelling exercise so far mounted by the RAF, 6.1.69, when ten F.6s, refuelled by Victor tankers, deployed to Tengah, Singapore (staging through Muharraq and Gan) and back, a distance of 18,500m. F.6s retro-fitted, 1970, with twin 30mm Aden

cannon in the front section of the ventral fuel tank.

Replaced at Leuchars, 22.3.72, by Phantom FG.1s of 43 Squadron, moving to Binbrook, 22.6.72, following the departure of 85 Squadron to West Raynham, to continue in the IAF role. Deployed to Akrotiri, Cyprus, June 1972 for one-month detachment, relieving 56 Squadron, which completed APC at Valley. Six F.6s sent to Cyprus, January 1974, following the Turkish invasion. Began receiving additional Lightnings from 226 OCU, mid-1974, following its closure, and from other F.3 squadrons which began re-equipping with the Phantom FGR.2. 'C' Flight assumed the training task of Lightning Conversion, 1974, the Lightning Training Flight taking over at Binbrook, October 1975.

11 Squadron finally disbanded, 30.4.88 (reforming as a Tornado F.3 Squadron at Leeming, 1.11.88). Sqn Ldr Aldington had the distinction of making the final RAF Lightning flight when he delivered one of three aircraft to RAF Cranfield, 30.6.88.

19 Squadron

Motto: *Possunt quia posse videntur* (They can because they think they can)
Command Assignments: Fighter Command Interceptor Alert Force; UK Air Defence Region (Southern) (1962–9.65); RAF Germany (23.9.65–31.12.76)
Aircraft: F.2 (12.62–10.69); F.2A (1.68–12.76)
Stations: Leconfield 12.62–1.68; Gütersloh 1.68–12.76

History

Began conversion from the Hunter F.6 to the Lightning F.2 at Leconfield, October

This BAe publicity photo of two F.3s at Wattisham in July 1970 shows XP738/E of 111 Squadron (note the F-1049-equipped JG71 'Richthofen zap' on the nose) fitted with Firestreaks, while the Lightning in the foreground is armed with Red Tops. Lightnings always flew with two missile 'bodies' fitted, a weighted drill round on the port side and an acquisition round on the starboard. It was always that way round to protect the glass seeker head from being damaged by the access ladder being fitted and removed. Sometimes, a metal cover was fitted over the glass to protect it when the aircraft was going to be used for inflight refuelling as it was expensive to replace the seeker if it was smashed by a flailing refuelling hose. Pilots also preferred to have missiles fitted as the aircraft was better balanced with them there. BAe

1962, the first RAF unit so to do. T.4 XM988 first aircraft to arrive, 29.10.62. First F.2, XN755/D, received 17.12.62.

Became operational as an all-weather unit, March 1963 with 12 F.2s and one T.4 Took part, July 1965, in in-flight refuelling trials with the new Victor K.1 tankers, winning, that same year, for the second time, the Dacre Trophy (awarded to the top UK fighter squadron in weapons proficiency). Transferred from Fighter Command, 23.9.65, to Second Tactical Air Force, RAF Germany, at Gütersloh (less than 100m from East Germany), becoming fully operational in 1966. F.2A Lightnings, able to carry four 30mm Aden cannon or twin Firestreak AAMs, or (more usually) twin Aden and two Firestreaks, began arriving, February 1968, the F.2s being progressively returned to BAC Warton, 1968–69, for modification to F.2A standard and re-issue to RAF Germany.

Disbanded, 31.12.76, at Gütersloh. Reformed, Wildenrath, 1.1.77, with the Phantom FGR.2.

23 Squadron

Motto: *Semper agressus* (Always on the attack)

Command Assignments: Fighter

163

Command Interceptor Alert Force; UK Air Defence Region (Northern)
Aircraft: F.3 (8.64–11.67); F.6 (5.67–10.75)
Stations: Leuchars, 8.64–31.10.75

History

Re-equipped from the Javelin to the Lightning F.3, at Leuchars, August 1964. XP707 and XP708, first to arrive, 18.8.64. Full squadron complement reached, end of October 1964.

Became operational early in 1965, when in-flight refuelling exercises with USAF KC-135 tankers took place. Replacement with the (interim) F.6, from May 1967, followed by full production standard F.6s. Won Dacre Trophy that same year (and again, 1969 and 1975, also winning the Aberporth Trophy 1970 and 1971). F.6 SX938, the last Lightning to be built for the RAF, was flown from Warton to Leuchars, 28.8.67.

Squadron fully equipped with F.6s by beginning of 1968. XR725/A and XS936/B flew non-stop to Toronto, Canada, in 7hr 20mins, August 1968, using in-flight refuelling, returning to Leuchars, 3.9.68.

Became operational with Red Top missile that same month. Detachments flown to Beauvechain, Belgium, July 1969, Malta, April 1970, Sweden, 1971, and to Cyprus, February 1971, this to take part in practice air defence of Cyprus and ACM. First successful trial of twin 30mm Aden gun packs, 26.3.71.

Replaced in the QRA role at Leuchars by Phantom FGR.2s of 111 Squadron, and disbanded, 31.10.75, before reforming as a Phantom FGR.2 squadron at Coningsby, 1.11.75., moving to RAF Wattisham, 25.2.76.

29 Squadron

Motto: *Impiger et acer* (Energetic and Keen)
Command Assignments: Fighter Command Interceptor Alert Force; UK Air Defence Region (Southern)
Aircraft: F.3 (5.67–12.74).
Stations: Wattisham, 5.67–12.74

History

Equipped with Javelins, was relieved of air defence duties on Cyprus, May 1967, by 56 Squadron's Lightning F.3s, which had arrived from RAF Wattisham that April. Returning to England, 29 Squadron reformed at Wattisham, 1.5.67, to become the last RAF unit to equip with the Lightning.

The first aircraft, XV328, a T.5, was taken on charge, 10.5.67, followed, 8.66–5.67, by F.3s, mostly 'hand-me-downs' from 74 and 23 Squadrons at Leuchars, then beginning conversion to the F.6. Fully operational by September 1967. Awarded Dacre Trophy, 19.7.74.

Disbanded, 31.12.74 at Wattisham, reforming as a Phantom FGR.2 squadron at Coningsby, 1.1.75.

56 (Punjab) Squadron

Motto: *Quid si coelum ruat* (What if heaven falls)
Command Assignments: Fighter Command Interceptor Alert Force; UK Air Defence Region (Southern); and to Cyprus (1975)

XR760/H was built as an F.3 and was delivered to 5 Squadron on 15 February 1966. After full F.6 modification on 3 January 1967 it was assigned to 23 Squadron as 'H', pictured here in 1970. This aircraft also served with 56 Squadron and the LTF at Binbrook. via Peter Winning

Aircraft: F.1 (12.60–4.65); F.1A (1961); F.3 (3.65–12.71); F.6 (9.71–6.76)
Stations: Wattisham, 12.60–28.6.76; Akrotiri, 5.67–12.64; Wattisham, 1975–28.6.76

History

Conversion to the Lightning F.1 began, December 1960, to become only the second Lightning squadron in the RAF, and the first to receive the F.1A (XM172 being the first to arrive, December 1960).

Work-up to operational status took place at Wattisham, then, while the runways were resurfaced, continued at Coltishall. Full complement of F.1As were received by March 1961. Undertook intensive in-flight refuelling trials, 1962, first using USAFE F-100Cs tanking from KC-50s, then with their Lightning F.1As with Valiants. Two F.1As flew non-stop to Cyprus on 23.7.62, in 4hr 22min, refuelled from two Valiants of Nos. 90 and 214 Squadrons. Became the official Fighter Command aerobatic team, 1963, being named the 'Firebirds'. First AAR detachment to Cyprus, *Forthright One*, took place, 2.64. F.3s began arriving at Wattisham, 2.65, the F.1As being transferred to 226 OCU at Coltishall. Took part in *Unison* 65 in September 1965, and a year later, in the Malta air defence exercise *ADEX 66*. Moved to Akrotiri, Cyprus, April 1967, replacing 29 Squadron's Javelins; a posting which lasted seven years (5.67–9.74). Meanwhile, F.6s had been acquired from 74 Squadron, which disbanded at Tengah, Singapore, 8.71. Following the Turkish invasion of Cyprus, 1974, 200 operational sorties were flown to protect the Sovereign Base Area airspace. Finally returned to Wattisham, the first of thirteen F.6s (and the Squadron's three Canberra TTs) arriving at Wattisham, 21.1.75. Awarded Dacre Trophy, 6.75.

56 (Designate) Squadron formed on the Phantom FGR.2 at Coningsby, 22.3.76, the actual squadron disbanding, 28.6.76 at Wattisham, being reformed the next day at Coningsby on the Phantom.

74 (Trinidad) Squadron

Motto: I Fear No Man
Command Assignments: Fighter Command Interceptor Alert Force; UK Air Defence Region (Southern and Northern) 1960–5.67; FEAF air defence, 6.67–25.8.71
Aircraft: F.1 (6.60–4.64); F.3 (4.64–9.67); F.6 (9.66–8.71)
Stations: Coltishall, 6.60–4.64; Leuchars, 2.6.64–5.67; Tengah, 6.67–1.9.71

History

Became the first RAF squadron to introduce the Lightning into service. XM165, the first F.1, taken on charge at Coltishall, 29.6.60.

In September 1960 Sqn Ldr John F.G. Howe led formation flypasts of four aircraft at the Farnborough Air Show. A nine-ship formation was flown at Farnborough 1961, when the first public demonstration of nine Lightnings rolling in tight formation took place. In 1962, the *Tigers* became the official Fighter Command aerobatic team.

Moved to Leuchars, 28.2.64, then, in April, became the first operational RAF squadron to operate the F.3, XP700 being the first to arrive, on 14.4.64. From 1965 onwards shared the northern IAF defensive duties at Leuchars with 23 Squadron's F.3s. Air-to-air tanking became a feature of these interception missions, operational range and endurance being improved from August 1966, by the introduction of the Lightning F.6, XR768/A being the first. From August 1966 full production F.6s, the first to reach an operational squadron, were received.

In June 1967, thirteen Lightnings transferred to Tengah, Singapore, in Operation *Hydraulic*, the longest and largest in-flight refuelling operation hitherto flown, staging through Akrotiri, Masirah, and Gan, and using seventeen Victor tankers from Marham, for a four-year tour of duty in the tropics. During this time, three 2,000m deployments were made to Australia non-stop using Victor tankers, the major one being Exercise *Town House* 16.6–26.6.69. Also participated in *Bersatu Padu* (Complete Unity), a five-nation exercise in Western Malaya and Singapore, July 1969. Regular exchanges were also flown with RAAF Mirages at Butterworth, Malaysia, and two Lightnings were flown to Thailand for a static display in Bangkok.

Squadron finally disbanded, Tengah, 25.8.71. All remaining Lightnings were flown on the 6,000m, thirteen-hour trip, to Akrotiri, Cyprus, from 2.9.71, staging through Gan and Muharraq and completing seven in-flight refuellings with Victor tankers, for transfer to 56 Squadron. Reformed as a Phantom F-4J squadron at Wattisham, 19.10.84.

92 (East India) Squadron

Motto: *Aut pugna aut morere* (Either fight or die)
Command Assignments: Fighter Command Interceptor Alert Force; UK Air Defence Region (Southern) 1963–65; RAF Germany, 29.12.65–31.3.77
Aircraft: F.2 (4.63–7.71); F.2A (8.68–3.77)
Stations: Leconfield, 4.63–12.65; Geilenkirchen, 29.12.65–12.67; Gütersloh 24.1.68–31.3.77

History

Late in 1962, began equipping with the Lightning F.2, the first, XN783/A, arriving on the squadron 17.4.63. Declared fully operational that summer, a team of F.2s displayed at Farnborough that September. Movement to Geilenkirchen, Germany began in December 1965, replaced 11 Squadron's Javelins. Moved to Gütersloh, February 1968, to join 19 Squadron. Re-equipment with the F.2A followed and was concluded in 1969.

Disbanded, 31.3.77, reforming as an FGR.2 Phantom squadron at Wildenrath, 1.4.77.

111 Squadron

Motto: *Adstantes* (Standing by)
Command Assignments: Fighter Command Interceptor Alert Force; UK Air Defence Region (Northern)
Aircraft: F.1A (4.61–2.65); F.3 (12.64–9.74); F.6 (5.74–9.74)
Stations: Wattisham, 4.61–30.9.74

History

Re-equipment, with the Lightning F.1A, began 6.3.61, when it took delivery of XM185. XM216, the last F.1A built, was delivered in August. Re-equipment with the F.3 began in late 1964.

In 1.65, formed the leading box in a formation of sixteen aircraft for a final salute and flypast over the funeral barge of Sir Winston Churchill. In 1965, formed a formation aerobatics team, of twelve

Lightnings. USAF U-2 reconnaissance aircraft from Lakenheath, previously thought immune to fighter interception, were successfully intercepted late that summer.

F.3s continued to be used until disbandment at Wattisham, 30.9.74, 111 Squadron (designate) forming on the Phantom FGR.2 at Coningsby, July 1974. Full squadron complement followed, 1.10.74.

AFDS (Air Fighting Development Squadron)/CFE (Central Fighter Establishment)

Command Assignments: CFE (Central Fighter Establishment)
Aircraft: F.1/F.1A//F.2/F.3/T.4
Stations: Coltishall, 8.59–9.62; Binbrook, 10.62–1.2.66

History

Formed, 1.9.59 under the command of Wg Cdr Jimmy Dell, after moving from West Raynham, whose runways were unsuitable for Lightning operations. Its role was to carry out tactical and operational trials of all new fighter aircraft types and to investigate all equipment and aircraft systems.

First F.1 aircraft – XG334 (lost 5.3.60), 335 and 336 – delivered, December 1959. Four more F.1s delivered, May 1960, and used in Exercise *Yeoman* that same month while on detachment to Leconfield. Moved to Binbrook, 1962, with the CFE. First F.2 (XN771) delivered, November 1962, followed by three more (XN726, 729 and 777 (lost 21.12.62). XP695, first F.3 to enter service, arrived, 1.1.64. First interim version F.6 (XR753), arrived, 16.11.65.

T.55 55-410/G-27-78 of the Kuwait Air Force, one of two purchased by Kuwait, and which was flown to Kuwait via Akrotiri and Jeddah in December 1969 by Flt Lt Terry Adcock and Sqn Ldr Bruce Hopkins. Kuwait operated Lightnings for seven years before replacing them with the French-built Mirage. *Aeroplane*

T.55 55-410/G-27-78 of the Kuwait Air Force nearest the camera, with XR759 and F.53 G-27-56/53-686 of
the Royal Saudi Air Force behind. F.6 XR759 was originally built as an F.3 and joined 56 Squadron on 18
January 1966, and was modified to full F.6 standard in July 1967, later serving in 5 and 11 Squadrons.
53-686 was flown to Saudi Arabia in April 1969. BAe

CFE disbanded, 1.2.66, AFDS becoming the FCTU (Fighter Command Trials Unit).

FCTU (Fighter Command Trials Unit)

Command Assignments: Fighter/Strike Command
Aircraft: F.2/F.3/T.4
Stations: Binbrook, 1.2.66–30.6.67

History

Renamed from the disbanded AFDS, 1.2.66. Developed the concept of supersonic targets for the front-line Lightning squadrons. Continued to operate from Binbrook until disbandment, 30.6.67, all aircraft going to the Binbrook Station Target Facility Flight.

LCS (Lightning Conversion Squadron)

Aircraft: F.1A/F.3/T.4/T.5
Stations: Middleton St. George, 29.6.62–31.5.63.

History

Formed, 29.6.62, using, initially, a few single-seat Lightnings from Nos. 56,74 and 111 Squadrons, on a daily/return basis. The first Lightning T.4, (XM970), arrived, 29.6.62, and the LCS had equipped with nine more by late 1962. Became 226 OCU, 1.6.63.

LCU (Lightning Conversion Unit)/LTF (Lightning Training Flight)

Aircraft: F.3/T.5/F.6
Stations: Binbrook, 10.74–3.76; Coningsby, 3.76–1977; Binbrook, 1977–1.8.87.

History

LCU formed from 'C' Flight, No.11 Squadron, September 1974, becoming the LTF, beginning of October 1974.

Using, initially, four F.3s and four T.5s

(from 1979, F.6 was added for target facilities purposes with a radar reflector usually carried in place of AI 23 radar), directed to provide conversion training for new pilots arriving from Tactical Weapons Units with fast-jet experience on Hawks, for onward posting to front-line Lightning squadrons. A T.5 flight was followed by two weeks of ground school, including approximately fourteen 'flights' in a simulator, followed by five flights in T.5, before first solo in the F.3. First phase of conversion training involved concentrated flying up to IRS (Instrument Rating Standard), followed by a series of exercises, including battle formation flying, culminating in a handling test on the T.5. A weapons phase, involving air combat training with Red Top aquisition rounds, followed, before a final check ride, normally with the CO. After about forty-two Lightning flying hours, the new pilot was assigned to either 5 or 11 Squadrons. In addition to conversion training, shorter, refresher courses for lapsed Lightning pilots were run.

Flt Lt Ian Black, a former Phantom navigator, became the last pilot to be trained to fly the Lightning before the Flight disbanded, 1.8.87. Some of the aircraft were operated by Nos. 5 and 11 Squadrons for some months after.

226 OCU (Operational Conversion Unit)

Motto: *We Sustain*
Command Assignments: CFE
Aircraft: F.1A/F.3/T.4/T.5.
Stations: Coltishall, 4.1.60–8.61; Middleton St. George, 8.61–12.4.64; Coltishall, 4.64–17.6.74 (Leconfield (1966) and Binbrook (1972) used during runway repairs at Coltishall.)

History

Formed at Coltishall, 4.1.60, under the aegis of CFE with the task of training Lightning pilots, with aircraft borrowed from 74 Squadron.

Moved to Middleton St. George, 8.61, to become the Lightning Conversion Squadron (LCS), using mainly Lightnings from Nos. 56 and 111 Squadrons. First T.4 (XM970) received, 27.6.62. followed by seven more before the end of 10.62. Retitled 226 OCU, 1.6.63, receiving seven

ex-74 Squadron F.1 aircraft shortly thereafter. Now took designation 145 (Shadow) Squadron (disbanded, 5.71, 65 (Shadow) Squadron being formed in its place).

226 OCU moved to Coltishall, 13.4.64. First T.5 (XS419) arrived, 20.4.65, being followed by fourteen more. Became last unit in the RAF to receive the F.3 (XP696, XP737, XR716 and XR718), during 6–7.80.

Formed within 226 OCU, 4.5.71, were: No.1 (Conversion) squadron, with T.4s/F.1As (adopting markings of 65 Squadron); No.2 (Weapons) Squadron, using T.4s/F.1As/T.5s (also adopting 65 Squadron markings); and No.3 (Advanced) Squadron, using F.3s/T.5s in No.2T Squadron markings.

226 OCU disbanded, 17.6.74 and was replaced by the LTF. Reactivated, late 1974, at Lossiemouth, as the Jaguar Conversion Unit.

Binbrook TFF (Target Facility Flight)

Command Assignments: FCTU
Aircraft: F.1
Stations: Binbrook

History

Formed, 1966 on disbandment of the FCTU. Two F.1s (XM164 and XM137) being delivered, 22.2.66 and 15.3.66, respectively. Disbanded, December 1973.

Wattisham TFF (Target Facility Flight)

Command Assignments: FCTU
Aircraft: F.1/F.1A
Stations: Wattisham

History

Formed, April 1966. Complement of three Lightnings, two pilots, one engineering officer and fifty groundcrew. Disbanded, December 1973.

Leuchars TFF (Target Facility Flight)

Command Assignments: FCTU
Aircraft: F.1/F.1A
Stations: Leuchars

History

Formed, April 1966. Complement of three Lightnings, two pilots, one engineering officer and fifty groundcrew. Absorbed into 23 Squadron, 1970. Disbanded, December 1973.

60 MU Leconfield

Command Assignments:
Aircraft: All marks
Stations: Leconfield

History

Carried out all major servicing at all marks of Lightning.

Akrotiri Station Flight

Command Assignments:
Aircraft: T.5
Stations: Akrotiri, Cyprus

History

Formed from 'C' Flight, 11 Squadron, 1974.

Lightning Conversion Unit (RSAF)

Command Assignments: Saudi Arabia
Aircraft: T.5
Stations: Khamis Mushayt Air Base

History

Operated as the Lightning Conversion Unit for the RSAF.

2 Squadron RSAF

Command Assignments: Saudi Arabia (Eastern and North-Western Sectors)
Aircraft: F.53, T.55

Stations: Tabuk Air Base, 1969–?; King Abd al-Aziz Air Base, Dhahran, ?–1976; King Feisal Air Base, 8.76–1986.

History

Formed, mid-1969, from a small number of pilots trained at 226 OCU Coltishall, 1968. These were supplemented by officers who had graduated from the transitional training course. F.53s, delivered by RAF and BAC pilots, began to arrive, 1.7.68. A Canberra was used to tow targets for firing practice. Joint exercises, aimed at the air defence of the Eastern Sector, were carried out. Last RSAF squadron to operate the Lightning, up until 22.1.86.

6 Squadron RSAF

Command Assignments: Saudi Arabia (Southern Zone)
Aircraft: F.52/F.53
Stations: King Abd al-Aziz Air Base, Dhahran, 1967–1978

History

Formed, 1967, from a group of Hunters and F.52 Lightnings. Used in air defence until the arrival of F.53 Lightnings. Lightning Flight declared operational, 13.11.66. From January 1967 onwards, used in air defence along the Yemini border area. Role changed to attack and defence, 1969, taking part in the defence of the Southern Zone until the other types were withdrawn, 1974. With the arrival of F.53 Lightnings, carried out the entire defence of the Southern Zone, 1974–78, by which time the Lightnings were redistributed between Nos.13 and 2 Squadrons.

13 Squadron RSAF

Command Assignments: Saudi Arabia (Eastern Zone and North-West Sector)
Aircraft: F.5, F.53, T.55
Stations: King Abd al-Aziz Air Base, Dhahran, 1978–1982; King Feisal Air Base, March 1982–

History

Formed, 1978, at the King Abd al-Aziz Air Base at Dhahran from the transitional Lightning training unit and part of 6 Squadron. Using F.53 and T.55 Lightnings, along with the F.5, shared in training and joint exercises in the defence of sectors of the Eastern Zone of Saudi Arabia. With the arrival of F-15s in 1981, Lightning operations began to diminish, and transfer to the King Feisal Air Base in the North-West Sector took place, 1981–3.82.

Kuwait Air Force

Command Assignments: Kuwait
Aircraft: T.55K/F.55K
Stations: Kuwait International Airport, Ahmed al Jaber and Jakra.

History

Deliveries of the first of twelve F.53 fighters begun December 1968. Operated Lightnings until 1977, when replaced by Mirage F.1Ks.

Lightning Production Airframes

Mark	Serial	Notes
P.1A	WG760	Preserved, Aerospace Museum, Cosford, Shropshire
P.1A	WG763	Preserved, Museum of Science and Industry, Manchester
P.1A	WG765	Structural test specimen
P.1B	XA847	Stored, Southampton area by Wensley Haydon Baillie
P.1B	XA853	First flown, 5.9.57. SOC 10.2.65
P.1B	XA856	First flown, 3.1.58. SOC 6.67
P.1B/F.1	XG307	First flown, 3.4.58. Bedford fire dump, 4.72
P.1B/F.1	XG308	First flown, 16.5.58. To Bedford 29.6.66
P.1B/F.1	XG309	First flown, 23.6.58. Dismantled 3.67 for scrap
P.1B/F.1	XG310	First flown, 17.7.58. Converted to serve as F.3 prototype
P.1B/F.1	XG311	Abandoned 31.7.63 after undercarriage failure. Crashed into the sea off Lytham. Test pilot, D.M.Knight, ejected safely, EE Co.
P.1B/F.1	XG312	First flown, 29.12.58. SOC 4.72
P.1B/F.1	XG313	First flown, 2.2.59. To Saudi Arabia as G-27-115. Preserved, Dhahran, Saudi Arabia
P.1B/F.1	XG325	First flown, 26.2.59. Used for Firestreak trials. Nose section at 1476 Sqn ATC, Rayleigh, Essex
P.1B/F.1	XG326	First flown, 14.3.59. SOC 1971
P.1B/F.1	XG327	First flown, 10.4.59. Modified to F.3 standard, 1960
P.1B/F.1	XG328	First flown, 18.6.59. Scrapped, 5.72
P.1B/F.1	XG329	First flown, 30.4.59. Preserved, Norfolk and Suffolk Aviation Museum, Flixton, Bungay, Suffolk
P.1B/F.1	XG330	First flown, 30.6.59. Last flown, 5.1.65
P.1B/F.1	XG331	Nose section in Gloucestershire Aviation Collection, Staverton, Glos
P.1B/F.1	XG332	Abandoned, 13.9.62, on approach to Hatfield, after double engine fire. Test pilot, George P. Aird, ejected safely but broke both legs crashing through a greenhouse. DH
P.1B/F.1	XG333	First flown, 26.9.59
P.1B/F.1	XG334	Abandoned, 5.3.60, off Wells-Next-the-Sea after hydraulics failure. Sqn Ldr Ron Harding ejected safely. AFDS
P.1B/F.1	XG335	Abandoned, 11.1.65, Larkhill Ranges after undercarriage failed to lower. Crashed, Woodborough, Wilts. Sqn Ldr J. Whittaker, A&AEE, ejected safely
P.1B/F.1	XG336	First flown, 25.8.59
P.1B/F.1	XG337	Preserved, Aerospace Museum, Cosford, Shropshire
T.4/P.11	XL628	(Prototype) Abandoned by Test Pilot, J.W.C. Squier, 1.10.59, over the Irish Sea
T.4/P.11	XL629	(Prototype) Gate guardian at RAF Boscombe Down, Wiltshire
F.1	XM131	Static test airframe
F.1	XM132	Static test airframe
F.1	XM133	Static test airframe
F.1	XM134	Abandoned, 11.9.64, after starboard undercarriage leg failed to fully lower. Crashed off Happisburgh, Norfolk. Flt Lt Terry Bond, 226 OCU test pilot, ejected safely
F.1	XM135	Preserved, at IWM Duxford, Cambridge
F.1	XM136	Abandoned, 12.9.67, after cockpit fire. Crashed, Scottow near RAF Coltishall. Jock Sneddon, Wattisham TFF, ejected and landed safely
F.1	XM137	First flown, 14.12.59
F.1	XM138	Written-off after engine fire on runway at RAF Coltishall, 16.12.60. Flt Lt Bruce Hopkins, AFDS, evacuated aircraft safely

Mark	Serial	Notes
F.1	XM139	First flown, 12.1.60
F.1	XM140	First flown, 25.1.60
F.1	XM141	Damaged in take-off accident, 16.5.61. Subsequently reduced to spares
F.1	XM142	Abandoned, 26.4.63, after hydraulic power loss. Crashed off Cromer, Norfolk. Flt Lt J.M. Burns, 74 sqdn, ejected safely
F.1	XM143	First flown, 27.2.60
F.1	XM144	Nose section with South-West Aviation Heritage, Eaglescott Airfield, Devon
F.1	XM145	First flown, 18.3.60
F.1	XM146	First flown, 29.3.60. Scrapped, 11.66
F.1	XM147	First flown, 7.4.60
F.1	XM148	Cancelled
F.1	XM149	Cancelled
F.1	XM163	First flown, 23.4.60
F.1	XM164	First flown, 13.6.60
F.1	XM165	First flown, 30.5.60. Scrapped, 10.66
F.1	XM166	First flown, 1.7.60. Scrapped, 10.66
F.1	XM167	First flown, 14.7.60. SOC, 10.66
F.1	XM168	Structural test airframe. Cancelled?
F.1A	XM169	Preserved, nose section with North Yorks Aircraft Recreation Centre and Museum, Chop Gate, N. Yorks
F.1A	XM170	Mercury spillage caused by heavy landing on first flight, 12.9.60. Written off. E.E. Co.
F.1A	XM171	Abandoned, 6.6.63, after a collision over Great Bricett with XM179. Flt Lt 'Mo' Moore, 56 Sqdn, safe
F.1A	XM172	Preserved, gate guard, RAF Coltishall, Norfolk
F.1A	XM173	Preserved, RAF Bentley Priory, Greater London

F.53 53-686 of the Royal Saudi Air Force rolling on take-off with re-heat lit and carrying 1,000lb (450kg) practice bombs. *Aeroplane*

Mark	Serial	Notes
F.1A	XM174	Abandoned, 29.11.68, after fire in air, aircraft crashing into a quarry at Bulmullo, nr Leuchars, Flt Lt Edward Rawcliffe, Leuchars TFF, ejected safely
F.1A	XM175	First flown, 23.11.60
F.1A	XM176	First flown, 1.12.60
F.1A	XM177	First flown, 20.12.60
F.1A	XM178	Preserved with the *Assoc des Amis du Musee du Chateau*, Savingny-Les-Beaune, France
F.1A	XM179	Lost, 6.6.63, in mid-air collision with XM171, during practice formation aerobatics. Crashed Great Bricett near Wattisham. Flt Lt Mike Cooke, 56 Sqdn, seriously injured during ejection sequence
F.1A	XM180	First flown, 23.1.61
F.1A	XM181	First flown, 25.1.61
F.1A	XM182	First flown, 6.2.61
F.1A	XM183	First flown, 9.2.61
F.1A	XM184	Fire on landing, RAF Coltishall, 17.4.67. Flt Lt Gerry Crumbie, 226 OCU, safe
F.1A	XM185	Abandoned near Wattisham 6.3.61 after undercarriage failed to lower. Fg Off P. Ginger, 56 Squadron, ejected safely
F.1A	XM186	Lost, 18.7.63, over Wittering during aerobatic presentation. Flg Off Alan Garside, 111 Sqdn, killed
F.1A	XM187	Undercarriage collapsed at Wattisham, 24.4.61
F.1A	XM188	At RAF Coltishall, 21.6.68, Sqn Ldr Arthur Tilsley, 226 OTU, taxied in with no brakes and ran off taxiway before striking No.1 Hangar
F.1A	XM189	First flown, 30.3.61
F.1A	XM190	Abandoned, 15.3.66, after ECU fire. Crashed in North Sea off Cromer. Capt Al Peterson USAF, 226 OCU, Coltishall, ejected safely
F.1A	XM191	Crashed on landing at RAF Wattisham, 9.6.64, after in-flight fire. Flt Lt N. Smith, 111 Sqdn, uninjured. Nose section now used as a travelling exhibit with RAF Exhibition, Production and Transport Unit
F.1A	XM192	Preserved by Charles Ross at Binbrook, Lincolnshire
F.1A	XM213	Crashed, 6.5.66, at RAF Coltishall after aborted take-off. Sqn Ldr Paul Hobley, 226 OCU, uninjured. Cat 5
F.1A	XM214	First flown, 29.6.61
F.1A	XM215	First flown, 11.7.61
F.1A	XM216	To 111 Sqn, 29.8.61
F.1A	XM217	Cancelled
F.1A	XM218	Cancelled
T.4	XM966	Crashed in the Irish Sea, 22.7.65, after fin disintegrated at Mach 2. Jimmy L. Dell and Graham Elkington, English Electric, ejected safely
T.4	XM967	First flown, 30.3.62
T.4	XM968	Abandoned 24.2.77 near Gütersloh, Germany, after total hydraulic failure led to loss of control. Sqn Ldr M.J. Lawrance, 92 Sqn and Sqn Ldr Christopher Glanville-White, Harrier Squadron CO, ejected safely
T.4	XM969	First flown, 28.3.61
T.4	XM970	First flown, 5.5.61. First T.4 in RAF service
T.4	XM971	Abandoned 2.1.67, RAF Coltishall, after radome collapsed and debris entered air intake. Crashed Tunstead. Sqn Ldr Terry Carlton, 226 OCU, and Flt Lt Tony Gross, student, ejected and landed safely
T.4	XM972	First flown, 29.4.61
T.4	XM973	First flown, 17.5.61
T.4	XM974	Abandoned 14.12.72 near Happisburgh, 14.12.72 after ECU/re-heat fire. Crashed in North Sea. Sqn Ldr John Spencer and Flg Off Geoffrey Philip Evans, 226 OCU, ejected safely
T.4	XM987	First flown, 13.7.61
T.4	XM988	Abandoned 5.6.73 near Great Yarmouth after Wg Cdr Christopher Bruce, 74 Sqn, entered a spin followed by loss of control
T.4/T.54	XM989/54-650	Converted from T.4 for *Magic Carpet*. Re-serialled as 54-607 in 1967
T.4	XM990	Crashed, South Walsham, Norfolk, 19.9.70, after aileron control failure during Battle of Britain Air Show at Coltishall. Both Flt Lt John Leslie Sims and Flt Lt Alfred Brian Fuller, 226 OCU, ejected safely

Mark	Serial	Notes
T.4	XM991	Written off (Cat.5) after ground fire at Gütersloh, 6.75
T.4/T.54	XM992/54-651	Converted from T.4 for *Magic Carpet*. Re-serialled as 54-608 in 1967. Written-off at Khamis Mushayt, 26.10.70 after starter fire
T,4	XM993	Written-off after overunning runway at Middleton St. George, 12.12.62. Al Turley and student, Wg Cdr C.M. Gibbs, escaped before aircraft caught fire and burned out. LCS
T.4	XM994	First flown, 12.3.62. To 19 Sqn, 6.11.62
T.4	XM995	First flown, 25.1.62. To 92 Sqn, 29.11.62
T.4/T.5	XM996	First flown, 13.4.62. To OCU, 8.1.63
T.4/T.5	XM997	First flown, 22.5.62. To OCU M.St.G, 14.1.63
T.4	XN103–112	10 a/c, cancelled
F.2/F.3	XN724	First flown, 11.9.61. To Boscombe Down, 22.5.62. Converted to F.2A. To 19 Sqn
F.2	XN723	Abandoned 25.3.64 near Hucknall after in-flight fire. Crashed Keynham, nr. Leicester, Mr D. Witham, Rolls-Royce, ejected safely
F.2/F.3	XN725	First flown, 31.3.62. Converted to F.3 prototype
F.2/F.2A	XN726	First flown, 29.9.61. To CFE, Binbrook, 14.2.63. To 19 Sqn, 7.6.68. Cat. 4 damaged by lightning strike 1972. Nose section now with the Cockpit collection, Rayleigh, Essex
F.2/F.2A	XN727	First flown, 13.10.61. To 92 Sqn
F.2/F.2A	XN728	First flown, 26.10.61. To 92 Sqn, 1.4.63. Undercarriage collapsed, 3.4.68. Now derelict at the former A1 Commercials Yard, Balderton, Notts
F.2/F.52	XN729/52-659 RSAF	Delivered 9.5.67 (as replacement for XN796/52-657). Re-serialled as 52-612 in 1967. Crashed near Khamis Mushayt, 2.5.70
F.2/F.2A	XN730	First flown, 23.11.61. To 19 Sqn, 12.3.63. Later 92 Sqn. Now preserved, *Luftwaffenmuseum*, Uetersen, Germany
F.2	XN731	First flown, 8.1.62. Later served with 92 and 19 Sqns
F.2	XN732	First flown, 19.1.62. To 92 Sqn, 30.4.63
F.2/F.2A	XN733	First flown, 1.2.62
F.2	XN734/G27-239	Converted from F.2 for *Magic Carpet* but never sent to Middle East
F.2/F.2A	XN735	First flown, 23.2.62
F.2/F.52	XN767/52-655 RSAF	Converted from F.2 for *Magic Carpet*. Delivered 1966. Re-serialled as 52-609 in 1967
F.2	XN768	First flown, 14.3.62
F.2	XN769	Nose section with Russell Carpenter, Sidcup, Greater London
F.2/F.52	XN770/52-656 RSAF	Converted from F.2 for *Magic Carpet*. Delivered 1966. Re-serialled as 52-610 in 1967
F.2/F.2A	XN771	First flown, 29.8.62
F.2/F.2A	XN772	Abandoned, 28.1.71, near Diepholz, Germany after entering spin at 36,000ft. Flg Off Peter George Hitchcock, 92 Squadron, ejected
F.2/F.2A	XN773	First flown, 13.6.62
F.2/F.2A	XN774	First flown, 27.9.62
F.2/F.2A	XN775	First flown, 1.10.62
F.2/F.2A	XN776	Preserved, Museum of Flight, East Fortune, Lothian
F.2/F.2A	XN777	Damaged 21.12.62, Binbrook, when nose leg broke off after overshooting runway. Air Cdr Millington, CC AFDS, uninjured
F.2/F.2A	XN778	First flown, 9.11.62
F.2/F.2A	XN779	First flown, 20.11.62
F.2/F.2A	XN780	Destroyed in ground fire at Gütersloh, 29.9.75
F.2/F.2A	XN781	First flown, 12.12.62
F.2/F.2A	XN782	*Luftfahrtausstellung* in Hermeskill Museum, Germany
F.2/F.2A	XN783	First flown, 26.1.63
F.2/F.2A	XN784	Preserved, Air Classic, Mönchengladbach, Germany
F.2/F.2A	XN785	Crashed, 27.4.64, on approach to disused airfield at Hutton Cranswick, East Yorkshire following a problem during an in-flight refuelling. Flg Off George Davey, 92 Squadron, did not eject and was killed
F.2/F.2A	XN786	Destroyed in ground fire at Gütersloh, 4.8.76. 19 Squadron
F.2/F.2A	XN787	First flown, 15.2.63
F.2/F.2A	XN788	First flown, 25.2.53
F.2/F.2A	XN789	First flown, 11.3.63
F.2/F.2A	XN790	First flown, 20.3.63
F.2/F.2A	XN791	First flown, 4.4.63
F.2/F.2A	XN792	First flown, 19.4.63

Mark	Serial	Notes
F.2/F.2A	XN793	First flown, 1.5.63
F.2/F.2A	XN794	First flown, 16.5.63
F.2/F.2A	XN795	Nose section, Cockpit Collection, Rayleigh, Essex
F.2/F.52	XN796/52-657 RSAF	Converted from F.2 for *Magic Carpet*. Delivered 7.66. Crashed on take off from Mushayt, 20.9.66.
F.2/F.52	XN797/52-658 RSAF	Converted from F.2 for *Magic Carpet*. Delivered 1966. Re-serialled as 52-611 in 1967. Crashed whilst practising single engine approaches to Khamis Mushayt, 28.11.68. Maj Essa Ghimlas killed
F.2	XN798–808	11 aircraft, cancelled
F.3/F.6	XP693	G–FSIX. Barry Pover, Exeter, Devon
F.3	XP694	Scrapped, 4.88. Used as target, Otterburn ranges, Northumberland
F.3	XP695	First flight, 20.6.63. Last flight, 15.3.84. Airfield decoy, then scrapped, 9.87
F.3	XP696	First flown, 2.7.63
F.3/F.6	XP697	First flown, 18.7.63
F.3	XP698	In collision with XP747, 16.2.72, off Harwich. Flt Lt Patrick 'Chile' Cooper, 29 Squadron, killed
F.3	XP699	Abandoned 3.3.67, Wethersfield, Suffolk, after fuel-line failure/fire. Crashed near Finchingfield, Essex. Flt Lt Ian Fenton, 56 Squadron, ejected safely
F.3	XP700	Abandoned, 7.8.72, on take-off from RAF Wattisham after engine fire. Crashed Great Waldingfield, Suffolk. Flt Lt George Nicol Fenton, 29 Squadron, ejected
F.3	XP701	First flight, 14.9.63. Scrapped late 87. Nose section, Robertsbridge Aviation Society, Robertsbridge, East Sussex
F.3	XP702	First flight, 19.9.63. Last flight, 28.8.82. Stored, then scrapped, 4.88. Remains used as target, Otterburn ranges, Northumberland
F.3	XP703	Nose section, W/Off Mick Jennings, RAF Coltishall
F.3	XP704	Crashed 28.8.64 near Leuchars after spinning during practice aerobatic display. Flt Lt Phil Owen, 74 Sqdn, killed
F.3	XP705	Abandoned near Akrotiri, Cyprus, 8.7.71 after jet fire. Flt Lt Graham H. Clarke, 29 Squadron, ejected safely
F.3	XP706	First flight, 28.10.63. Last flight, 7.85. Preserved, Lincolnshire Lightning Preservation Society, Strubby, Lincolnshire
F.3	XP707	First flight, 13.11.63. Crashed, 19.3.87 near Binbrook, during practice aerobatics. LTF
F.3	XP708	Target, Pendine ranges, Dyfed
F.3	XP735	First flown, 4.12.63
F.3	XP736	Crashed into the sea 30m off Lowestoft, 22.9.71. Flg Off Phil Mottershead, 29 Squadron, killed
F.3	XP737	Ditched in Irish Sea off Valley, Wales, 17.8.79, after port undercarriage failed to lower. Flg Off Raymond T. Knowles, 5 Squadron, ejected safely
F.3	XP738	Written off (Cat.5) after wheels-up landing at RAF Wattisham, 10.12.73. 111 Squadron
F.3	XP739	Abandoned, 29.9.65, on approach to Wattisham after a double engine flame-out. Flt Lt Hedley Molland, 111 Squadron, ejected safely.
F.3	XP740	First flown, 1.2.64
F.3	XP741	First flight, 4.2.64. Last flight, 9.87. Delivered to Manston for fire training
F.3	XP742	Abandoned, 7.5.70, in North Sea off Great Yarmouth, Norfolk, after ECU fire. Flg Off Stuart Richard Tulloch, 111 Sqn, ejected safely
F.3	XP743	First flown, 18.2.64
F.3	XP744	Abandoned, 10.5.71, near Akrotiri, Cyprus, after zonal fire warning. Flt Lt Robert David Cole, 56 Squadron, ejected safely. Crashed 8m South-East of Akrotiri
F.3	XP745	Nose section, Vanguard Haulage, Greenford, Greater London
F.3	XP746	First flown, 26.3.64
F.3	XP747	In collision 16.2.72 with XP698 over North Sea. Flt Lt Paul Reynolds, 29 Squadron, ejected safely
F.3	XP748	First flight, 4.5.64. Last flight, 2.75.Stored for two years. Used as gate guardian until summer 1988. Target, Pendine ranges, Dyfed
F.3	XP749	First flight, 11.12.63. Last flight, 10.86. Scrapped 12.87
F.3	XP750	First flight, 3.1.64. Last flight, 11.84. Scrapped, 12.87
F.3	XP751	First flight, 16.3.64. Last flight, 10.86. Scrapped, 12.87

Mark	Serial	Notes
F.3	XP752	Collided with FAF Mirage IIIE near Colmar, France, 20.5.71. Flt Lt Tony Alcock, 111 Squadron, landed safely but aircraft written-off (Cat 5) due to damage
F.3	XP753	Crashed into the sea off Scarborough 26.8.83, during unauthorized aerobatics. Flt Lt Mike Thompson, LTF, killed
F.3	XP754	First flown, 5.6.64
F.3	XP755	First flown, 15.6.64
F.3	XP756	Abandoned, 25.1.71, after re-heat fire. Crashed off Great Yarmouth. Capt Bill Povilus, USAF attached to 29 Squadron, ejected safely
F.3	XP757	First flown, 4.7.64
F.3	XP758	First flown, 10.7.64
F.3	XP759	First flown, 14.8.64
F.3	XP760	Abandoned 24.8.66. ECU failure. Crashed North Sea 35nm off Seahouses, Fife. Flt Lt Al Turley, 23 Squadron, ejected safely
F.3	XP761	First flight, 3.11.64. Last flight, 14.10.74. Scrapped, 1.88
F.3	XP762	First flown, 3.9.64
F.3	XP763	First flown, 11.9.64
F.3	XP764	First flight, 19.9.64. Last flight, 10.86. Scrapped, 1.88
F.3	XP765	First flown, 26.9.64
F.3/F.6	XR711	Crashed on take-off at RAF Wattisham, 29.10.71. Flt Lt Eric Steenson, 111 Squadron, uninjured
F.3/F.6	XR712	Crashed, 26.6.65, near Padstow, Cornwall, after shedding pieces of tailpipe during Exeter Air Show. Flt Lt Tony Doyle, 111 Sqdn, ejected safely
F.3/F.6	XR713	First flight, 21.10.64. Last flight, 11.3.87. Preserved, RAF Leuchars,Fife. 111 Squadron
F.3/F.6	XR714	Crashed, 27.7.66, on runway at RAF Akrotiri, after being caught in jet blast during formation take-off. 111 Squadron
F.3/F.6	XR715	Abandoned, 13.2.74, after ECU fire forced Flt Lt Terence 'Taff' A. Butcher, 29 Squadron, to eject. Aircraft crashed at Watermill Farm, Mells, near Halesworth, Suffolk
F.3/F.6	XR716	First flight, 19.11.64. Last flight, 9.87. Fire training, RAF Cottesmore
F.3/F.6	XR717	First flown, 25.11.64
F.3/F.6	XR718	First flight, 14.12.64. Last flight, 2.2.87. Battle damage repair aircraft at Wattisham. Preserved, Blythe Valley Aviation Collection, Walpole, Suffolk

The formidable weapons load options available to the F.53. Two Firestreak or two Red Top, plus two 30mm Aden cannon with 130 rounds each (housed in the forward section of the ventral tank), forty-four 2in (51mm) spin-stabilized rockets in the fuselage forward weapon bay in place of missile pack and two 1,000lb (450kg) HE bombs. The rockets are housed within the fuselage in twin retractable launchers that automatically extended outwards and downwards in one second for firing and closed again after attack. The rockets were designed to fire with optimum dispersion for hitting the target. They fired in 'ripple' salvos whereby two were fired automatically every twenty-five milliseconds. Single 'ripple' salvos could be fired from first one and then the other launcher, or twin 'ripple' salvos could be fired from both launchers simultaneously. Each Matra Type 155 launcher (two proposed twins shown here) could carry eighteen 8mm SNEB 13½lb (6kg) rockets. BAC

Mark	Serial	Notes
F.3/F.6	XR719	First flown, 18.12.64. 56 Squadron 16.3.65–8.66. Used at Shoeburyness 9.8.66–1973. Declared Cat.5 after heavy landing at Coltishall, 5.6.73
F.3/F.6	XR720	First flight, 24.12.64. Last flight, 6.2.85. Scrapped, 1.88
F.3	XR721	Crashed, 5.1.66, in the garden of Elm Tree Farm Cottages on the B1079, Otley to Helmingham Road, near Woodbridge, Suffolk, after engine flame-out. Flg Off Derek Law, 56 Squadron, tried to eject but the canopy jammed and he was killed by ejection after a successful belly landing
F.3	XR722	Converted to F.53 (53-656 RSAF) and allocated to 2 Squadron RSAF. Crashed, 6.2.72, while on loan to 6 Squadron, RSAF. Capt Mohammed Saud uninjured
F.3	XR723	Converted to F.6. Abandoned, 18.9.79, near Akrotiri, Cyprus, after engine fire. Gp Capt Pete Carter, Station CO, ejected safely. Crashed 15m south of Akrotiri
F.3/F.6	XR724	First flight, 10.2.65. Last flight, 29.7.92. G-BTSY. Preserved, Lightning Association, Binbrook Airfield, Lincolnshire
F.3/F.6	XR725	First flight, 19.2.65. Last flight, 17.12.87. Preserved, Charles Ross, Chestnut Farm, Binbrook, Lincolnshire
F.3/F.6	XR726	First flight, 26.2.65 Last flight, 24.8.87. Scrapped. Nose section, private collector, Harrogate, North Yorks
F.3/F.6	XR727	First flight, 8.3.65. Last flight, 10.5.88. Flown to RAF Wildenrath
F.3/F.6	XR728	First flight, 17.3.65. Last flight, 24.6.88. Preserved, Lightning Preservation Group, Bruntingthorpe, Leicestershire
F.3/F.6	XR747	First flight, 2.4.65. Last flight, 14.8.87. Nose section, Barry Plover, Plymouth, Devon
F.3	XR748	Abandoned 24.6.74 near Coltishall after total hydraulic failure. Crashed in North Sea off Great Yarmouth. Flg Off Kevin Mason, 111 Squadron, ejected
F.3/F.6	XR749	First flight, 30.4.65. Last flight, 9.82. Preserved, Ken Ward, Teeside Airport, Durham
F.3/F.6	XR750	First flown, 10.5.65
F.3/F.6	XR751	Preserved, Roy Flood, Lower Tremar, Cornwall
F.3A/F.6	XR752	First flight, 16.6.65. Last flight, 8.1.86. Suffered in-flight fire and was finally scrapped, 9.87
F.3A/F.6	XR753	First flight, 23.6.65. Last flight, 24.5.88. Preserved, 11 Squadron, RAF Leeming, North Yorks
F.3A/F.6	XR754	First flight, 8.7.65. Last flight, 24.6.88. Delivered to RAF Honington as battle damage repair airframe, scrapped 1992. Nose section preserved, Blythe Valley Aviation Collection, Walpole, Suffolk
F.3A/F.6	XR755	First flight, 15.7.65. Last flight, 12.87. Preserved, Ernie Marshall, private collector, Callington, Cornwall
F.3A/F.6	XR756	First flight, 11.8.65. Last flight, 12.87
F.3A/F.6	XR757	First flight, 19.8.65. Last flight, 12.87. Nose section, NATO Aircraft Museum, New Waltham, Lincolnshire
F.3A/F.6	XR758	First flight, 30.8.65. Last flight, 12.5.88. Used at RAF Laarbruch as battle damage repair airframe
F.3A/F.6	XR759	First flight, 9.9.65. Last flight, 29.9.87. Scrapped. Nose section, Andrew Eaton, Haxey, Lincolnshire
F.3A/F.6	XR760	Abandoned, 15.7.86 near Whitby after rear fuselage fire. Crashed in North Sea 7m north of Whitby. Bob Bees, 11 Squadron, ejected safely
F.3A/F.6	XR761	Abandoned, 8.11.84 over North Sea after pitch trim failure followed by re-heat fire. Crashed North Sea, 8m north of Spurn Head. Flt Lt Mike D. Hale, 5 Squadron, ejected safely
F.3A/F.6	XR762	Crashed into the sea off Akrotiri, Cyprus, 14.4.75, after Sqn Ldr Hampton, 11 Squadron, misjudged height above sea during tail chase. Pilot killed
F.3A/F.6	XR763	First flight, 15.10.65. Abandoned 1.7.87 near Akrotiri, Cyprus, during APC, after double engine flame-out following ingestion of part of the target banner. Flt Lt D.K.M. 'Charlie' Chan, 5 Squadron, ejected safely
F.3A/F.6	XR764	Abandoned 30.9.71 near Akrotiri, Cyprus after jet pipe fire. Crashed into Limasol Bay, south-east of Akrotiri. Flt Lt Richard Arthur Bealer, 56 Squadron, ejected safely
F.3A/F.6	XR765	Abandoned, 23.7.81 over North Sea after double re-heat fire. Crashed into the North Sea, 50m North East of Binbrook. Flt Lt J.G. Wild, 5 Squadron, ejected safely
F.3A/F.6	XR766	Abandoned 7.9.67 near Leuchars after uncontrollable spin. Crashed in North Sea, 20m east of Montrose. Sqn Ldr Ron Blackburn, 23 Squadron, ejected safely

Mark	Serial	Notes
F.3A/F.6	XR767	Lost, at night, 26.5.70, in the Straits of Malacca off Tengah, Singapore after Flt Lt John C. Webster of 74 Squadron became disorientated. Pilot killed
F.6	XR768	Abandoned, 29.10.74, near Saltfleet, Lincolnshire after possible double re-heat fire. Crashed, North Sea, 3m off Mablethorpe. Flt Lt T.W. Jones, 5 Sqdn, ejected safely
F.6	XR769	First flight, 1.12.65. Abandoned over the sea, 11.4.88, near Easington, Lincolnshire, after engine fire. Crashed 10m east of Spurn Head. Flt Lt Dick Coleman RAAF, attached to 11 Sqn, ejected safely
F.6	XR770	First flight, 16.12.65. Last flight, 4.88. Nose section, NATO Aircraft Museum, New Waltham, Lincolnshire
F.6	XR771	First flight, 20.1.66. Last flight, 4.88. Preserved, Midlands Air Museum, Coventry, Warwickshire
F.6	XR772	Abandoned, 6.3.85, off Spurn Head after possible structural failure. Crashed in North Sea, 20m north-east of Skegness. Martin 'Tetley' Ramsey, 5 Squadron, ejected safely
F.6	XR773	First flight, 28.2.66. Last flight, 23.12.92. G-OPIB. Lightning Flying Club, Barry Pover, Exeter, Devon
F.3	XR774/795	Twenty-two aircraft cancelled
T.5	XS416	First flight, 20.8.64. Last flight, 21.12.87. Preserved, NATO Aircraft Museum, New Waltham, Lincolnshire
T.5	XS417	First flight, 17.7.64. Last flight, 18.5.87. Preserved, Newark Air Museum, Winthorpe, Nottinghamshire
T.5	XS418	First flight, 18.12.64. Crashed, 23.8.68, while landing at Stradishall, when undercarriage retracted on landing. Flt Lt Henry Ploszek and SAC Lewis were uninjured. Last flight, 9.74. Used as surface decoy until scrapped, 9.87
T.5	XS419	First flight, 18.12.64. Last flight, 27.2.87. Scrapped 7.93
T.5	XS420	First flight, 23.1.65. Crashed on night take-off from Coltishall, July 1973. Capt Gary Catren, Instructor, and Flg Off George Smith, uninjured. Last flight, 5.83. Preserved, Fenland and West Norfolk Aviation Museum, Wisbech, Cambridgeshire
T.5	XS421	Nose section, Cockpit Collection, Rayleigh, Essex
T.5	XS422	Stored, Southampton area, Wensley Haydon-Baillie
T.5	XS423	First flight, 31.5.65. Last flight, 1974. Used as airfield decoy. Scrapped, 9.87
T.5	XS449	First flight, 30.4.65. Last flight, 9.74. 87. Used as airfield decoy. Scrapped, 9.87
T.5	XS450	First flight, 25.5.65. Last flight, 1.75. Scrapped, 9.87
T.5	XS451	G-LTNG. Barry Pover, Plymouth Devon
T.5	XS452	First flight, 30.6.65 Last flight, 30.6.88. Airworthy, for Mike Beachey-Head, South Africa
T.5	XS453	Abandoned 1.6.66 near Happisburgh, Norfolk, after hydraulics failure. Crashed into North Sea. 226 OCU. Flg Off Geoff Fish, on his first T-5 solo, ejected safely
T.5	XS454	First flight, 6.7.65. Cat. 3 damage, 7.3.67, when main undercarriage collapsed on Coltishall runway. Flt Lts Mike Graydon and Bob Offord unhurt. Last flight, 6.75. Used as decoy until 9.87. Scrapped
T.5	XS455	Abandoned near Spurn Head, 6.9.72, after hydraulic failure caused loss of control. Crashed in North Sea off Withensea. Sqn Ldr T.J.L. Gauvain, 226 OCU, and Lt R. Verbist, Belgian Air Force, both ejected, both injured
T.5	XS456	First flight, 26.10.65. Last flight, 1.87. Gate guardian, Elms Golf Centre, Wainfleet, Lincolnshire
T.5	XS457	First flight, 8.11.65. Written-off after undercarriage collapsed at Binbrook, 9.12.83. 5 Squadron. Nose section on display at NATO Aircraft Museum, New Waltham, Lincolnshire
T.5	XS458	First flight, 3.12.65. Last flight, 30.6.88. Preserved, Tony Hulls, Cranfield, Bedfordshire
T.5	XS459	First flight, 22.12.66. Crashed on approach to Binbrook, 21.3.81. LTF. Last flight, 15.3.87. Now at Fenland and W. Norfolk Aviation Museum, Wisbech, Cambridgeshire
T.5/T.55	XS460/55-710 for RSAF	Written-off in cross-wind landing accident at Warton, 7.3.67. Jimmy Dell and P. Williams, BAC, unhurt
T.5	XS851/855	Five aircraft cancelled
F.6	XS893	Ditched in sea off Tengah, Singapore, 12.8.70, when port undercarriage failed to lower. Flg Off Mike Rigg, 74 Squadron, ejected safely
F.6	XS894	Crashed in the sea 5m off Flamborough Head, 8.9.70. Major W.B. Schaffner, USAF attached to 5 Squadron, killed

177

Mark	Serial	Notes
F.6	XS895	First flight, 6.4.66. Last flight, 12.87. Scrapped. Used at Pendine ranges, Dyfed, as a target
F.6	XS896	Crashed on approach to Tengah, Singapore, 12.9.68, after fire in rear fuselage. Flg Off P.F. Thompson, 74 Squadron, killed
F.6	XS897	First flight, 10.5.66. To 74 Squadron, 21.12.66. Flown to 56 Squadron by Flt Lt Roger Pope, 4–6.9.71. Last flight, 14.12.87. Preserved, South Yorks Aviation Museum, Firbeck, South Yorkshire
F.6	XS898	First flight, 20.5.66. Last flight, 30.6.88. Scrapped at Cranfield, 12.94. Nose section, Tony Collins, Lavendon, Buckinghamshire
F.6	XS899	First flight, 8.6.66. Last flight, 30.6.88. Scrapped at Cranfield, 12.94. Nose section preserved by W/Off Mick Jennings, RAF Coltishall
F.6	XS900	Abandoned, 24.1.68 after take-off from Lossiemouth when controls were jammed by FOD caused by total loss of power. Flt Lt Stuart Miller, 5 Squadron, ejected safely
F.6	XS901	First flight, 1.7.66. Last flight, 12.5.88. Delivered to RAF Brüggen as battle damage repair airframe
F.6	XS902	Abandoned near Grimsby, 26.5.71 after re-heat fire. Crashed 9m east of Spurn Head. Flt Lt Alastair MacKay RCAF, attached to 5 Squadron, ejected safely
F.6	XS903	First flight, 17.8.66. Last flight, 10.5.88. Preserved, Yorkshire Air Museum, Elvington, North Yorkshire
F.6	XS904	First flight, 26.8.66. Last Lightning to fly. Preserved, Lightning Preservation Group, Bruntingthorpe, Leicestershire
F.6	XS918	Abandoned over the sea off Leuchars 4.3.70 after jet pipe fire. Crashed Firth of Forth. Flg Off Anthony David Doidge, 11 Squadron, ejected and was killed
F.6	XS919	First flight, 28.9.66. Last flight, 15.3.88. Dismantled in yard at Torpoint Shipping Co. Ltd, Torpoint, Devon
F.6	XS920	Crashed, 13.7.84 near Heuslingen, Germany, after hitting power cables during ACM. Flt Lt Frost, 5 Squadron, killed
F.6	XS921	Crashed 30m off Flamborough Head, 19.9.85, after uncontrolled spin
F.6	XS922	First flight, 6.12.66. Last flight, 14.6.88. Delivered to RAF Wattisham as battle damage aircraft, then scrapped. Nose section, Air Defence College, Salisbury, Wiltshire
F.6	XS923	First flight, 13.12.66. Last flight, 30.6.88. Scrapped at Cranfield 12.94. Nose section with Sue and Roy German, Welshpool, Powys
F.6	XS924	Stalled in stream turbulence during formation take-off for the RAF 50th Anniversary Display and crashed at Beelsby, near Binbrook, 29.4.68. Flt Lt Al Davey, 5 Squadron, killed
F.6	XS925	First flight, 28.2.67. Last flight, 9.87. Preserved (XS8961M) RAF Museum, Hendon
F6	XS926	Abandoned over North Sea, 22.9.69, after spinning during ACT. Crashed 51m E of Flamborough Head. Major Charles B. Neel USAF, attached to 5 Squadron, ejected safely
F.6	XS927	First flight, 15.2.67. Last flight, 10.86. Scrapped, by 3.88
F.6	XS928	First flight, 28.2.67. Last flight, 8.92. Gate guardian, BAe Warton, Lancashire
F.6	XS929	First flight, 1.3.67. Last flight, 20.5.88. Gate guardian, RAF Akrotiri, Cyprus
F.6	XS930	Crashed, 27.7.70, into Malay village following take-off from Tengah, Singapore, after Flt Lt Frank Whitehouse, 74 Squadron, climbed too steeply after take-off. Pilot killed. 100 buildings destroyed and two villagers injured
F.6	XS931	Abandoned 25.5.79 near Flamborough Head after control restriction after take-off caused by FOD. Crashed off Hornsea. Flg Off Pete Coker, 5 Squadron, ejected
F.6	XS932	First flight, 9.4.67. Last flight, 10.86. Nose section, Lightning Preservation Group, Bruntingthorpe, Leicestershire
F.6	XS933	First flight, 27.4.67. Last flight, 10.86. Nose section, Terrington Aviation Collection, Terrington St. Clement, Norfolk
F.6	SX934	Abandoned near Akrotiri, Cyprus, 3.4.73, after ECU fire. Flt Lt Frederick A. Greer, 56 Squadron, ejected safely
F.6	XS935	First flight, 29.5.67. Last flight, 9.87. Scrapped
F.6	XS936	First flight, 31.5.67. Last flight, 10.87. Preserved, Castle Motors, Liskeard, Cornwall
F.6	XS937	Ditched off Flamborough Head, 30.7.76, after undercarriage failure. Flg Off Simon C.C. 'Much' Manning, X11 Squadron, ejected safely

Mark	Serial	Notes
F.6	XS938	Abandoned, 28.4.71, near Leuchars after re-heat fire during take-off. Crashed into River Tay, Fife. Flg Off Alastair Cameron MacLean, 23 Squadron, ejected safely
F.6		Twelve aircraft cancelled
T.5	XV328	Cockpit section, Phoenix Aviation, Bruntingthorpe, Leicestershire
T.5	XV329	Sent by sea to Singapore from Sydenham, Belfast, June 1967, when 74 Squadron deployed to Tengah from Leuchars. Returned by sea to the UK, August 1971, and had to be written-off in December when it was discovered that acid spillage from the batteries had corroded the airframe
F.52	52-655 RSAF	(see XN767) to 52-609. Converted from F.2 for *Magic Carpet*. On display, Technical Services Institute, Dhahran
F.52	52-656 RSAF	(see XN770) to 52-610. Converted from F.2 for *Magic Carpet*. Stored for display, Riyadh
F.52	52-657 RSAF	(see XN796) Converted from F.2 for *Magic Carpet*. Written-off after excessive rotation at low speed 20.9.66. Pilot unhurt
F.52	52-658 RSAF	(see XN797) Converted from F.2 for *Magic Carpet*. Re-serialled as 52-611 in 1967. Crashed whilst practising single engine approaches to Khamis Mushayt, 29.11.68, inbound to Khamis. Maj Essa Ghimlas killed
F.52	52-659 RSAF	(see XN729) Converted from F.2 for *Magic Carpet*. To 52-612. Crashed, Khamis Mushayt, 2.5.70 after hydraulic failure
F.53	53-412 KAF G-27-80.	'C' Displayed, Kuwait International Airport
F.53	53-413 KAF G-27-81	
F.53	53-414 KAF G-27-82	Crashed, 10.4.71, after fire. Pilot Razzack died en route to hospital
F.53	53-415 KAF G-27-83	'H' Displayed on pole in vic formation, Al Jaber AFB
F.53	53-416 KAF G-27-84	'J' Displayed on pole in vic formation, Al Jaber AFB
F.53	53-417 KAF G-27-85	'K' Displayed on pole in vic formation, Al Jaber AFB

F.1 XM139 of the Wattisham TFF. On top of the wing is one of the ammunition tanks (the F.1 had a pair of 30mm Adens in the cheek positions behind the panel to the rear of the two red triangles, called 'elephant ears'). In the TFF rôle these were not fitted but the tanks were filled with ballast to compensate and maintain the aircraft trim. The black trolley on the left is an oxygen trolley (the F.1 and F.1A had a gaseous oxygen system). The badge on the fin is the later Wattisham TFF badge, a stylized rear view of a cat with its tail raised and its whiskers the horizontal points at the side. This badge was chosen by TFF pilots because that is what they showed the intercepting pilots – their backside! The cat's tail represented the fins and the whiskers, wings and tailplane. A puckered orifice was painted beneath the tail, in place of the No.2 jet pipe (No.2 was left off). Pete Nash

Mark	Serial	Notes
F.53	53-418 KAF G-27-86	Derelict, Al Salem
F.53	53-419 KAF G-27-87	Crashed, 2.8.71, on take-off from Rezayat. Lt. Nasser unhurt
F.53	53-420 KAF G-27-88	'N' Displayed at Kuwait Technology Institute
F.53	53-421 KAF G-27-89	'O' Presented to Air Museum, Kuwait International Airport
F.53	53-422 KAF G-27-90	'P' Badly damaged at Messila Beach and dumped at Ali El Salem AFB
F.53	53-423 KAF G-27-91	'R' gate guardian at Ali El Salem AFB
F.53	53-666 RSAF G-27-2	Lost, 6.2.72. Details unknown
F.53	53-667 RSAF G-27-37	Crashed, 3.9.85, 28m north of Tabuk. Double re-heat fire
F.53	53-668 RSAF G-27-38 ZF577	Portsmouth Marine Salvage (ex-Haydon-Baillie Collection)
F.53	53-669 RSAF G-27-39	Crashed, 21.4.79, near Tabuk after running out of fuel
F.53	53-670 RSAF G-27-40 ZF578	Ex-Wales Air Museum, Cardiff Airport, exhibit
F.53	53-671 RSAF G-27-41 ZF579	Portsmouth Marine Salvage (ex-Haydon-Baillie Collection)
F.53	53-672 RSAF G-27-42 ZF580	Gate guardian, BAe Samlesbury Airfield
F.53	53-673 RSAF G-27-43	Crashed, 22.9.80, Khamis Mushayt after colliding with 53-680
F.53	53-674 RSAF G-27-44	Crashed off coast of Bahrain, 28.9.72. Pilot, Abdul Jussef, killed
F.53	53-675 RSAF G-27-45 ZF581	Portsmouth Marine Salvage (ex-Haydon-Baillie Collection)
F.53	53-676 RSAF G-27-46 ZF582	Portsmouth Marine Salvage (ex-Haydon-Baillie Collection)
F.53	53-677 RSAF	Crashed at night, 4.9.83
F.53	53-677 RSAF G-27-47	Crashed at night, 4.9.83. Written-off
F.53	53-678 RSAF G-27-48	Crashed near Tabuk, 21.4.79, during sandstorm after running out of fuel
F.53	53-679 RSAF G-27-49 ZF590	Portsmouth Marine Salvage (ex-Haydon-Baillie Collection)
F.53	53-680 RSAF G-27-50	Crashed, 22.9.80, Khamis Mushayt after colliding with 53-673
F.53	53-681 RSAF G-27-51 ZF583	Solway Aviation Soc., Carlisle Airport, Cumbria
F.53	53-682 RSAF G-27-52 ZF584	Gate guard, GEC-Marconi Ltd, South Gyles Works, Edinburgh
F.53	53-683 RSAF G-27-53 ZF585	Portsmouth Marine Salvage (ex-Haydon-Baillie Collection)
F.53	53-684 RSAF G-27-54	Crashed on take-off from Dhahran, 30.6.80
F.53	53-685 RSAF G-27-55 ZF591	Portsmouth Marine Salvage (ex-Hadon-Baillie Collection)
F.53	53-686 RSAF G-27-56 ZF592	Portsmouth Marine Salvage (ex-Haydon-Baillie Collection)
F.53	53-687 RSAF G-27-57	On display, Khamis Mushayt
F.53	53-688 RSAF G-27-58 ZF586	Crashed Tabuk, 27.7.84. Portsmouth Marine Salvage (ex-Haydon-Baillie Collection)
F.53	53-689 RSAF G-27-59	
F.53	53-690 RSAF G-27-60	Crashed, 4.9.68, Stakepool, Pilling, 12m north of Warton, after total control failure. John Cockburn, BAC, ejected safely
F.53	53-691 RSAF G-27-61 ZF587	Portsmouth Marine Salvage (ex-Haydon-Baillie Collection)
F.53	53-692 RSAF G-27-62 ZF593	Robins AFB, Highway 247, near Macon, Ga. USA
F.53	53-693 RSAF G-27-63 ZF588	Midlands Aeropark, Castle Donnington Airport
F.53	53-694 RSAF G-27-64	Crashed, 11.9.76, 40m north of Khamis Mushayt after spin
F.53	53-695 RSAF G-27-65	Crashed 55m South East of Tabuk, 28.9.81, on training sortie
F.53	53-696 RSAF G-27-66 ZF594	North East Air Museum, Usworth, Sunderland, Tyne & Wear
F.53	53-697 RSAF G-27-67	Crashed, 3.5.70, near Yemeni border during reconnaissance sortie after being hit by ground fire. Pilot ejected
F.53	53-698 RSAF G-27-68	
F.53	53-699 RSAF G-27-69	On display, Tabuk
F.53	53-700* RSAF G-27-233 ZF589	Portsmouth Marine Salvage (ex-Haydon -Baillie Collection)
T.54	54-650 RSAF M989	First flown, 30.8.61. On display, Dhahran
T.54	54-651 RSAF XM992	First flown, 13.12.61
T.55	55-410 KAF G-27-78	First flown, 24.5.68
T.55	55-411 KAF G-27-79	First flown, 3.4.69
T.55	55-710	Crashed landing at Warton, 7.3.67, in strong crosswind. BAC
T.55	55-711 RSAF G-27-70 ZF597	Damaged, 13.3.71, Portsmouth Marine Salvage (ex-Haydon-Baillie Collection)
T.55	55-712 RSAF G-27-71	Crashed, 21.5.74, into Half Moon Bay after inverted low-level pass over sand dunes. Col Ainousa and Lt Otaibi killed
T.55	55-713 RSAF G-27-72 ZF598	Midland Air Museum, Coventry Airport
T.55	55-714 RSAF G-27-73 ZF595	Portsmouth Marine Salvage (ex-Haydon-Baillie Collection)
T.55	55-715 RSAF G-27-74 ZF596	Portsmouth Marine Salvage (ex-Haydon-Baillie Collection)
T.55	55-716 RSAF G-27-75	First flown, 14.7.69. Scrapped, 1985

*Last Lightning built

RAF/RSAF/KAF Transfers

RAF Registration	Model	RSAF Registration	RAF Registration	Model	RSAF Registration
Aircraft Transferred from the RAF to the RSAF					
XM989	T.54	54-650 RSAF	XM992	T.54	54-651 RSAF
XN729	F.52	52-612/52-659 RSAF	XN734 G-27-239	F.3A	
XN767	F.52	52-609/52-655 RSAF	XN770	F.52	52-610/52-656 RSAF
XN796	F.52	52-657/52-657 RSAF	XN797	F.52	52-611/52-658 RSAF
Aircraft Transferred from the RSAF to the RAF					
ZF577 G-27-38	F.53	53-668 RSAF	ZF578 G-27-40	F.53	53-670 RSAF
ZF579 G-27-41	F.53	53-671 RSAF	ZF580 G-27-42	F.53	53-672 RSAF
ZF581 G-27-45	F.53	53-675 RSAF	ZF582 G-27-46	F.53	53-676 RSAF
ZF583 G-27-51	F.53	53-681 RSAF	ZF584 G-27-52	F.53	53-682 RSAF
ZF585 G-27-53	F.53	53-683 RSAF	ZF586 G-27-58	T.55	53-688 RSAF
ZF587 G-27-61	F.53	53-691 RSAF	ZF588 G-27-63	F.53	53-693 RSAF
ZF589 G-27-233	F.53	53-700 RSAF	ZF590 G-27-49	F.53	53-679 RSAF
ZF591 G-27-55	F.53	53-685 RSAF	ZF592 G-27-56	F.53	53-686 RSAF
ZF593 G-27-62	F.53	53-692 RSAF	ZF594 G-27-66	F.53	53-696 RSAF
ZF595 G-27-73	T.55	55-714 RSAF	ZF596 G-27-74	T.55	55-715 RSAF
ZF597 G-27-70	T.55	55-711 RSAF	ZF598 G-27-72	T.55	55-713 RSAF

Civilian Registrations

G-AWON	F.53	53-686 RSAF	G-A	F.53	53-687 RSAF
G-A	F.53	KAF	G-B	F.3A	XN734
G-B	F.6	XR724	G-FSIX	F.3	XP693

Maintenance Codes

	Model	RAF Registration		Model	RAF Registration
7755M	P.1A	WG760	7816M	P.1A	WG763
8050M	P.1B	XG329	7854M	F.1A	XM191
8056M	P.1B	XG337	8188M	P.1B	XG327
8346M	F.3A	XN734	8371M	P.1B	XA847
8402M	F.2	XN769	8411M	F.1	XM139
8412M	F.1	XM147	8413M	F.1A	XM192
8414M	F.1A	XM173	8415M	F.1A	XM181
8416M	F.1A	XM183	8417M	F.1	XM144
8418M	F.1A	XM178	8422M	F.1A	XM169
8427M	F.1A	XM172	8438M	F.3	XP761
8496M	F.2	XN730	8513M	F.2	XN724
8539M	F.2	XN782	8540M	F.2	SN784
8546M	F.2	XN728	8551M	F.2	XN774
8590M	F.1A	XM191	8592M	T.4	XM969
8924M	F.3	XP701	8935M	F.3	XR713
8940M	F.3	XR716	8972M	F.6	XR754
8973M	F.6	XS922			

Class B Markings

	Mark	RSAF/KAF Registration	RAF Registration		Mark	RSAF/KAF Registration	RAF Registration
G-27-2	F.53	53-666 RSAF		G-27-37	F.53	53-667 RSAF	
G-27-38	F.53	53-668 RSAF	ZF577	G-27-39	F.53	53-669 RSAF	
G-27-40	F.53	53-670 RSAF	ZF578	G-27-41	F.53	53-671 RSAF	ZF579
G-27-42	F.53	53-672 RSAF	ZF580	G-27-43	F.53	53-673 RSAF	
G-27-44	F.53	53-674 RSAF		G-27-45	F.53	53-675 RSAF	ZF581
G-27-46	F.53	53-676 RSAF	ZF582	G-27-47	F.53	53-677 RSAF	
G-27-48	F.53	53-678 RSAF		G-27-49	F.53	53-679 RSAF	7F590
G-27-50	F.53	53-680 RSAF		G-27-51	F.53	53-681 RSAF	ZF583
G-27-52	F.53	53-682 RSAF	ZF584	G-27-53	F.53	53-683 RSAF	ZF585
G-27-54	F.53	53-684 RSAF		G-27-55	F.53	53-685 RSAF	ZF591
G-27-56	F.53	53-686 RSAF	ZF592	G-27-57	F.53	53-687 RSAF	
G-27-58	F.53	53-688 RSAF	ZF586	G-27-59	F.53	53-689 RSAF	
G-27-60	F.53	53-690 RSAF		G-27-61	F.53	53-691 RSAF	ZF587
G-27-62	F.53	53-692 RSAF	ZF593	G-27-63	F.53	53-693 RSAF	ZF588
G-27-64	F.53	53-694 RSAF		G-27-65	F.53	53-695 RSAF	
G-27-66	F.53	53-696 RSAF	ZF594	G-27-67	F.53	53-697 RSAF	
G-27-68	F.53	53-698 RSAF		G-27-69	F.53	53-699 RSAF	
G-27-70	T.55	55-711 RSAF	ZF597	G-27-71	T.55	55-712 RSAF	
G-27-72	T.55	55-713 RSAF	ZF598	G-27-73	T.55	55-714 RSAF	ZF595
G-27-74	T.55	55-715 RSAF	ZF596	G-27-75	T.55	55-716 RSAF	
G-27-78	T.55	55-410 KAF		G-27-79	T.55	55-411 KAF	
G-27-80	F.53	53-412 KAF		G-27-81	F.53	53-413 KAF	
G-27-82	F.53	53-414 KAF		G-27-83	F.53	53-415 KAF	
G-27-84	F.53	53-416 KAF		G-27-85	F.53	53-417 KAF	
G-27-86	F.53	53-418 KAF		G-27-87	F.53	53-419 KAF	
G-27-88	F.53	53-420 KAF		G-27-89	F.53	53-421 KAF	
G-27-90	F.53	53-422 KAF		G-27-91	F.53	53-423 KAF	
G-27-233			ZF589				

F.3 XP757/M of 29 Squadron formates on Chipmunk T.10 WD289. Apocryphal it may be, but it is said that 29 Squadron's three 'X's are a result of the originator being told to paint two 'X's followed by 'one X' (it should of course have been 'IX'!). RAF Wattisham

Glossary

ADEX	Air Defence Exercise
AFCS	Automatic Flight Control System
AFDS	Air Fighting Development Squadren
AI 23B	Airborne Intercept Radar
Air Cdre	Air Commodore
AGL	Above Ground Level
APC	Armament Practice Camp
ASI	Airspeed Indicator
ASR	Air Sea Rescue
ATC	Air Traffic Controller/Control
AVM	Air Vice Marshal
AVPIN	isopropylnitrate (starter fuel)
BAC	British Aircraft Corporation
'Badger'	Soviet Tupolev Tu–16 bomber
'Bear'	Soviet Tupolev Tu–20(95) bomber
'Brackets'	inflight refuelling
Categories (of military accidents)	Cat 3: The aircraft damage is considered to be beyond unit resources but may be repairable on site by a Service working party or a contractor's working party. Cat 4: The aircraft is considered to need special facilities or equipment for repair which is not available on site. Cat 5: The aircraft is considered to be damaged beyond economical repair.
CGI	Chief Ground Instructor
Chief Tech	Chief Technician
C-in-C	Commander-in-Chief
CFI	Chief Flying Instructor
CI	Chief Instructor
'cobblestones'	buffeting caused by compressibility
dive circle	Recovery area centered on a point 18nm from the airfield, on the extended centreline of the duty runway. Its radius in nm equated to approximately the altitude of the aircraft in thousands of feet (where the pilot would descend from 36,000ft to 3,000ft)
DOCFW	Deputy Officer Commanding Flying Wing
ECU	Engine Control Unit
Firestreak	air-to-air heat-seeking missile
Flt Lt	Flight Lieutenant
Flg Off	Flying Officer
F-100	USAF Super Sabre fighter aircraft
g	acceleration of free fall due to gravity
GCI	Ground Controlled Interception
GCA	Ground Controlled Approach
Gp Capt	Group Captain
HE	High Explosive

IAS	Indicated Air Speed
IIFIS	Interim Integrated Flight Instrument System
ILS	Instrument Landing System approach aid
IWI	Interceptor Weapons Instructor
JPT	Jet Pipe Temperature
KAF	Kuwait Air Force
KC–50	Boeing in-flight refuelling aircraft
knot	unit of speed of 1nm (about 1.15 statute miles or 1.85km) per hour
LAC	Leading Aircraftsman
LOX	liquid oxygen
'linies'	flight line crewmen
LCU	Lightning Conversion Unit
LCS	Lightning Conversion Squadron
Mach	System of speed measurement using the Mach number devised by Ernst Mach, an Austrian physicist (1838–1916). Mach 1.0 is speed of sound, about 760mph (1223km/h) at sea level and 660mph (1062km/h) at altitude
Magic Carpet	first delivery of Lightnings to RSAF, in 1966
Magic Palm	second phase of the delivery programme to RSAF begun in 1968.
MPC	Missile Practice Camp
MU	Maintenance Unit
NATO	North Atlantic Treaty Organisation
nm	nautical miles
OC	Officer Commanding
OCU	Operational Conversion Unit
ORP	Operational Readiness Platform
OPs	operations
'overburgers'	overwing fuel tanks
'overcook'	apply too much power
PI	Practice Intercept
'plumbers'	armourers
'prod'	air-to-air refuelling using a probe and drogue
PSP	Personal Survival Pack
QFI	Qualified Flying Instructor
QRA	Quick Reaction Alert
QWI	Qualified Weapons Instructor
Rad-ex	radar exercise
RSAF	Royal Saudi Air Force
RCDI	Rate of Climb & Descent Indicator
Red Top	air-to-air heat-seeking missile
reheat	to add fuel to the exhaust gases of a jet engine to generate extra thrust
Riggers	airframe mechanics
RPMs	Revolutions Per Minute

R/T	radio telegraphy	TANKEX	In-flight refuelling exercise
SAC (RAF)	Senior Aircraftsman	Ten Ton Club	members belonging to the 1,000 mph Club
SAC (USAF)	Strategic Air Command	TFF	Target Facility Flight
SACEUR	Supreme Allied Commander Europe	TFW	Tactical Fighter Wing
SAR	Search and Rescue	TMN	True Mach Number
SATCO	Senior Air Traffic Control Officer	'trappers'	Examining Team of instructors
'sooties'	engine fitters	tropopause	The height at which the stratosphere begins. It varies with latitude and season but can be taken as approximately 36,000ft above which the temperature remains constant.
SOC	struck off charge		
SOP	Standard Operating Procedure		
SPH	seat pan handle		
Sqn Ldr	Squadron Leader	USAF	United States Air Force
TACAN	Tactical Air Navigation	Wg Cdr	Wing Commander
TACEVAL	Tactical Evaluation		

Bibliography

BAC Lightning, Arthur Reed (Ian Allan, 1980)
British Military Aircraft Accidents. The Last 25 Years, David Oliver (Ian Allan, 1990)
EE/BAC Lightning, Bryan Philpott (PSL, 1984)
EE/BAC Lightning, Bruce Barrymore Halpenny (Osprey, 1984)
English Electric P1 Lightning, Roland Beamont (Ian Allan, 1985)
The Lightning Conversion Units 1960–1987. Compiled by Sqn Ldr Gordon Moulds MBE RAF (Prospect Litho, 1993)
The History and Development of Martin-Baker Escape Systems (Martin-Baker, 1978)
Lightning Review July 1991–July 1996. Edited and published by Charles Ross

Lightnings Live On! Hugh Trevor (Lightning Preservation Group, 1996)
No.226 OCU Lightning Instructors Handbook RAF Gütersloh, Marc Tecklenborg & Werner Rydzynski (Flottmann Verlag GmbH, 1995)
RAF Nuclear Deterrent Forces, Humphrey Wynn (HMSO/MoD Air Historical Branch (RAF), 1994)
Sir James Martin, Sarah Sharman (PSL, 1996)
Spreading My Wings, Diana Barnato Walker MBE (PSL, 1994)
Tigers: The story of No.74 Squadron RAF, Bob Cossey (Arms & Armour Press, 1992)

F.6s of 111 Squadron in the early 1970s. *Aeroplane*

Index